MAYBE AN
Artist

A Graphic Memoir by
LIZ MONTAGUE

RANDOM HOUSE **STUDIO**
NEW YORK

All rights reserved. Published in the United States by Random House Studio,
an imprint of Random House Children's Books,
a division of Penguin Random House LLC, New York.

Random House Studio with colophon is a registered trademark of
Penguin Random House LLC.
Visit us on the Web! GetUnderlined.com
Educators and librarians, for a variety of teaching tools,
visit us at RHTeachersLibrarians.com

Library of Congress Cataloging-in-Publication Data is available upon request.
ISBN 978-0-593-30781-6 (hardcover) — ISBN 978-0-593-30782-3 (pbk.) —
ISBN 978-0-593-30784-7 (ebook)

The text of this book is set in 13-point Liz's Font.
The illustrations were rendered digitally.
Book design by Carol Ly and Juliet Goodman

MANUFACTURED IN CHINA
10 9 8 7 6 5 4 3 2 1
First Edition

TO MY FAMILY, MY HUSBAND,
AND MY NINE-YEAR-OLD SELF.
THANK YOU (FOR EVERYTHING).

I'm a person who was born in a certain place,
in a certain time, and I can be unsure about everything,
but I am not unsure of what I have lived. I know it.

—MARJANE SATRAPI

INTRODUCTION

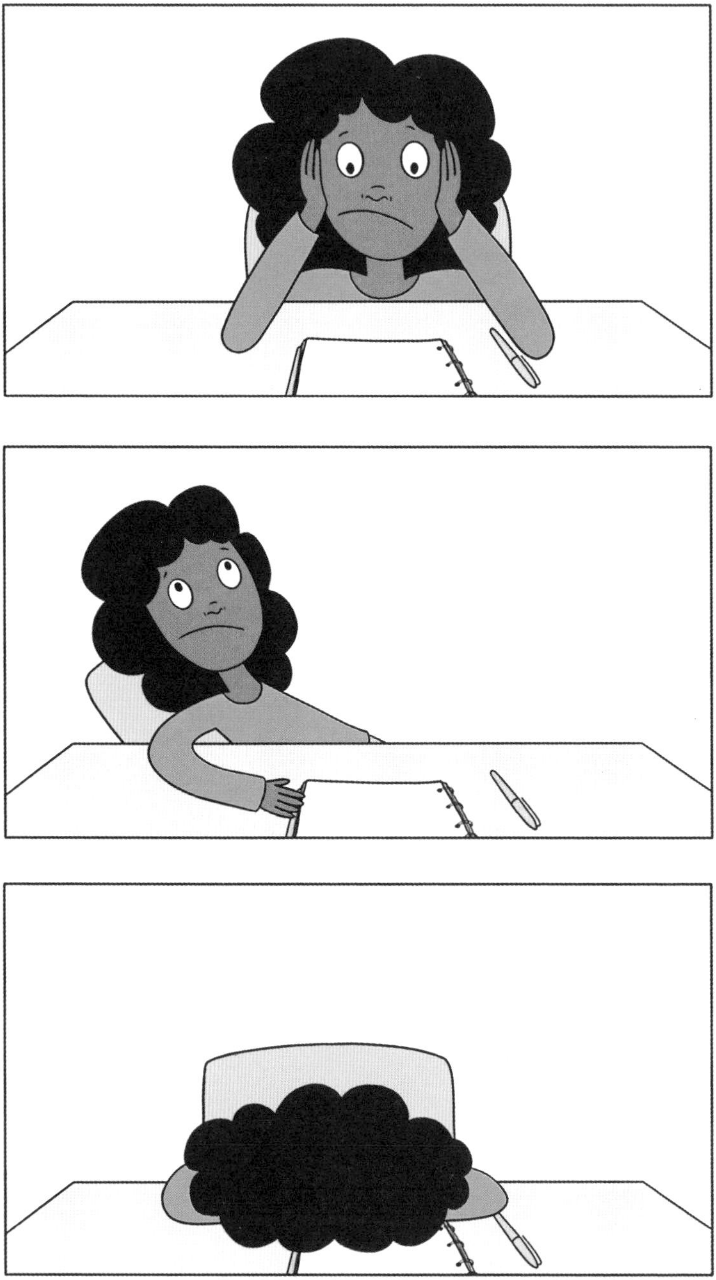

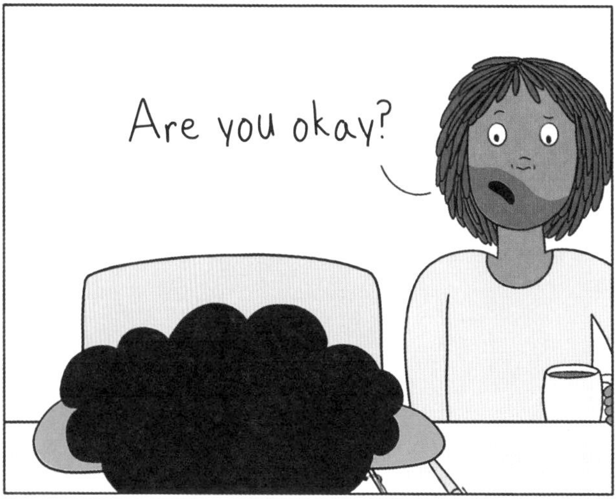
Are you okay?

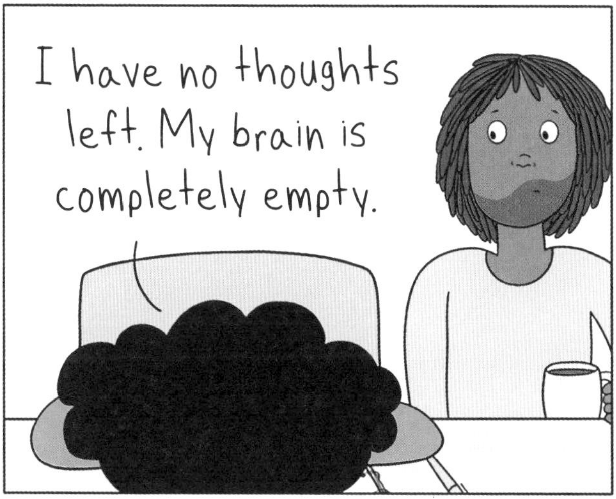
I have no thoughts left. My brain is completely empty.

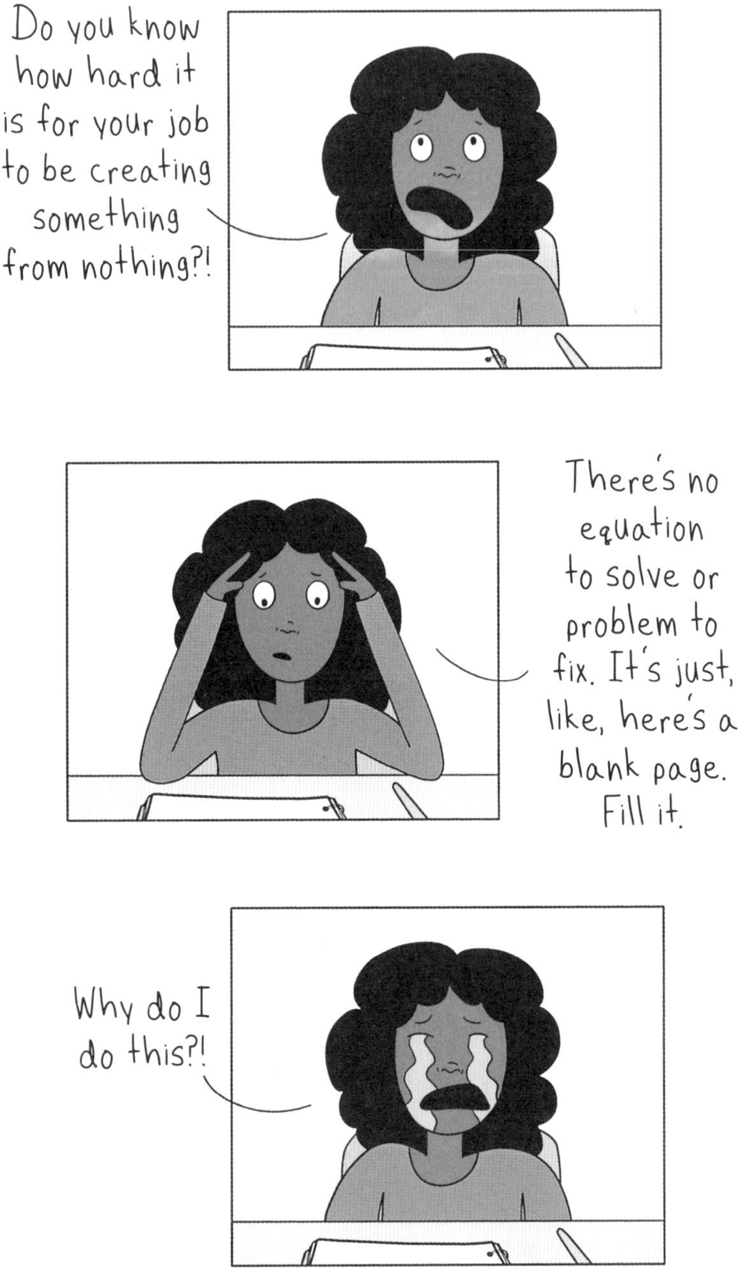
Do you know how hard it is for your job to be creating something from nothing?!
There's no equation to solve or problem to fix. It's just, like, here's a blank page. Fill it.
Why do I do this?!

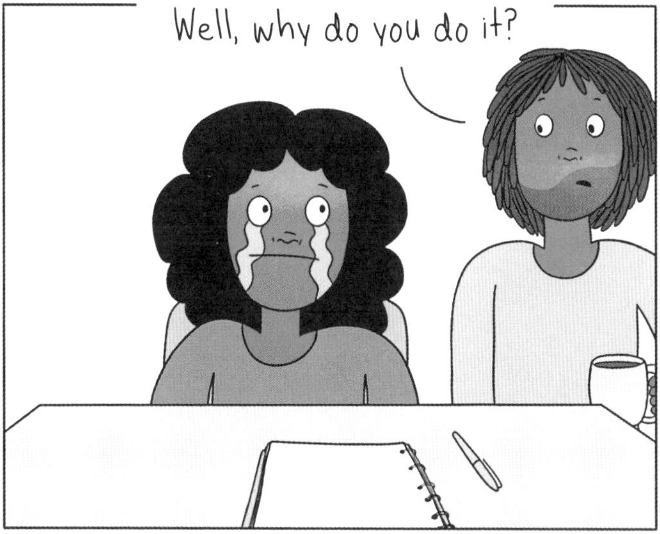
Well, why do you do it?

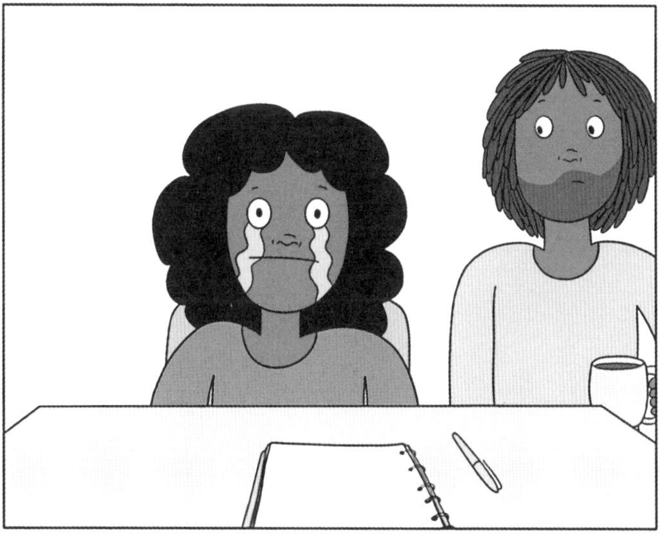

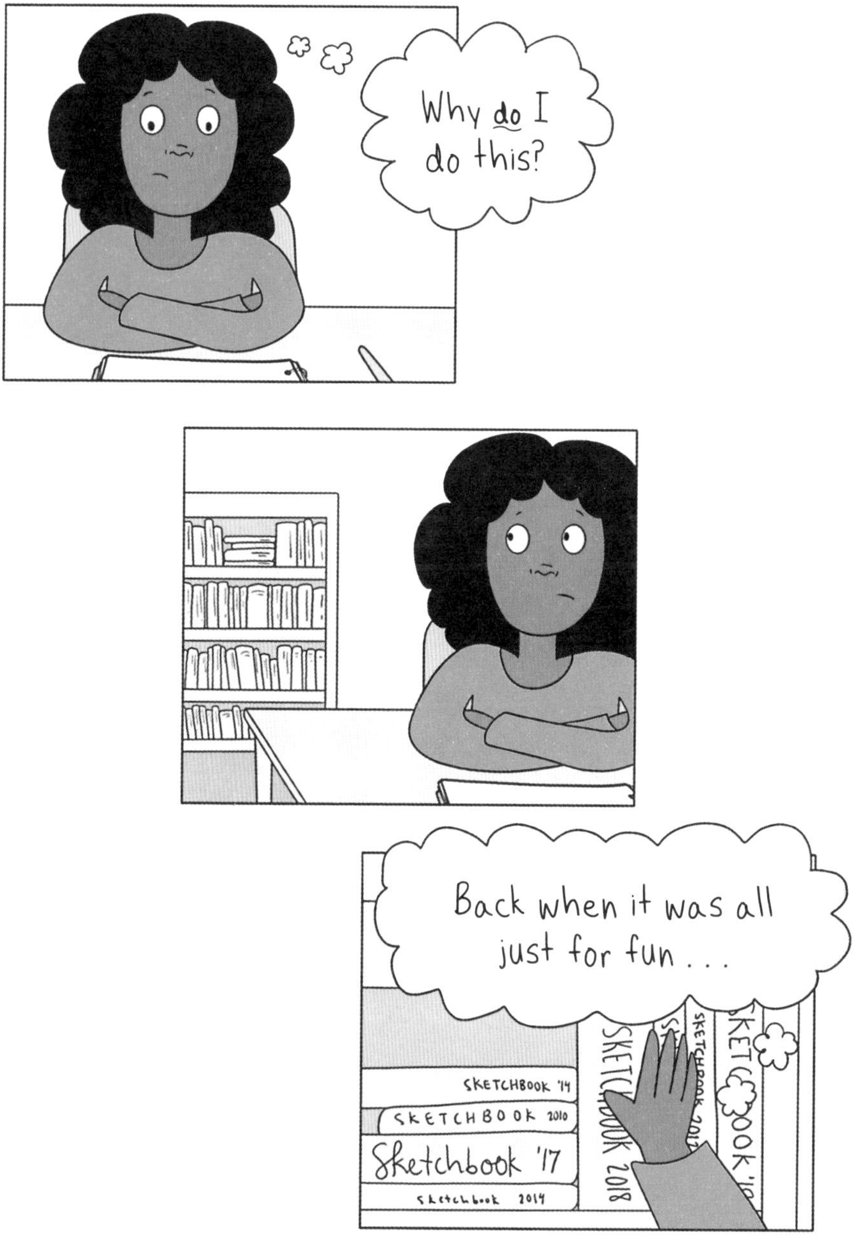
Why do I do this?
Back when it was all just for fun . . .
SKETCHBOOK '14
SKETCHBOOK 2010
Sketchbook '17
Sketchbook 2014
SKETCHBOOK 2018

2017
'13
2017
Liz Montague

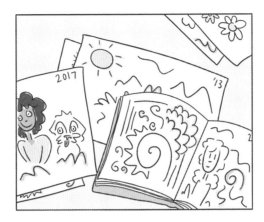

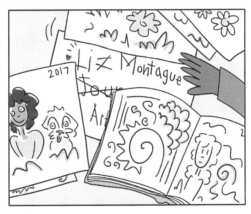

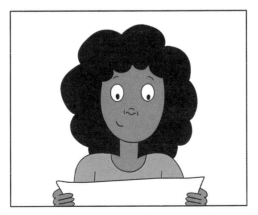

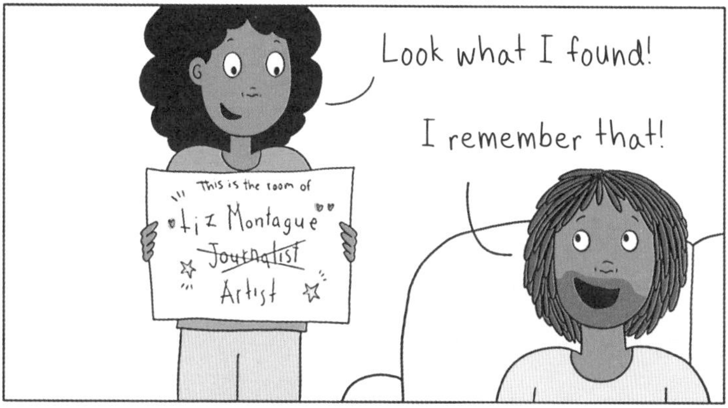
Look what I found!
I remember that!
This is the room of
Liz Montague
Journalist
Artist

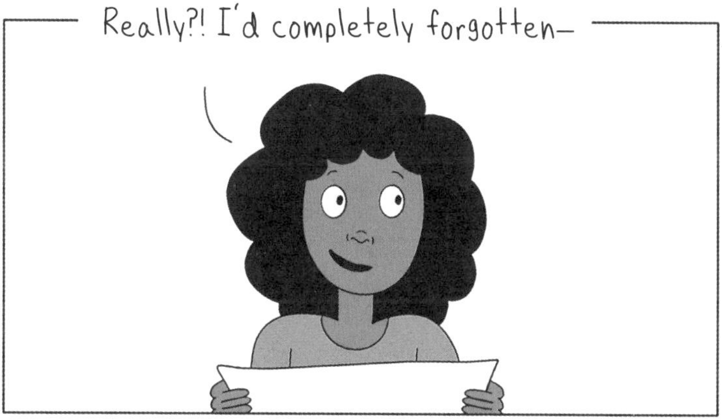
Really?! I'd completely forgotten—

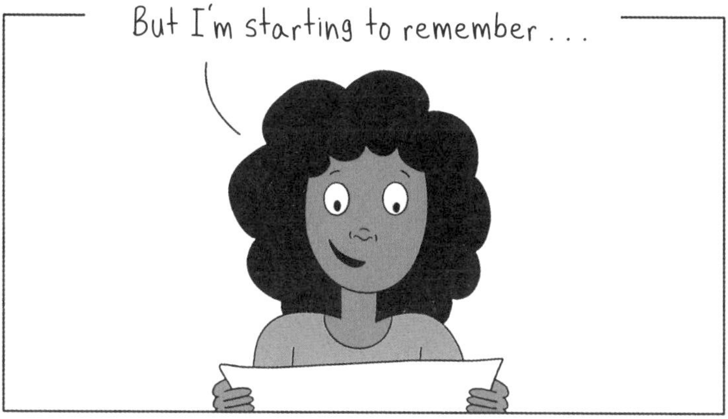
But I'm starting to remember . . .

GOLDFINCH ELEMENTARY SCHOOL

MARLTON, NEW JERSEY
2001–2007

On September 11, 2001, I was five years old and lived in Marlton, New Jersey, with my parents and two older sisters. That day there was a plane crash two hours away in New York City.

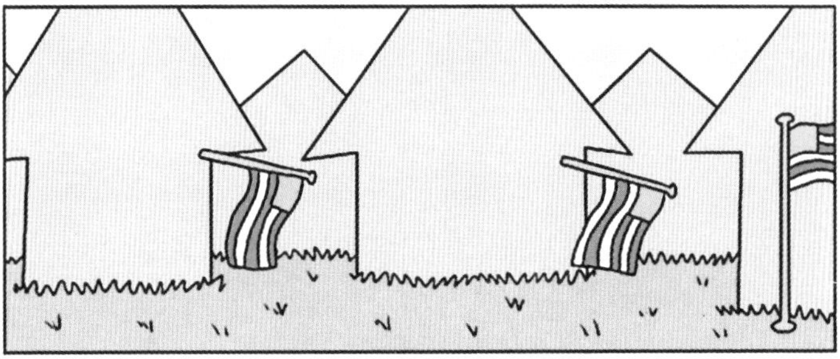

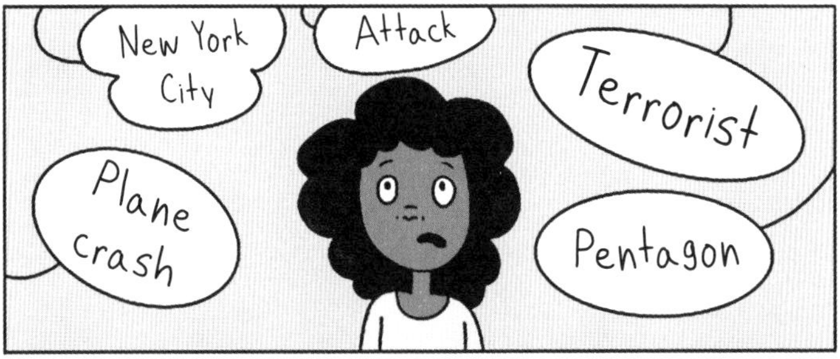
New York City
Attack
Terrorist
Plane crash
Pentagon

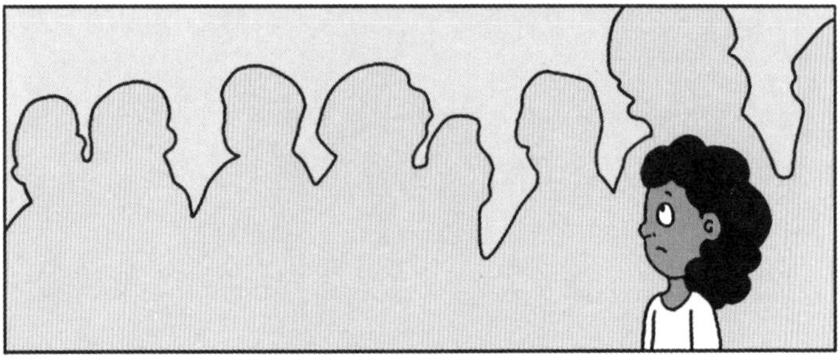

At first, I really didn't think it was a big deal. September 12 felt like any other day.

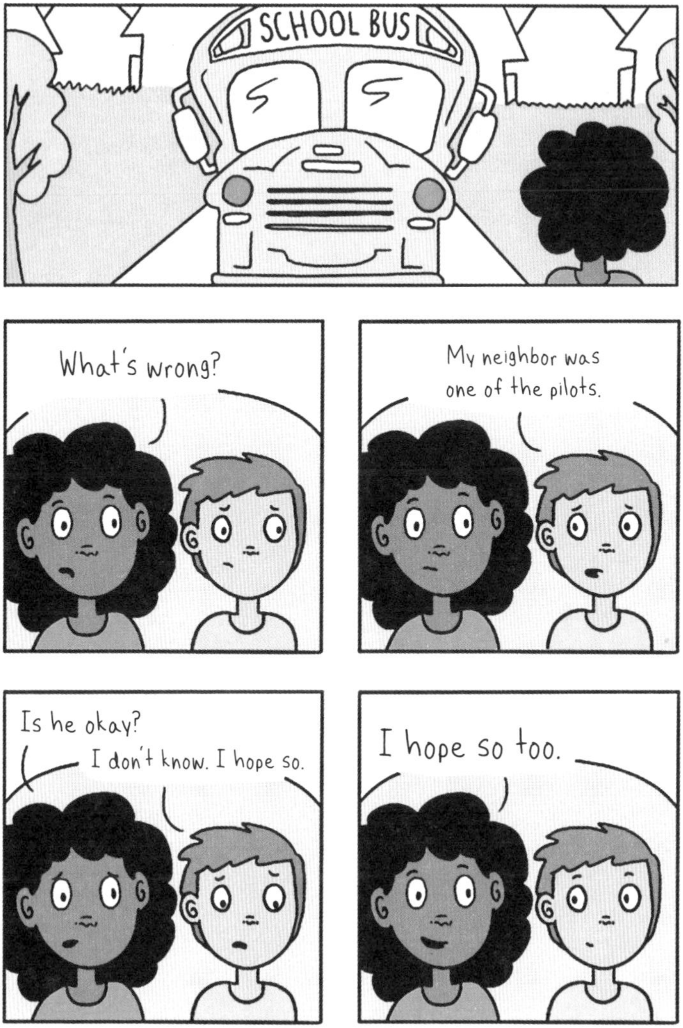
SCHOOL BUS
What's wrong?
My neighbor was one of the pilots.
Is he okay?
I don't know. I hope so.
I hope so too.

But things changed the way a day goes to sleep as fall and wakes up as winter. When one leaf on the ground becomes a million leaves.

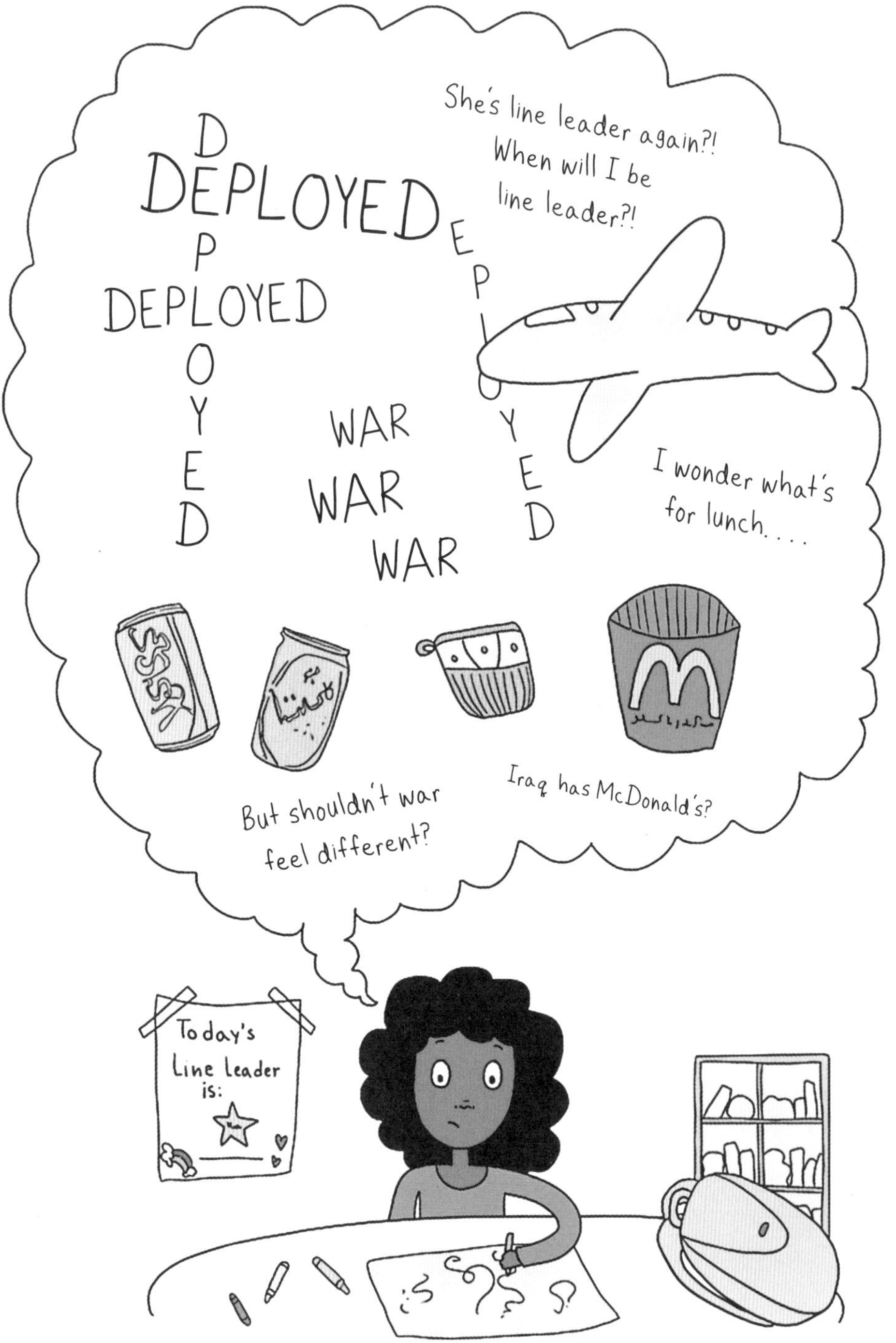
D
DEPLOYED
P
DEPLOYED
O
Y
E
D
E
P
L
O
Y
E
D
WAR
WAR
WAR
She's line leader again?!
When will I be line leader?!
I wonder what's for lunch....
But shouldn't war feel different?
Iraq has McDonald's?
Today's Line Leader is:

I got the majority of my news updates from the older kids after school while I waited for the bus home.

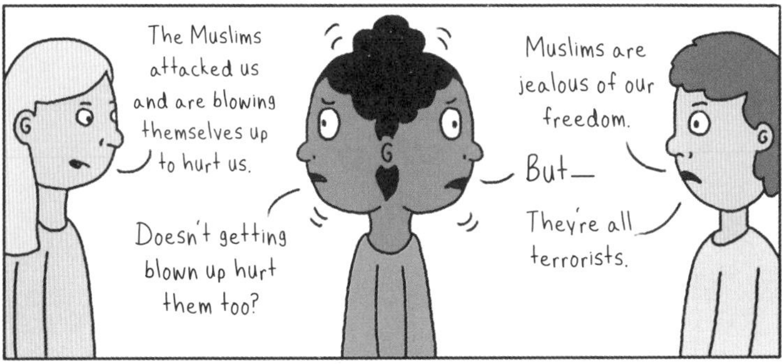
The Muslims attacked us and are blowing themselves up to hurt us.
Doesn't getting blown up hurt them too?
Muslims are jealous of our freedom.
But—
They're all terrorists.

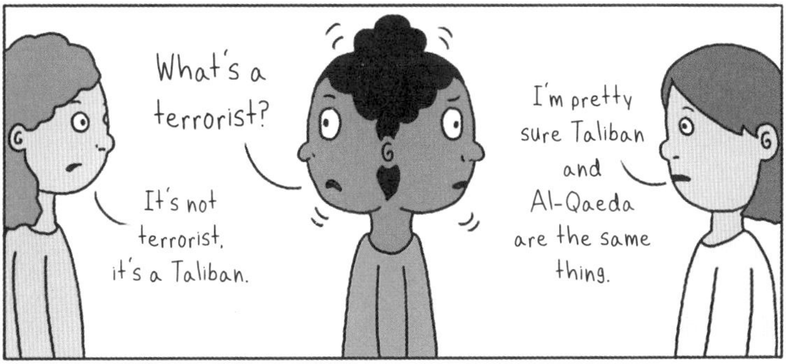
What's a terrorist?
It's not terrorist, it's a Taliban.
I'm pretty sure Taliban and Al-Qaeda are the same thing.

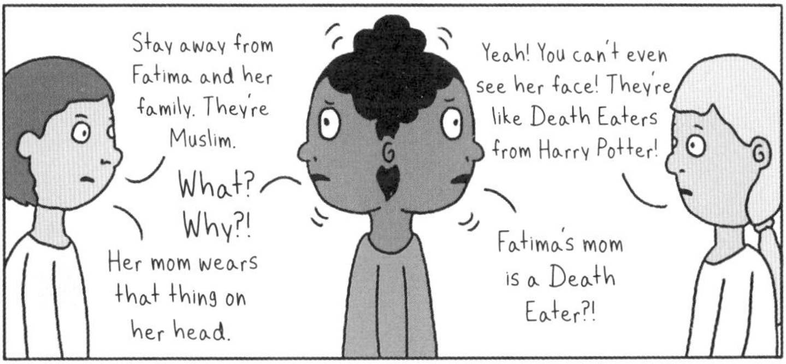
Stay away from Fatima and her family. They're Muslim.
What? Why?!
Her mom wears that thing on her head.
Yeah! You can't even see her face! They're like Death Eaters from Harry Potter!
Fatima's mom is a Death Eater?!

I tried to fact-check with my parents, but they didn't understand.

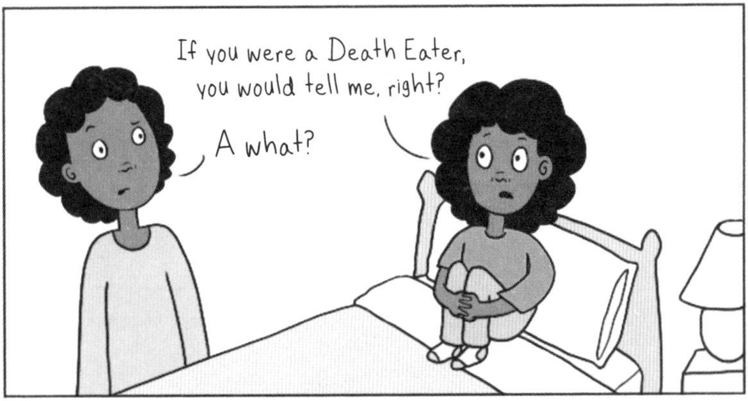
If you were a Death Eater, you would tell me, right?
A what?

And my teachers didn't understand that my parents didn't understand.

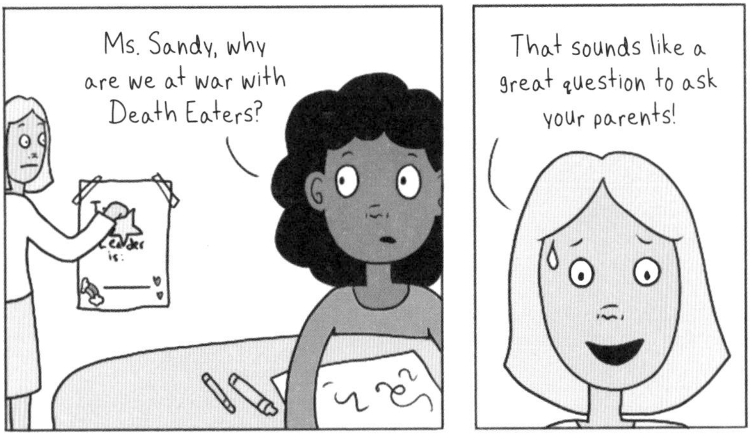
Ms. Sandy, why are we at war with Death Eaters?
That sounds like a great question to ask your parents!

WAK WAK WAK   WAK WAK WAK WAK
ЯAW ЯAW ЯAW ЯAW   ЯAW ЯAW ЯAW
WAR   WAR WAR WAR   WAR WAR WAR WAR
ЯAW ЯAW WAR ЯAW ЯAW ЯAW   ЯAW
WAR   WAR WAR   WAR WAR WAR WAR
ЯAW ЯAW ЯAW ЯAW ЯAW   ЯAW
AR WAR

By third grade, the war was old news.

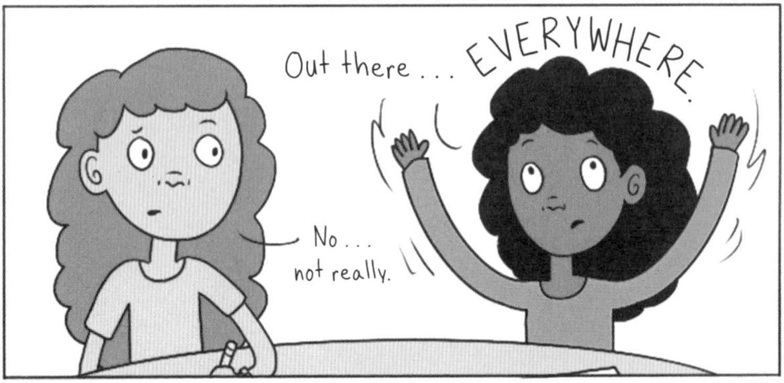
Out there . . . EVERYWHERE.
No . . .
not really.

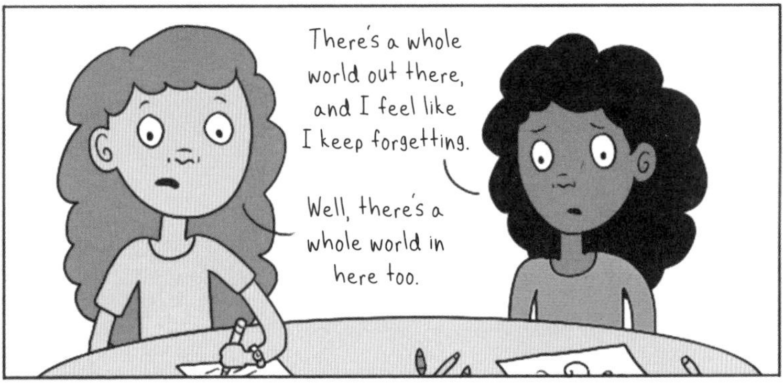
There's a whole world out there, and I feel like I keep forgetting.
Well, there's a whole world in here too.

She had a point. Time was marching on in our little world.

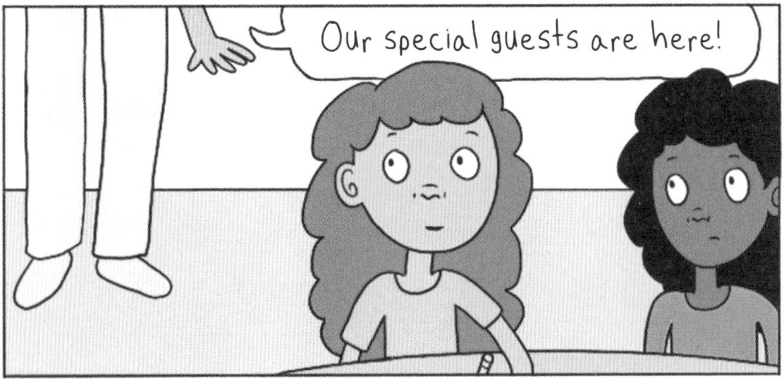
Our special guests are here!

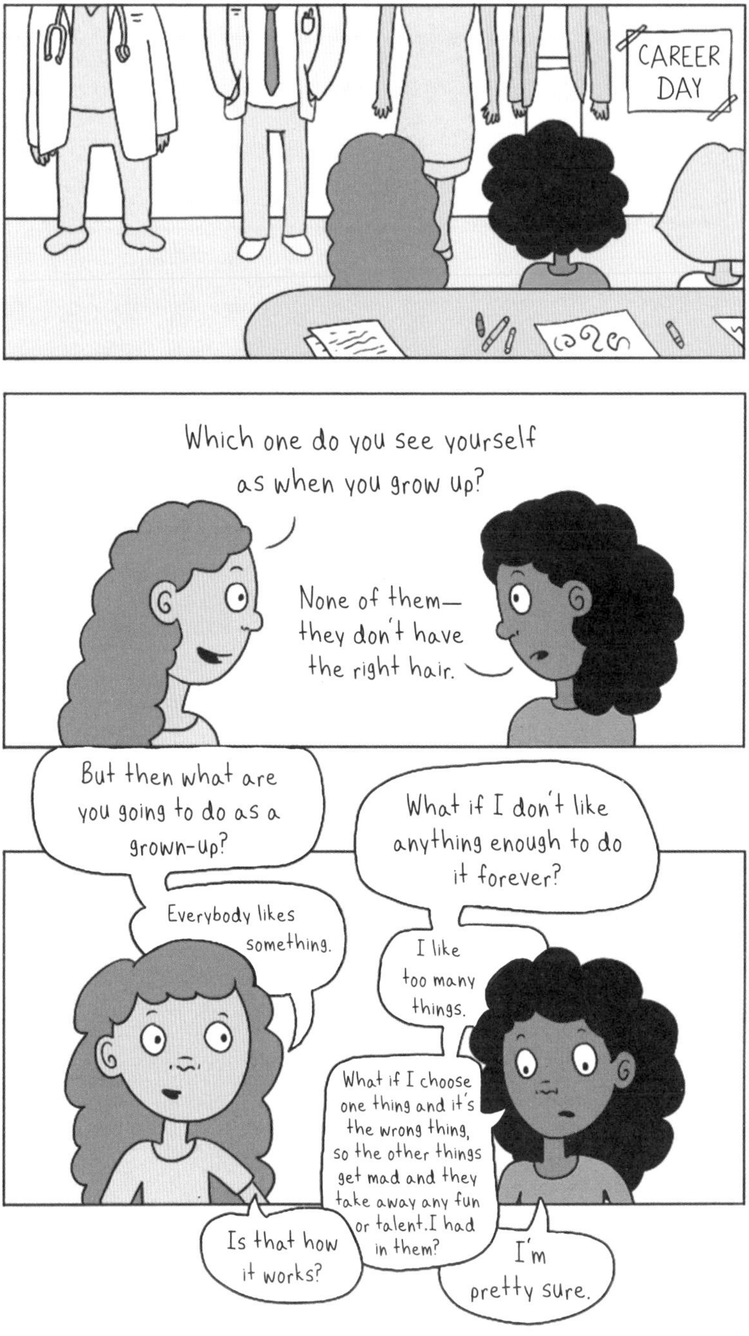
CAREER DAY
Which one do you see yourself as when you grow up?
None of them— they don't have the right hair.
But then what are you going to do as a grown-up?
Everybody likes something.
What if I don't like anything enough to do it forever?
I like too many things.
What if I choose one thing and it's the wrong thing, so the other things get mad and they take away any fun or talent I had in them?
Is that how it works?
I'm pretty sure.

When I got home from school, I kept thinking about career day.

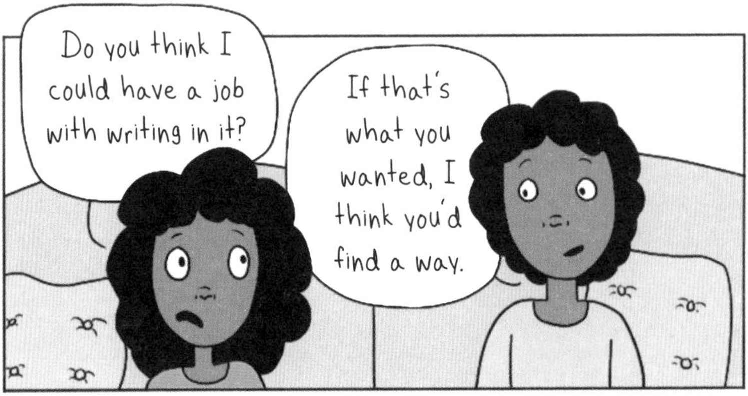
Do you think I could have a job with writing in it?
If that's what you wanted, I think you'd find a way.

Other people had a hard time reading my writing. My parents used a mirror to read it.

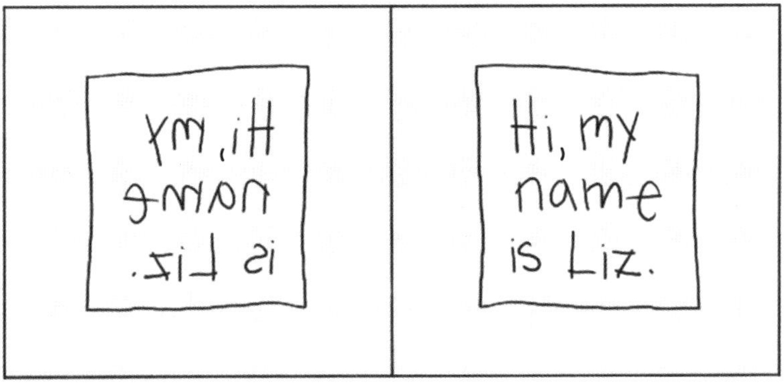
Hi, my name is Liz.

My sisters thought my writing was really weird.

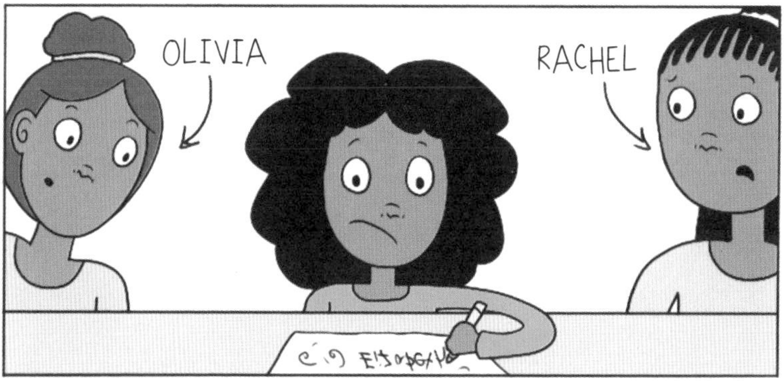
OLIVIA
RACHEL

Olivia was two years older than me and already in middle school, and Rachel, who was six years older than me, was in high school.

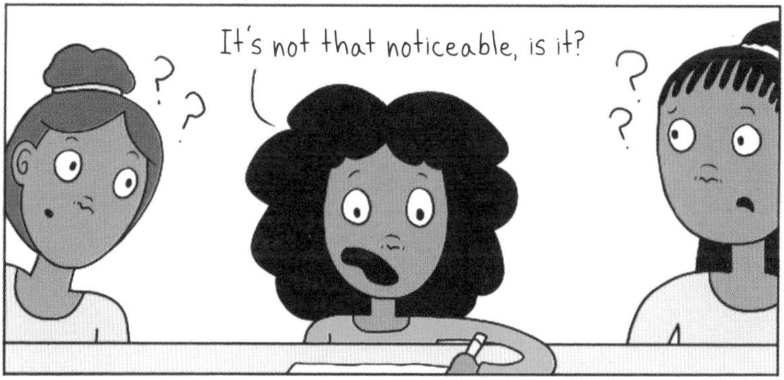
It's not that noticeable, is it?

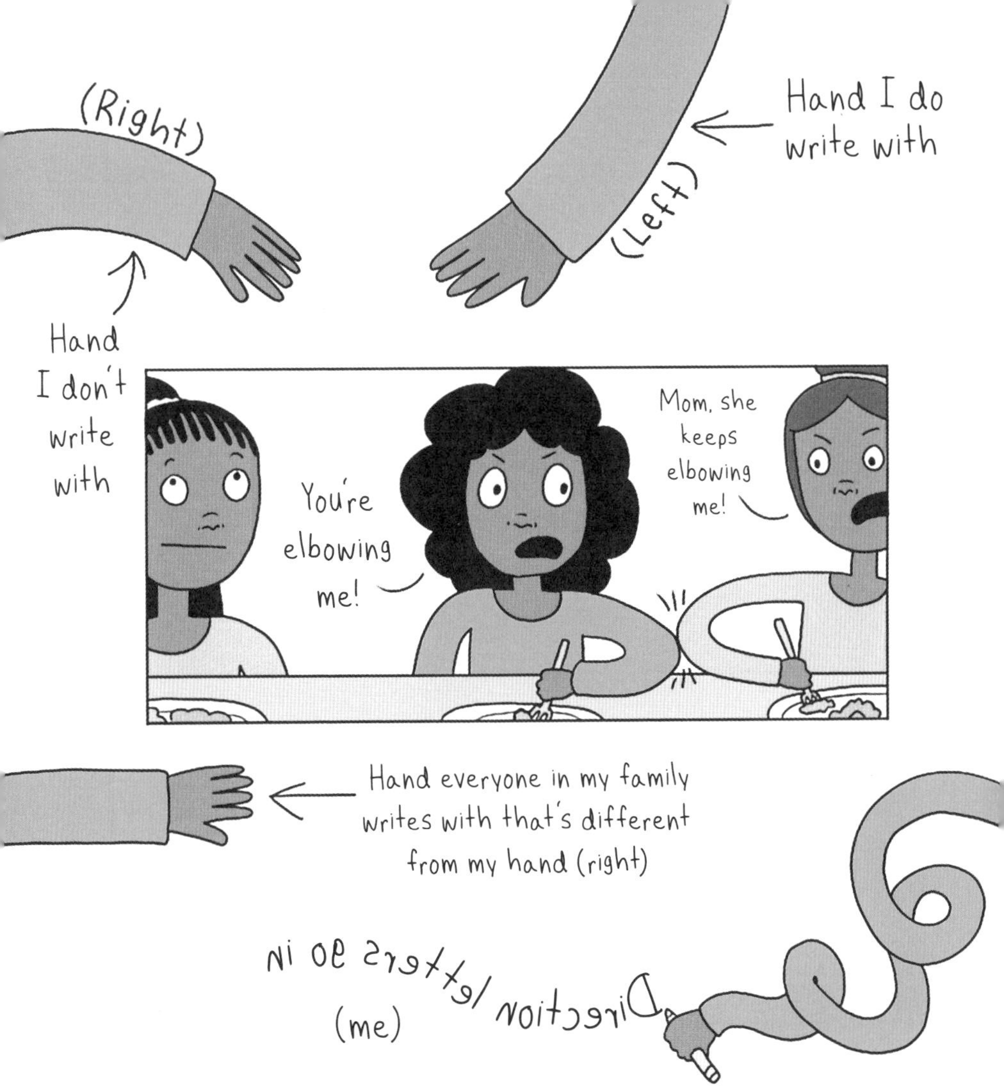
(Right)
Hand I don't write with
(Left)
Hand I do write with
You're elbowing me!
Mom, she keeps elbowing me!
Hand everyone in my family writes with that's different from my hand (right)
Direction letters go in
(me)

I didn't really notice the direction letters faced. They looked the same both ways to me.

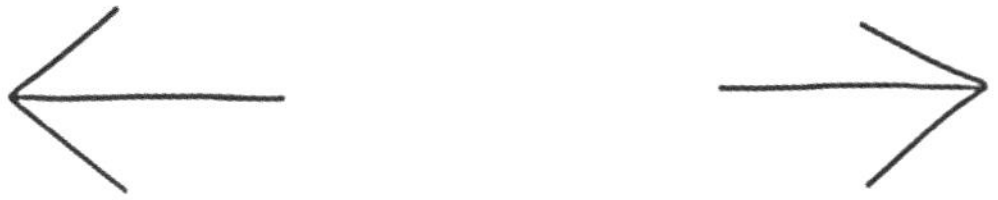

But I didn't just read differently. I spoke differently too.

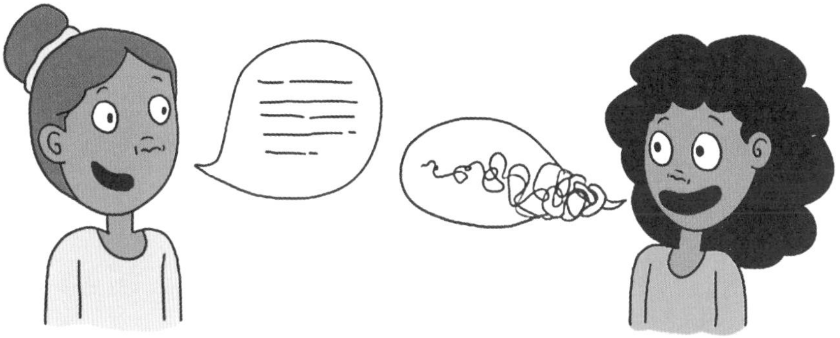

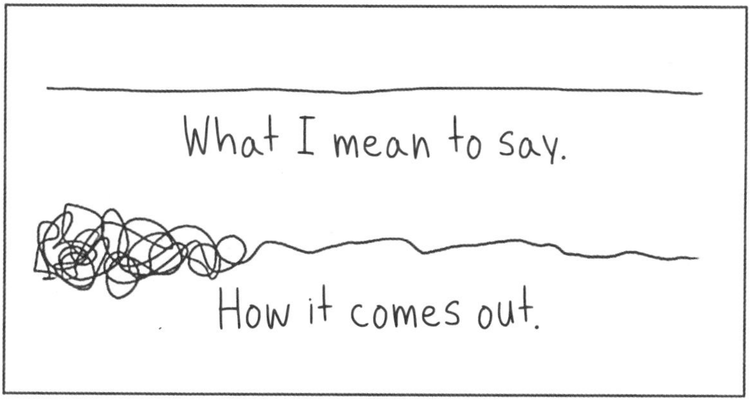
What I mean to say.
How it comes out.

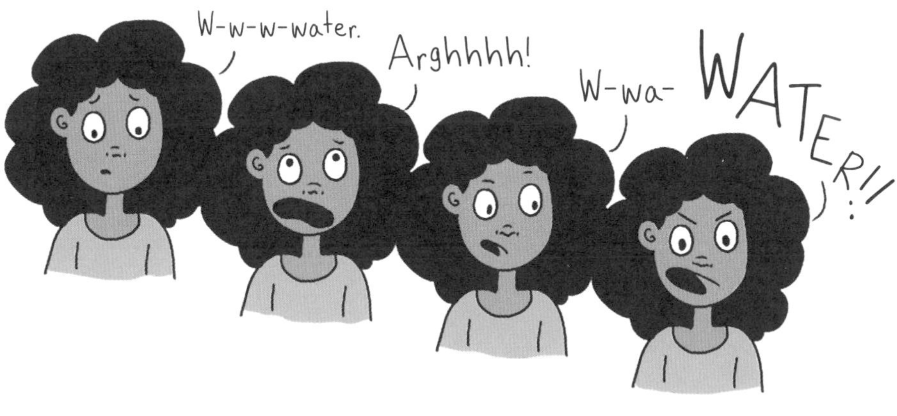
W-w-w-water.
Arghhhh!
W-wa-
WATER!!

I became determined to write and speak like everyone else.
I didn't want to fight with my mouth in front of the whole class.

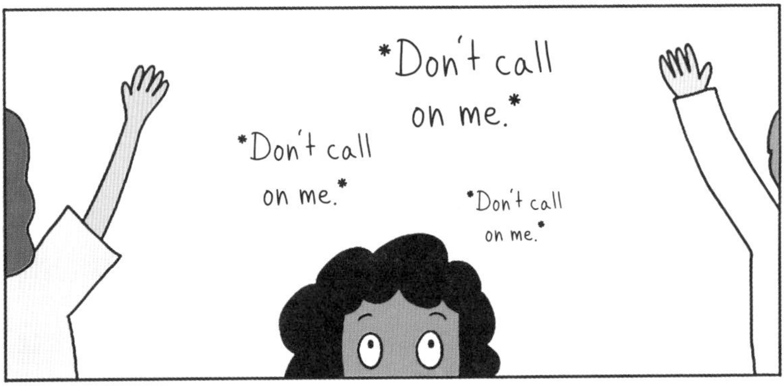
Don't call on me.
Don't call on me.
Don't call on me.

Letters were hard, but shapes were easy. I was really good at shapes.

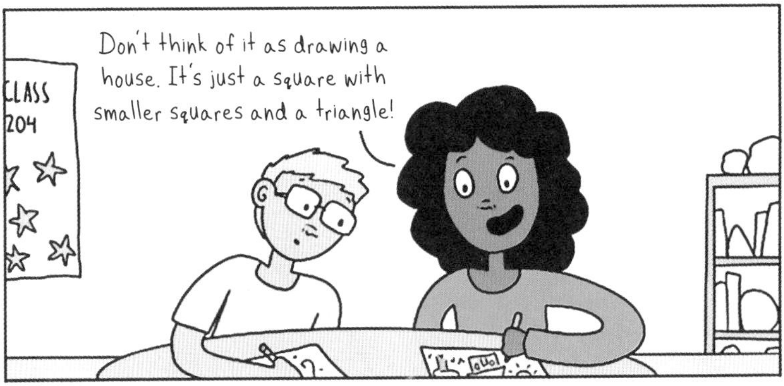
CLASS 204
Don't think of it as drawing a house. It's just a square with smaller squares and a triangle!

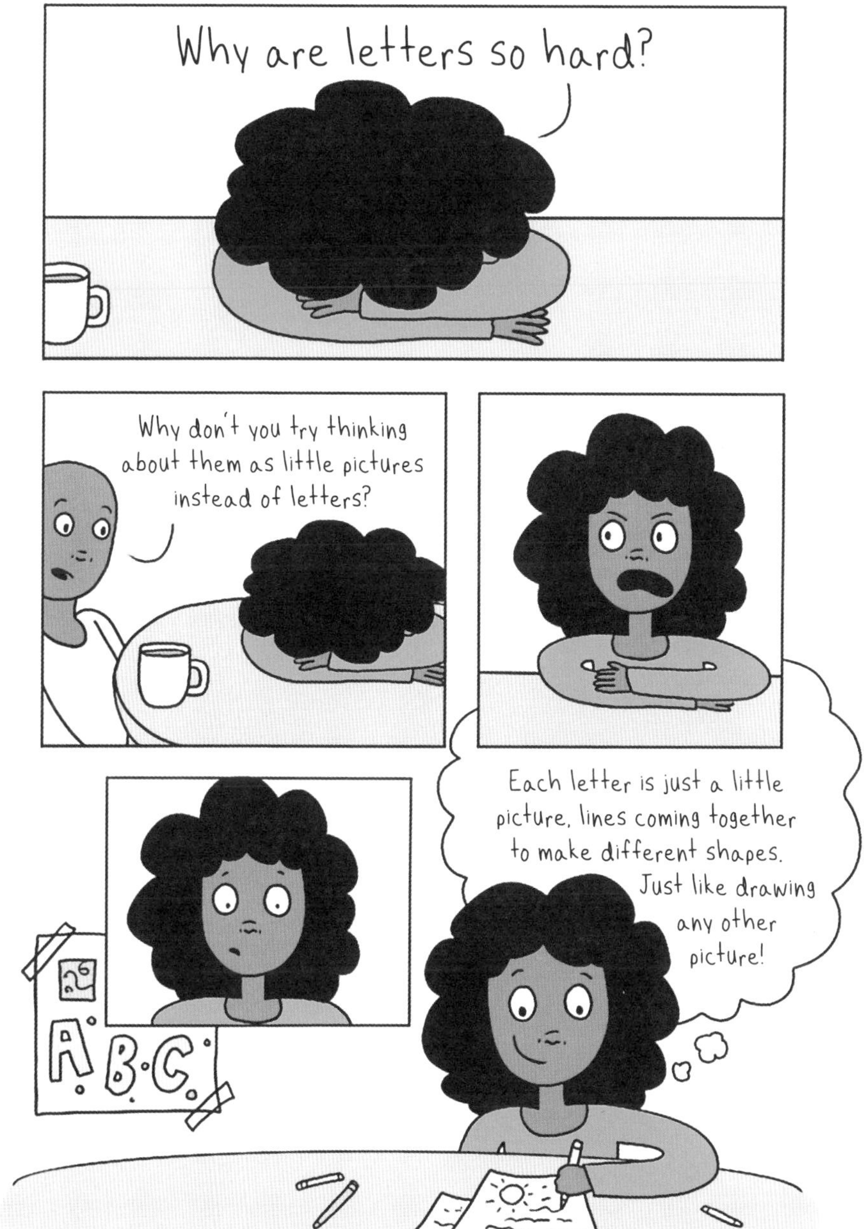
Why are letters so hard?
Why don't you try thinking about them as little pictures instead of letters?
Each letter is just a little picture, lines coming together to make different shapes. Just like drawing any other picture!
ABC

By the end of fifth grade, I'd gotten the hang of it.

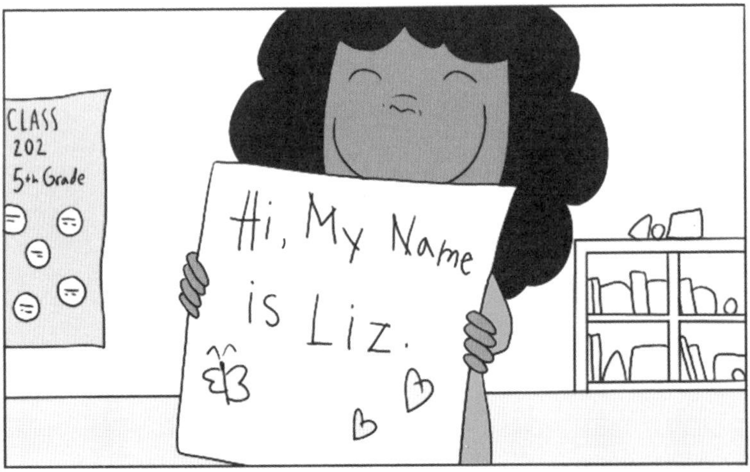
CLASS
202
5th Grade
Hi, My Name is Liz.

Mostly.

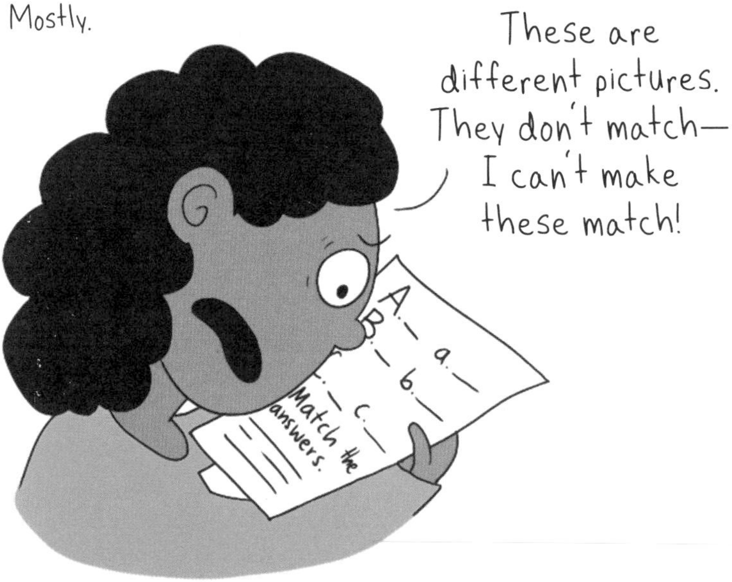
These are different pictures. They don't match— I can't make these match!
A
B
C
a
b
c
Match the answers.

Seeing letters as little pictures meant I had trouble finding connections between capital and lowercase letters.

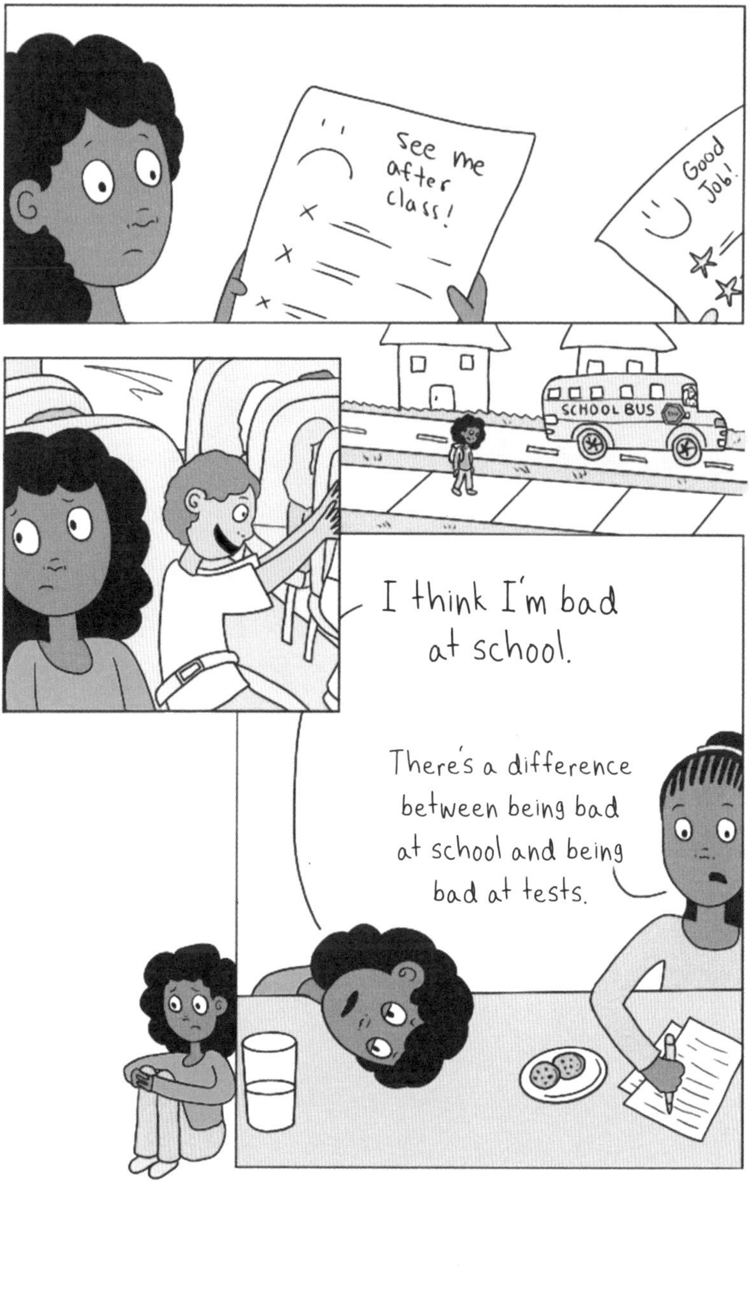
See me after class!
Good Job!
SCHOOL BUS
I think I'm bad at school.
There's a difference between being bad at school and being bad at tests.

Once elementary graduation came, I hoped I was leaving tests behind once and for all. Middle school would have a more sophisticated system—I was sure of it.

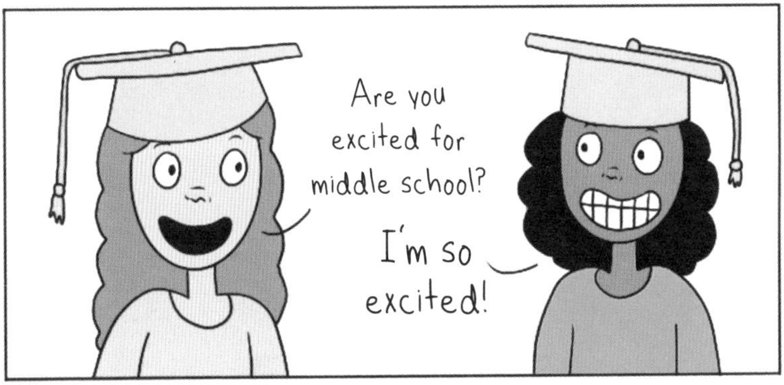
Are you excited for middle school?
I'm so excited!

Only, I wasn't excited, I was nervous. Elementary school felt nice and worn in, like a cozy sweater.

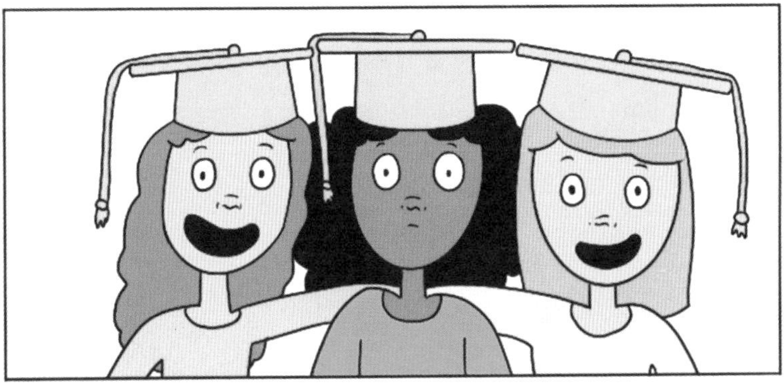

Hurston Middle would be stiff and new. I wasn't sure I would fit.

But first came summer. Summer was the best. Summer meant track practice and Girl Scouts and that tight feeling your skin gets after a really hot day.

Summer also meant camp. Rachel, Olivia, and I all went to the same local camp, called the Blue Barn.

We wore bright yellow shirts and mostly ran around outside. Sometimes the older kids hung out with us, like our family friend Joe.

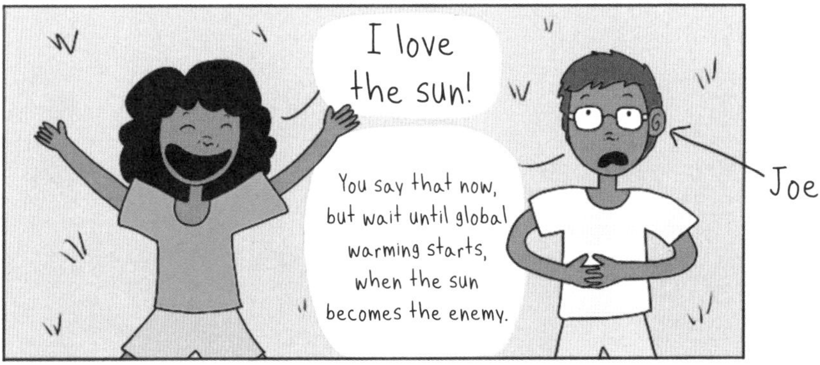
I love the sun!
You say that now, but wait until global warming starts, when the sun becomes the enemy.
Joe

I learned a lot at camp.

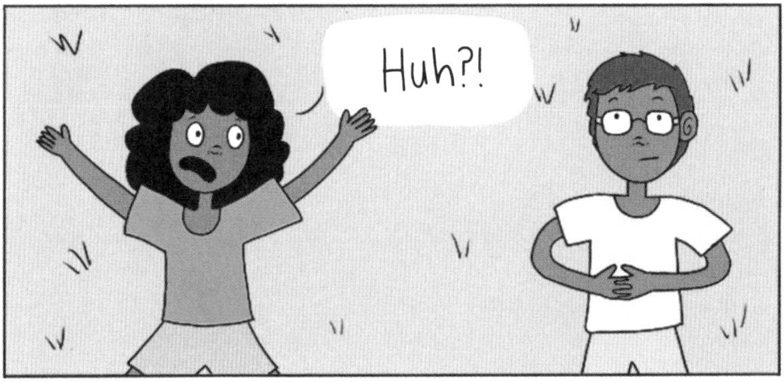
Huh?!

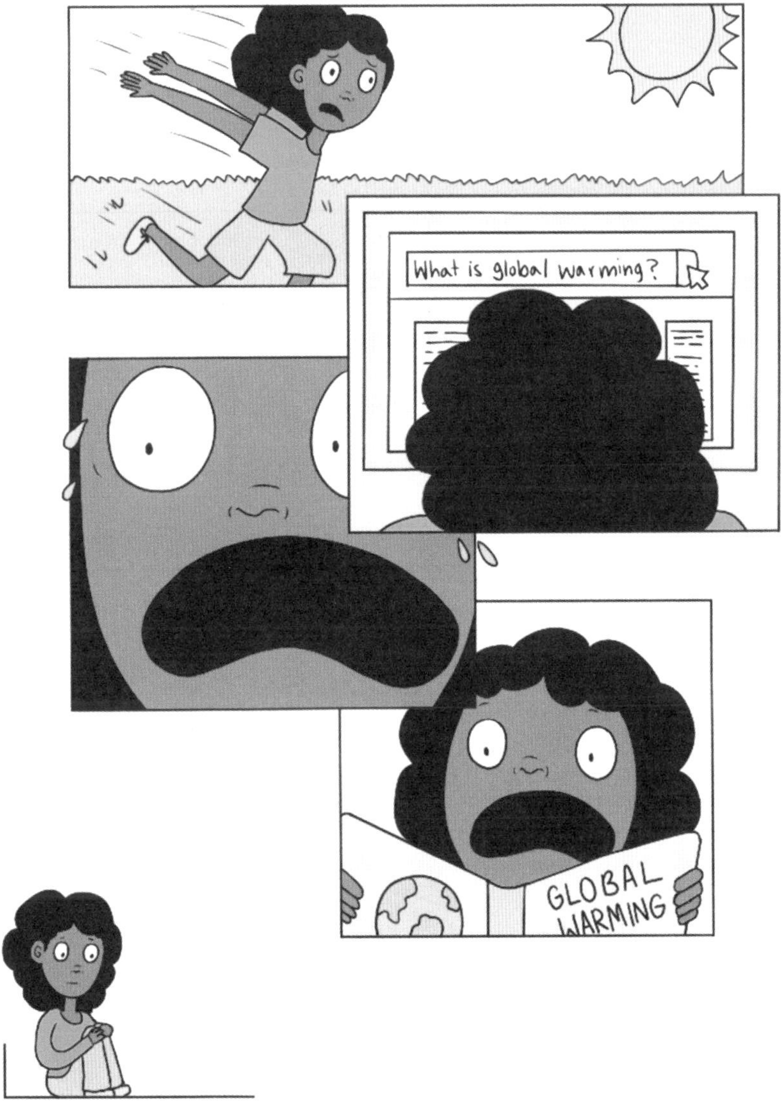
What is global warming?
GLOBAL WARMING

That night, I held a family meeting.

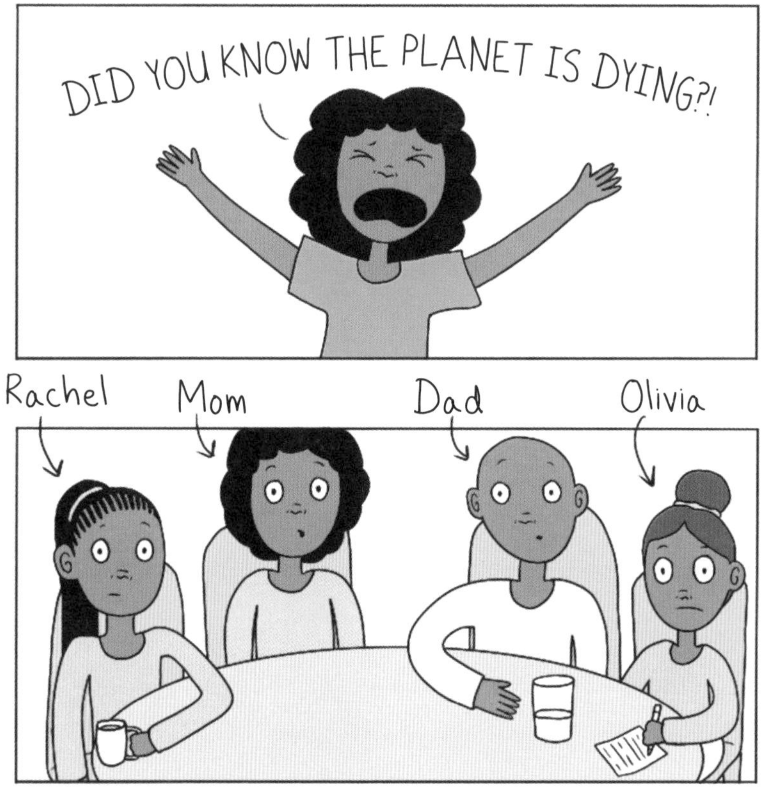
DID YOU KNOW THE PLANET IS DYING?!
Rachel
Mom
Dad
Olivia

I had to do something, anything. I grabbed my markers and got to work. I loved making signs, especially now that other people could easily read my words.

That weekend, with Olivia as my assistant, I hit the streets.

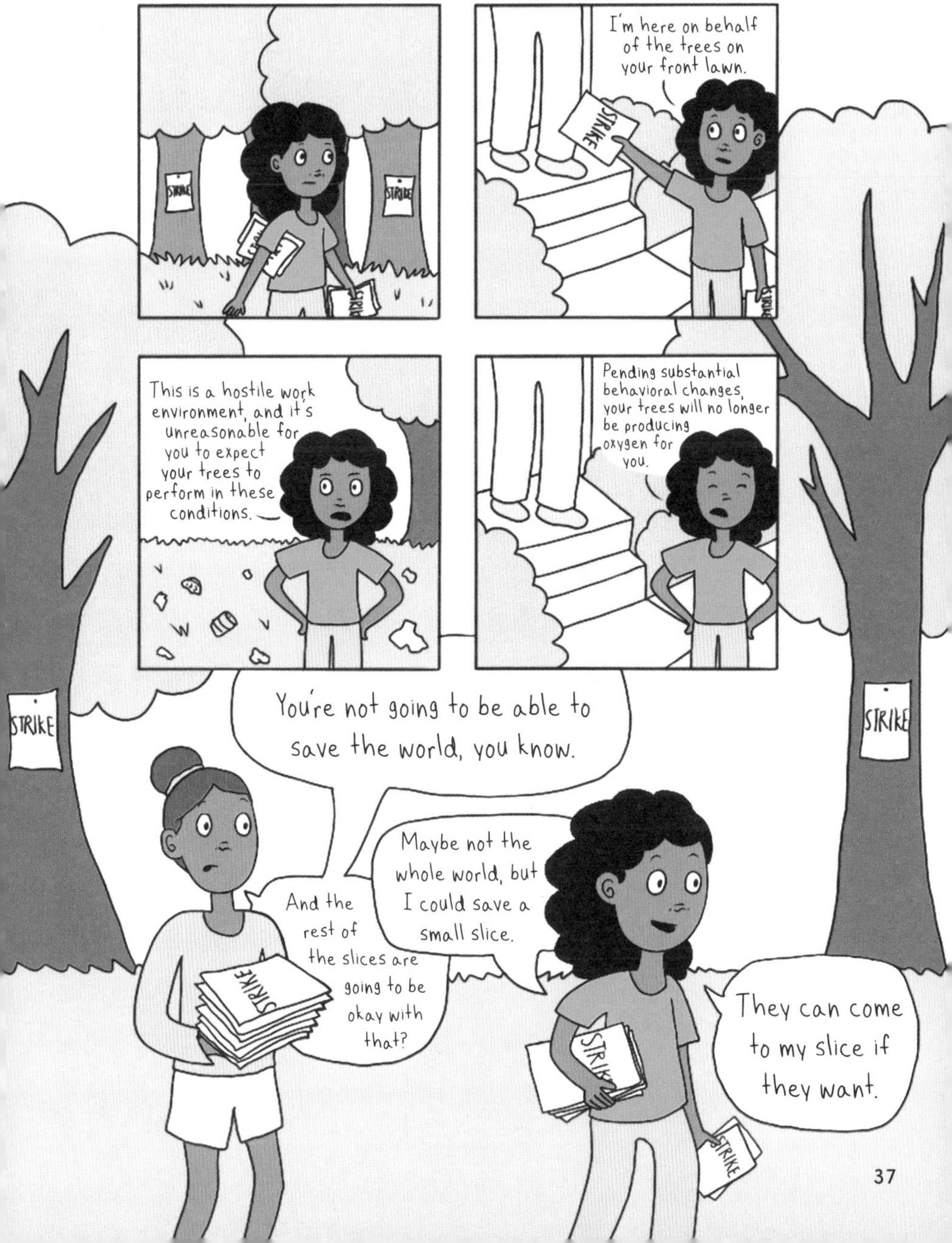
STRIKE
STRIKE
I'm here on behalf of the trees on your front lawn.
STRIKE
This is a hostile work environment, and it's unreasonable for you to expect your trees to perform in these conditions.
Pending substantial behavioral changes, your trees will no longer be producing oxygen for you.
STRIKE
STRIKE
You're not going to be able to save the world, you know.
Maybe not the whole world, but I could save a small slice.
And the rest of the slices are going to be okay with that?
They can come to my slice if they want.
STRIKE
STRIKE
STRIKE

I couldn't understand how grown-ups had let things get __so__ bad. Naturally, I wanted answers.

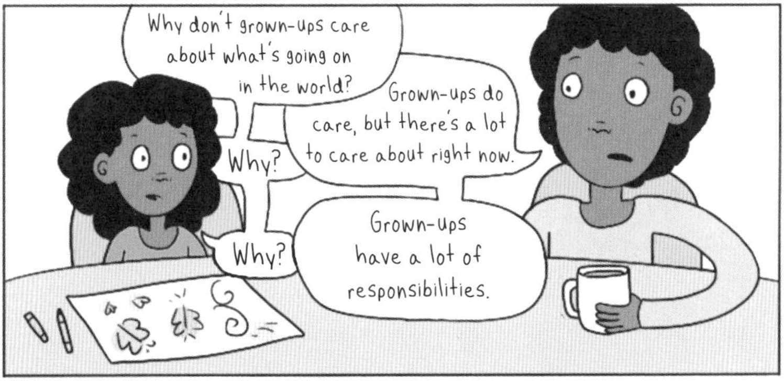
Why don't grown-ups care about what's going on in the world?
Grown-ups do care, but there's a lot to care about right now.
Why?
Grown-ups have a lot of responsibilities.
Why?

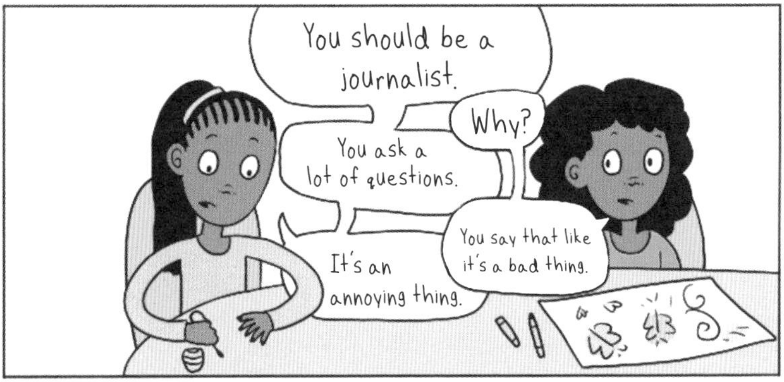
You should be a journalist.
Why?
You ask a lot of questions.
You say that like it's a bad thing.
It's an annoying thing.

I had never thought much about journalism before. I didn't read the newspapers my dad had lying around—the spacing between letters and words was too small. Sometimes I read global warming articles on my mom's laptop.

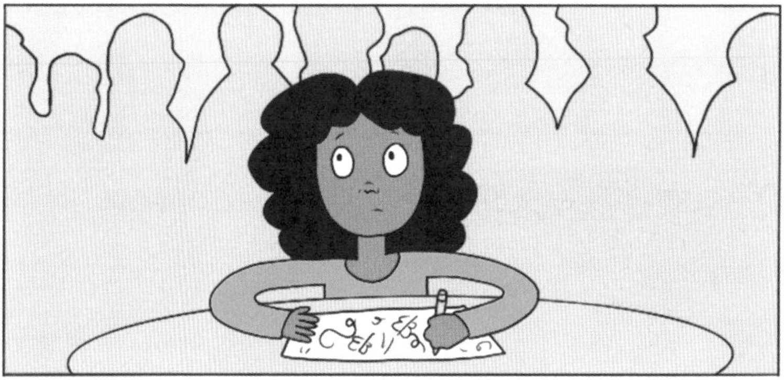

I wanted to understand the bigger things going on in the world. Being a journalist seemed like a good way of doing that.

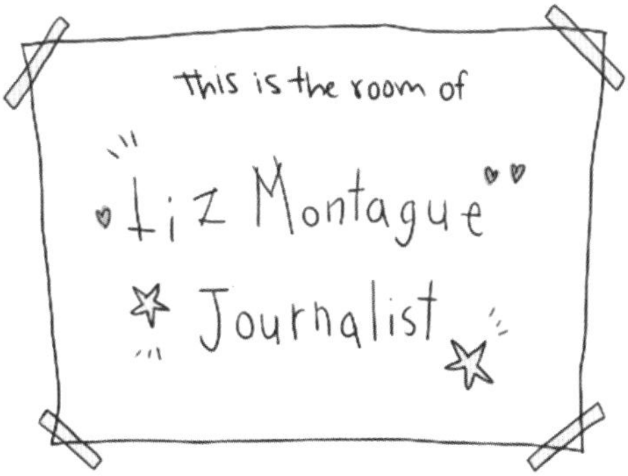
This is the room of
Liz Montague
Journalist

But I wasn't going to write tiny-spaced articles. I would make signs. That way everyone could read them.

I spent the rest of the summer mastering my craft.

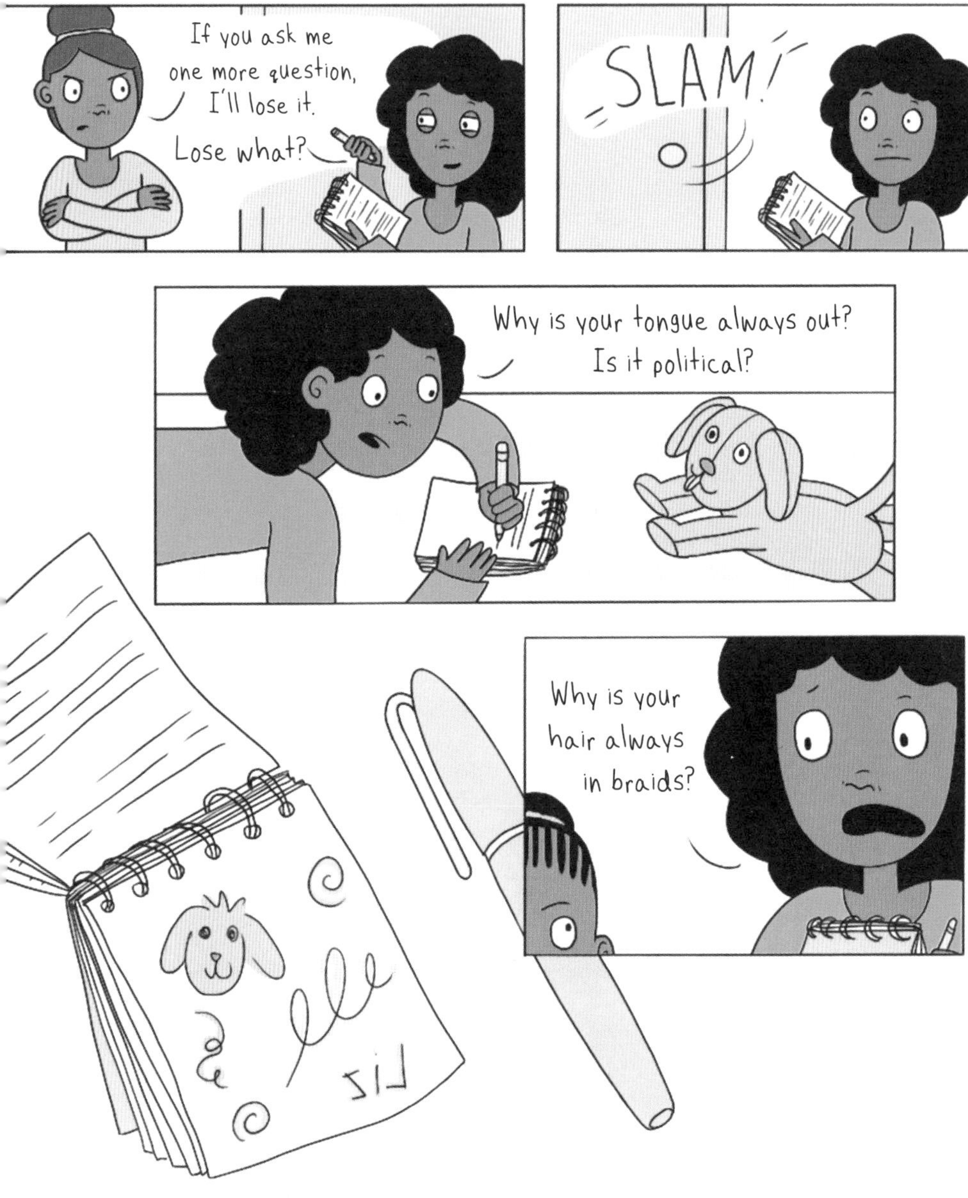

If you ask me one more question, I'll lose it.
Lose what?
SLAM!
Why is your tongue always out? Is it political?
Why is your hair always in braids?

You never know when you're going to come across a story, so I had to be prepared at all times.

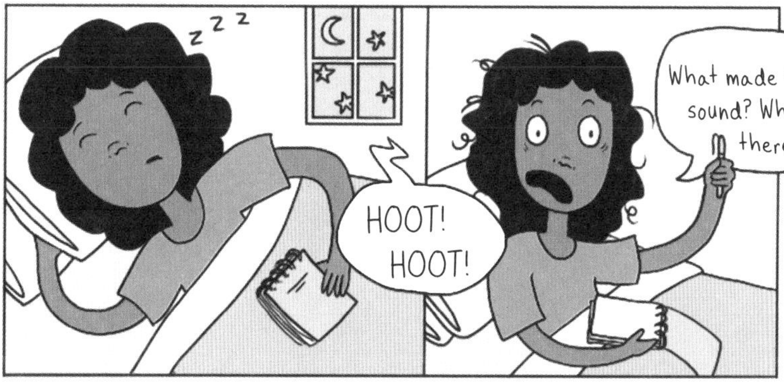

z z z
HOOT! HOOT!
What made that sound? Who's there?!

I took journalism so seriously, I even investigated Rachel's room to look for potential stories.

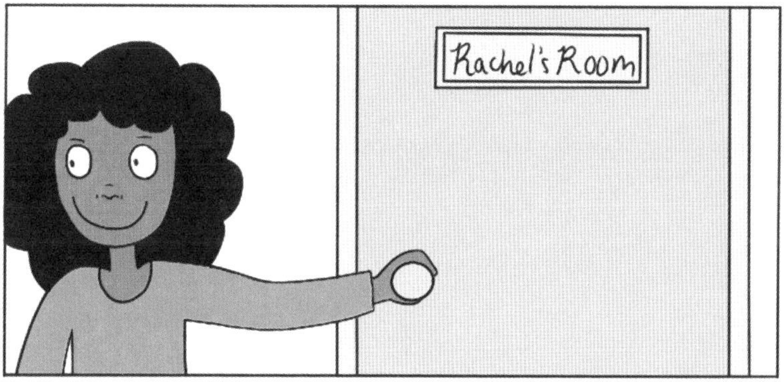

Rachel's Room

The biggest book on her shelf immediately caught my eye.

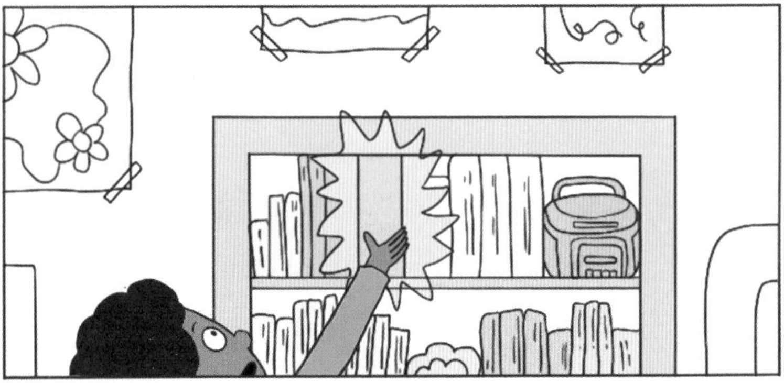

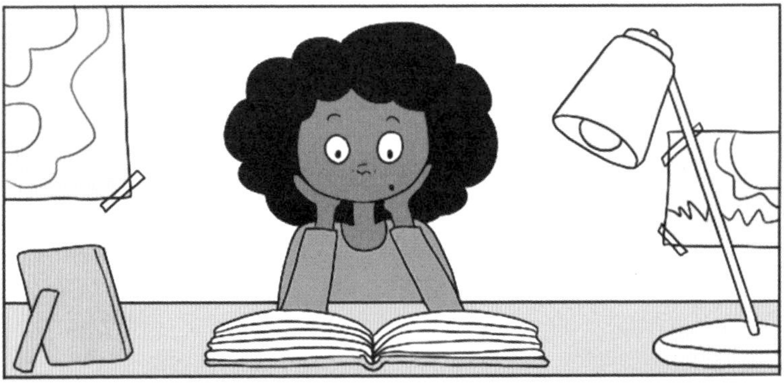

I didn't read the whole book, and I didn't finish most of the paragraphs I read, but I understood the gist of it enough to be outraged.

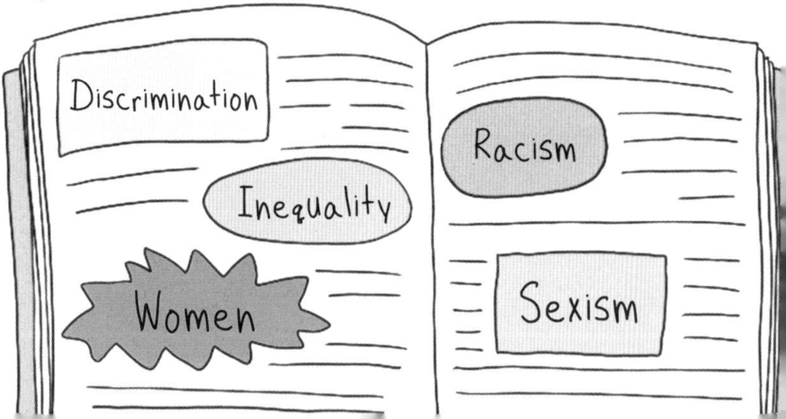

Discrimination
Racism
Inequality
Women
Sexism

Sadly, my investigation was cut short.

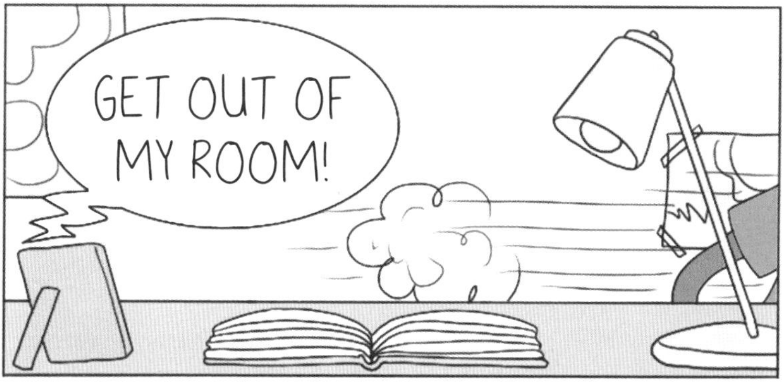
GET OUT OF MY ROOM!

But I had seen plenty.

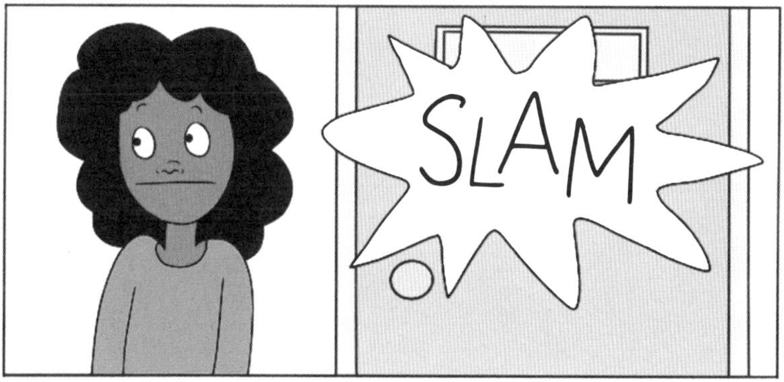
SLAM

It was my duty as a journalist to share my newfound information with the public. I ran to my crayon box and worked tirelessly. It felt like years passed.

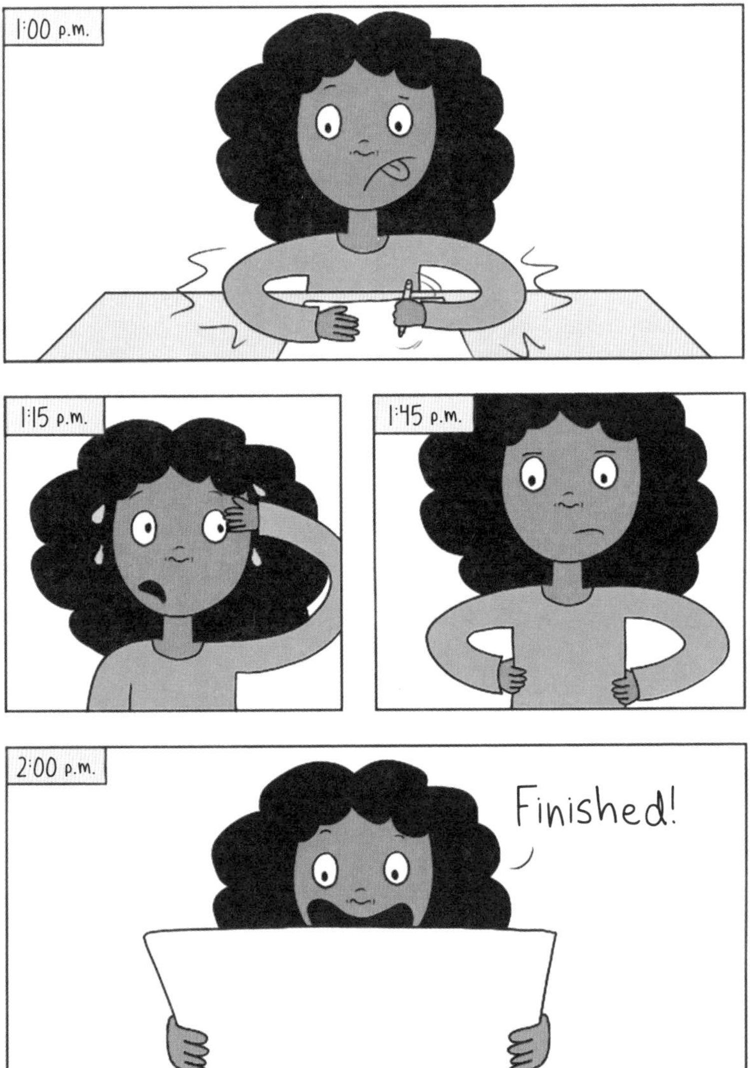
1:00 p.m.
1:15 p.m.
1:45 p.m.
2:00 p.m.
Finished!

With this piece, I wanted to communicate injustice, toxic beauty standards, the ethics of capitalism, and so much more.

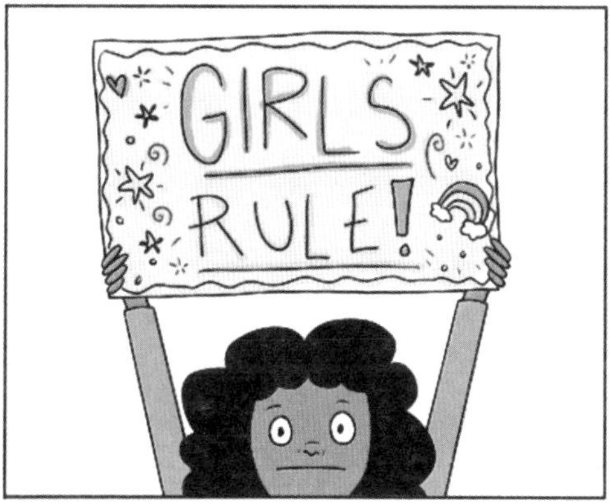
GIRLS RULE!

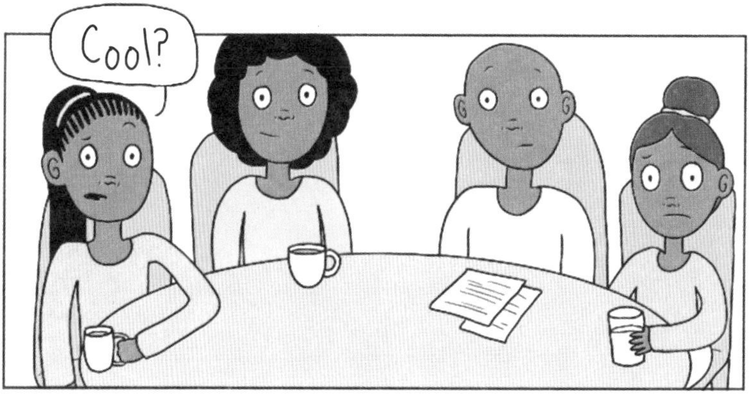
Cool?

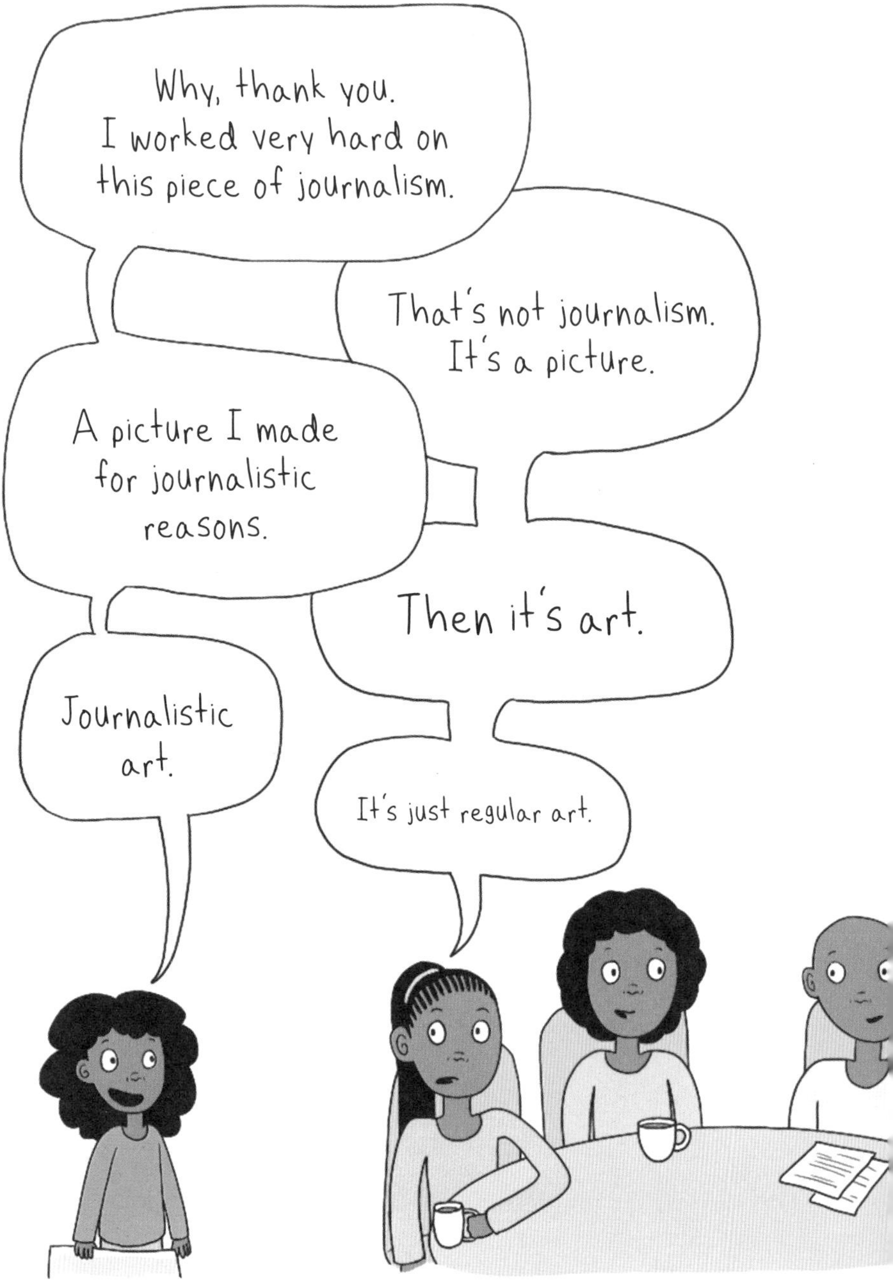
Why, thank you. I worked very hard on this piece of journalism.
That's not journalism. It's a picture.
A picture I made for journalistic reasons.
Then it's art.
Journalistic art.
It's just regular art.

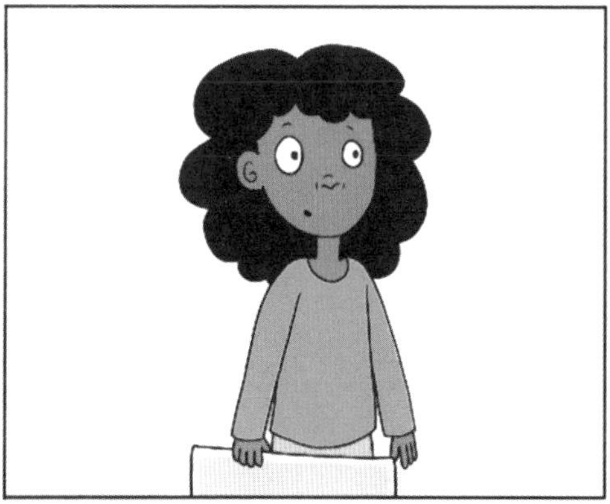

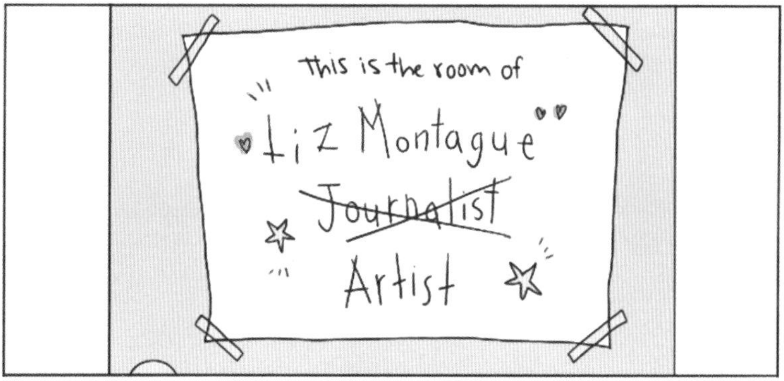
This is the room of
Liz Montague
~~Journalist~~
Artist

HURSTON MIDDLE SCHOOL

MARLTON, NEW JERSEY
2007–2010

A lot changed over the summer. All the brunettes in my class were now blond and had things called highlights.

I had grown two inches and was now offensively tall. And there was a new pause between when I thought something and when I said it.

Every action I took now felt observed, so I began to observe myself. I wasn't walking to math—I was watching myself walk to math. Nothing but bony legs and long strides that became even longer and quicker when I realized everyone else was also watching me walk to math.

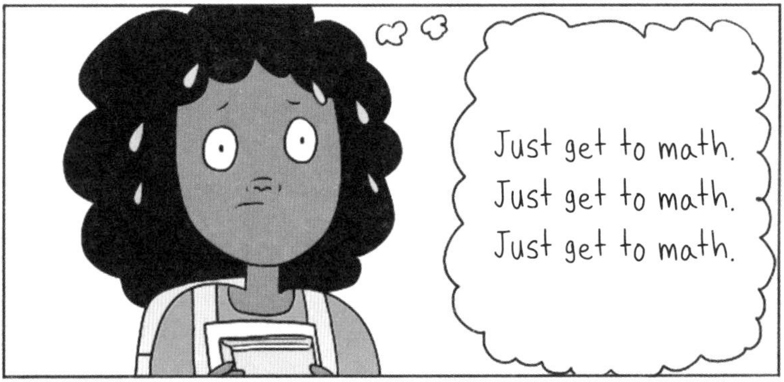
Just get to math.
Just get to math.
Just get to math.

I was on display against my will. I stood out from all the other girls in my classes.

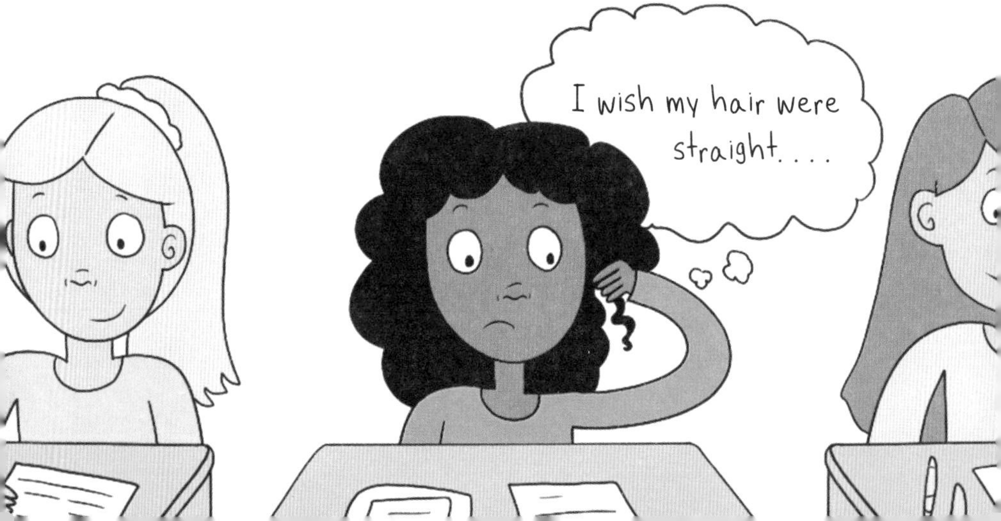
I wish my hair were straight. . . .

After school, I borrowed Olivia's hair straightener. I wanted my hair to be flippy and bouncy like the other girls'.

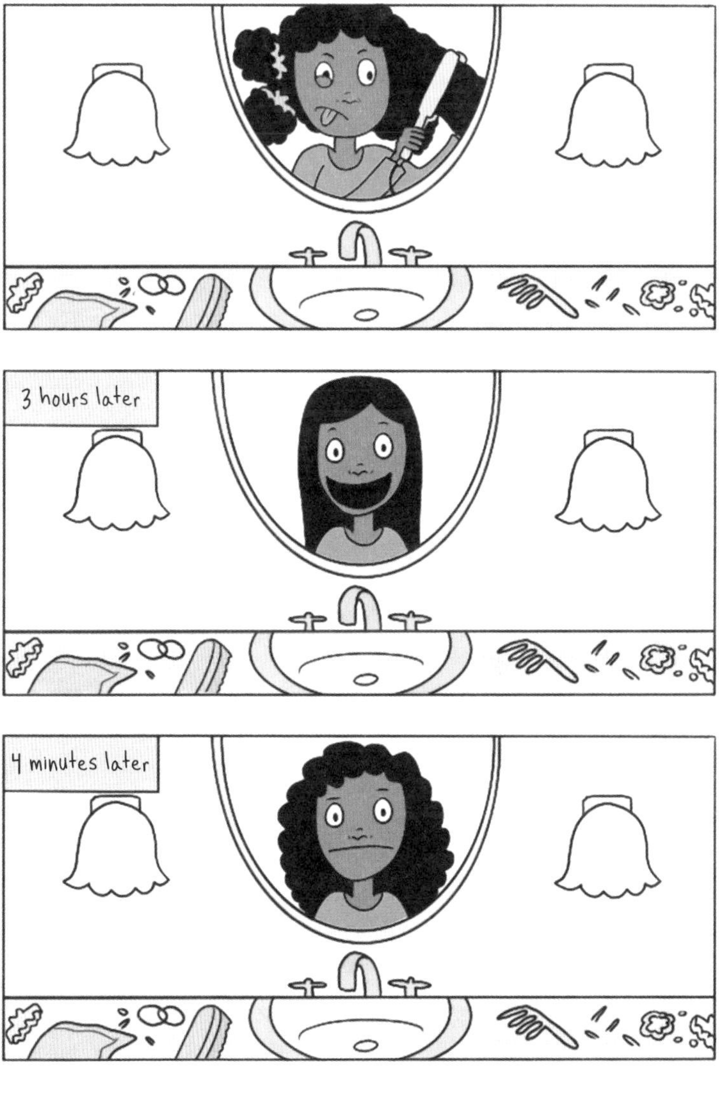
3 hours later
4 minutes later

The next morning, my hair looked awful. I was sure my day couldn't get any worse.

Then, to my horror, I was handed a Scantron test.

Sixth grade was not off to a great start.

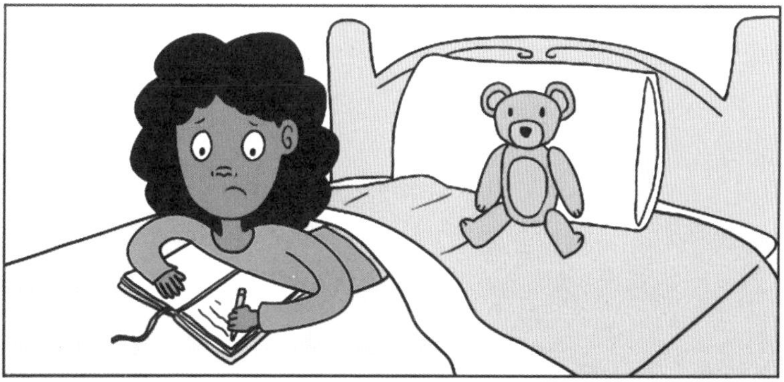

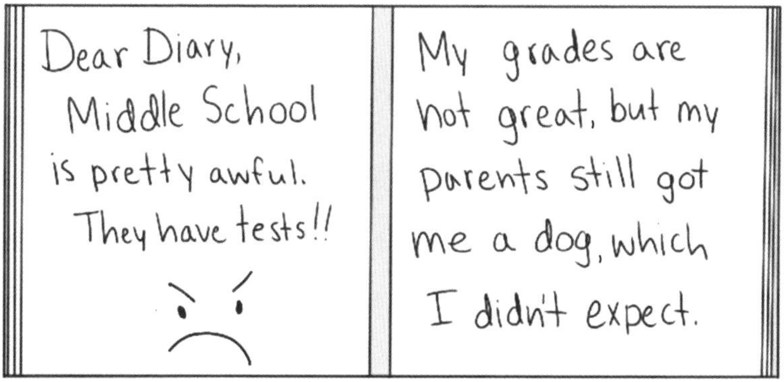
Dear Diary,
Middle School is pretty awful. They have tests!!
My grades are not great, but my parents still got me a dog, which I didn't expect.

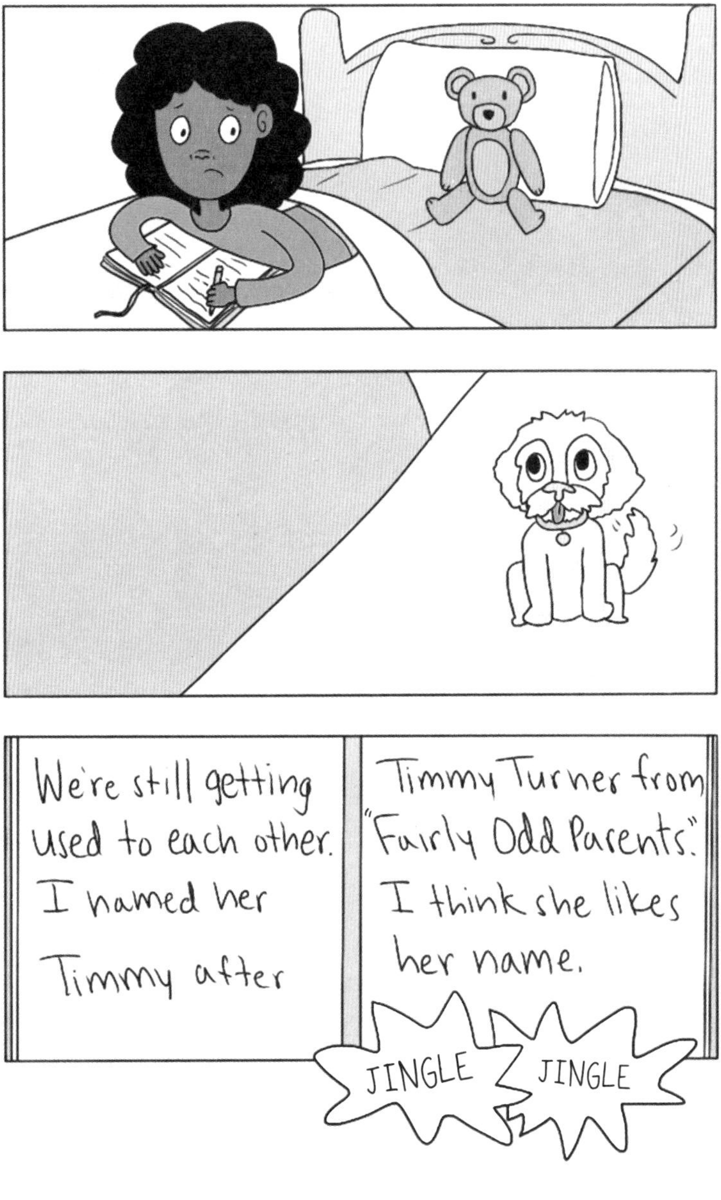
We're still getting used to each other. I named her Timmy after
Timmy Turner from "Fairly Odd Parents." I think she likes her name.
JINGLE
JINGLE

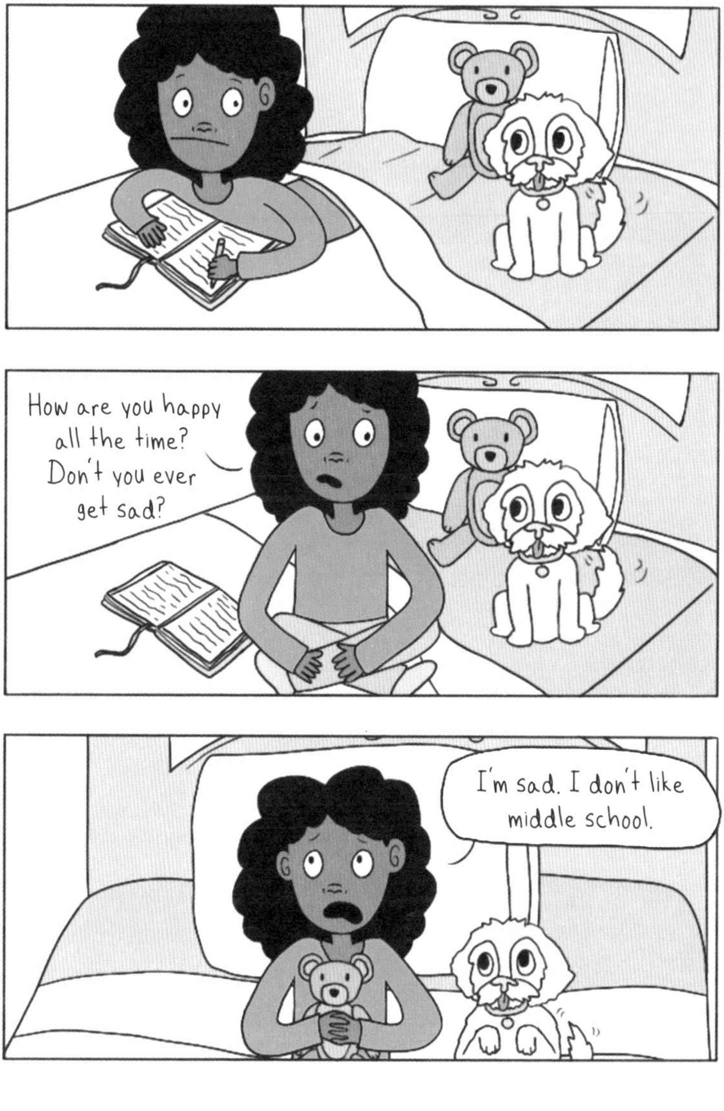
How are you happy all the time? Don't you ever get sad?
I'm sad. I don't like middle school.

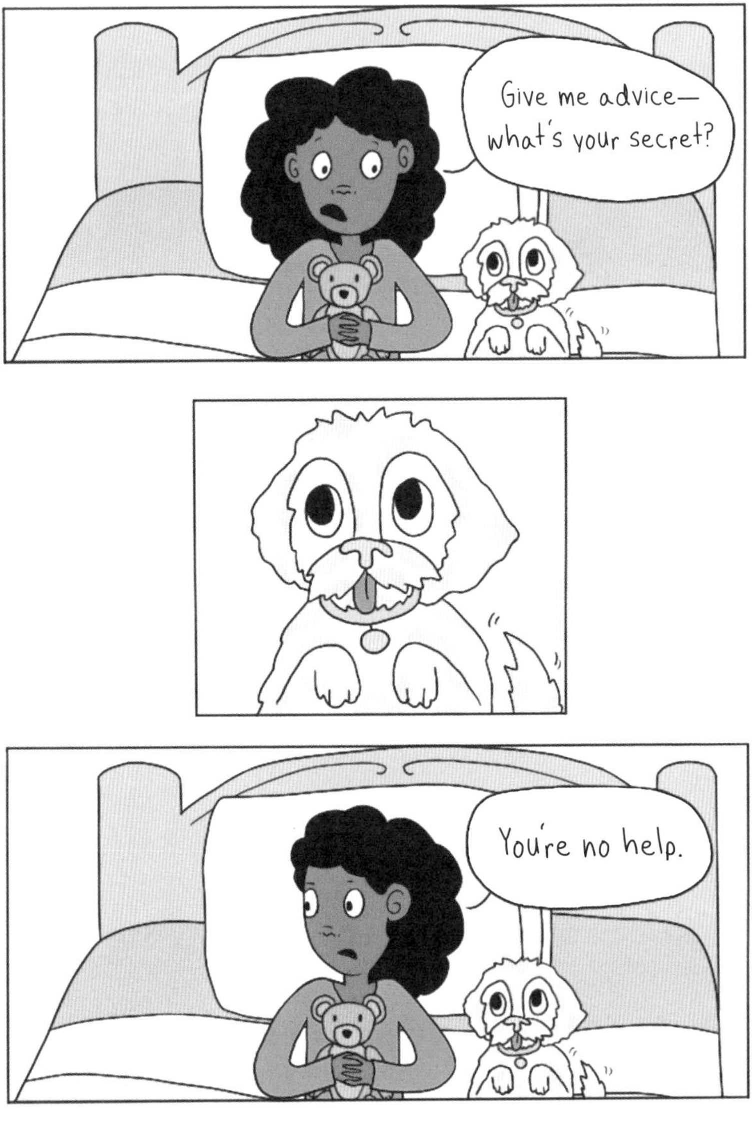
Give me advice—
what's your secret?
You're no help.

The next day at lunch, I decided sixth grade was officially the worst.

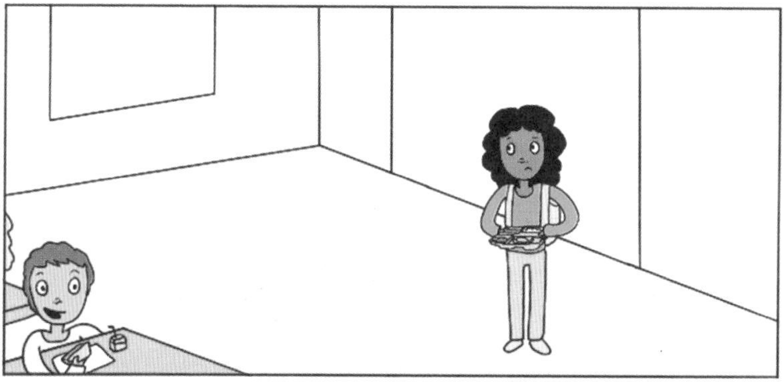

Usually I sat at a back table with girls I knew from Girl Scouts, but that day their table was full.

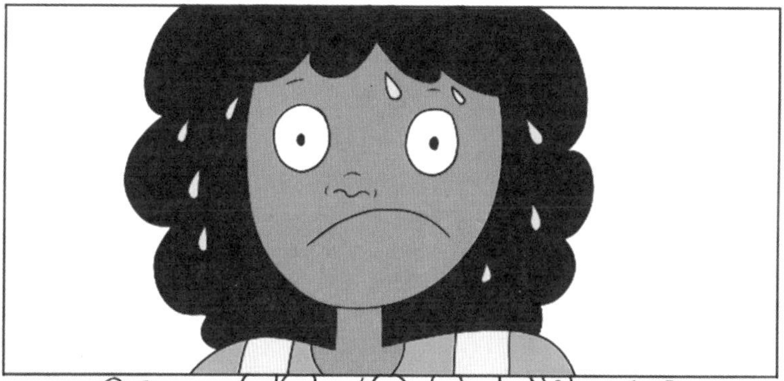

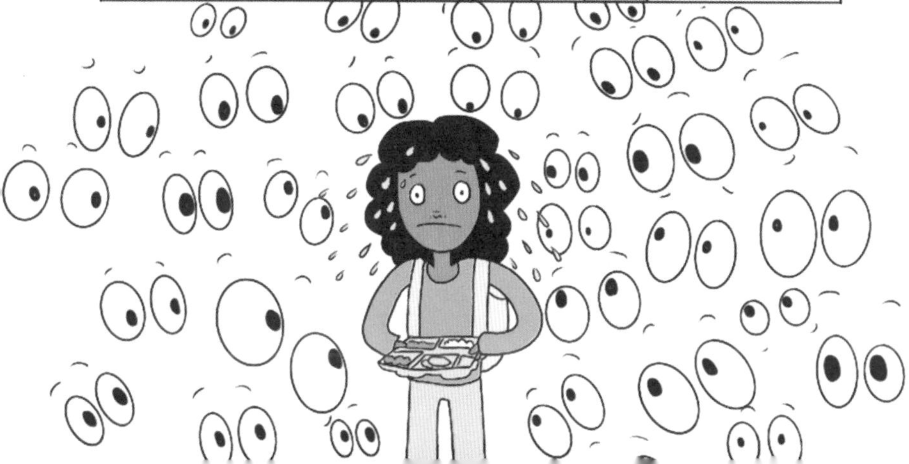

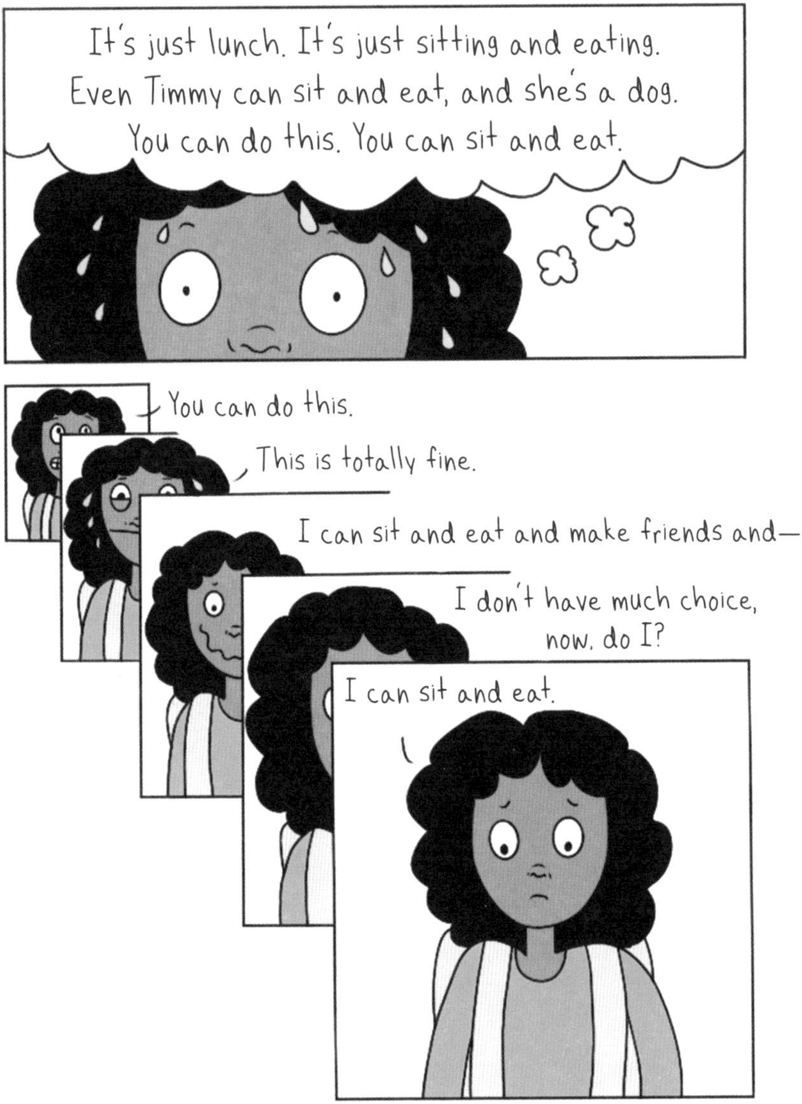
It's just lunch. It's just sitting and eating. Even Timmy can sit and eat, and she's a dog. You can do this. You can sit and eat.
You can do this.
This is totally fine.
I can sit and eat and make friends and—
I don't have much choice, now, do I?
I can sit and eat.

Hey, can I sit and eat here?

Sure!

I sat in the same spot every day for a few weeks, and it officially became My Table. I, Elizabeth Montague, had a table. I even started making friends with the girls who sat there.

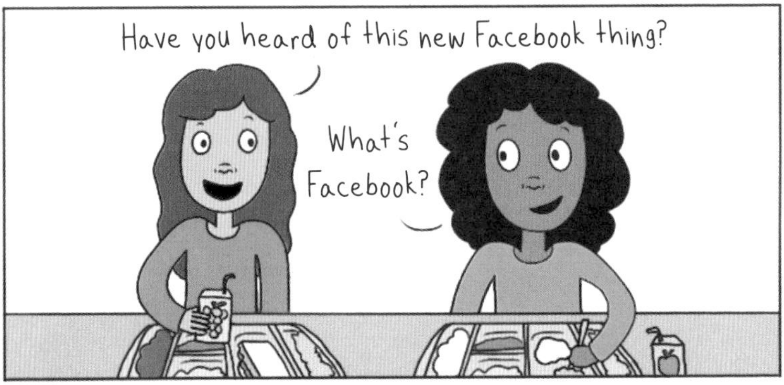
Have you heard of this new Facebook thing?
What's Facebook?

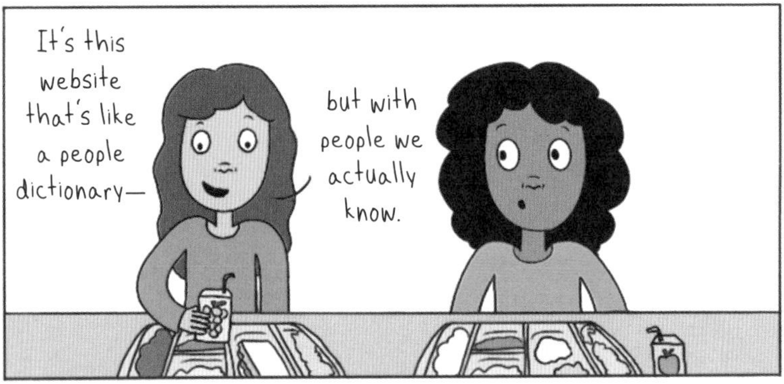
It's this website that's like a people dictionary—
but with people we actually know.

My older sisters had Myspace, but I'd never had any interest in that. As soon as I got home, though, I checked out Facebook. It was an entirely new frontier.

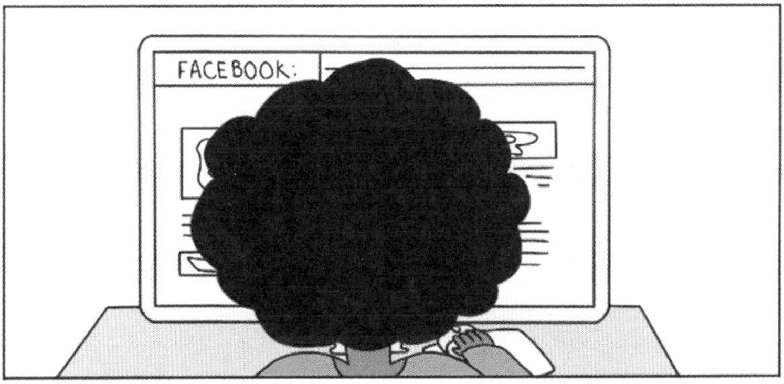
FACEBOOK:

It was nice being able to meet people without actually having to meet them and know things about them without actually having to talk to them.

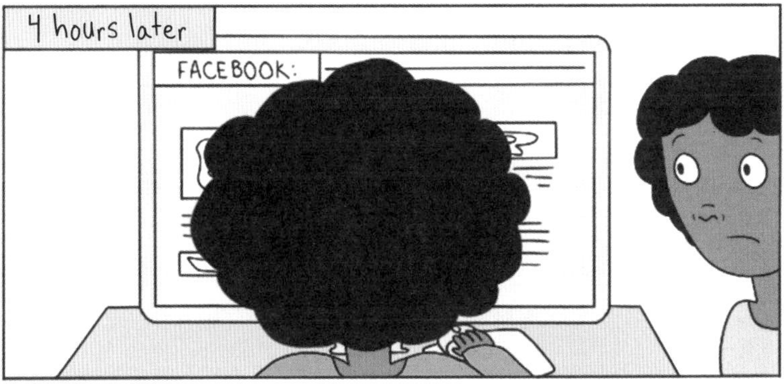
4 hours later
FACEBOOK:

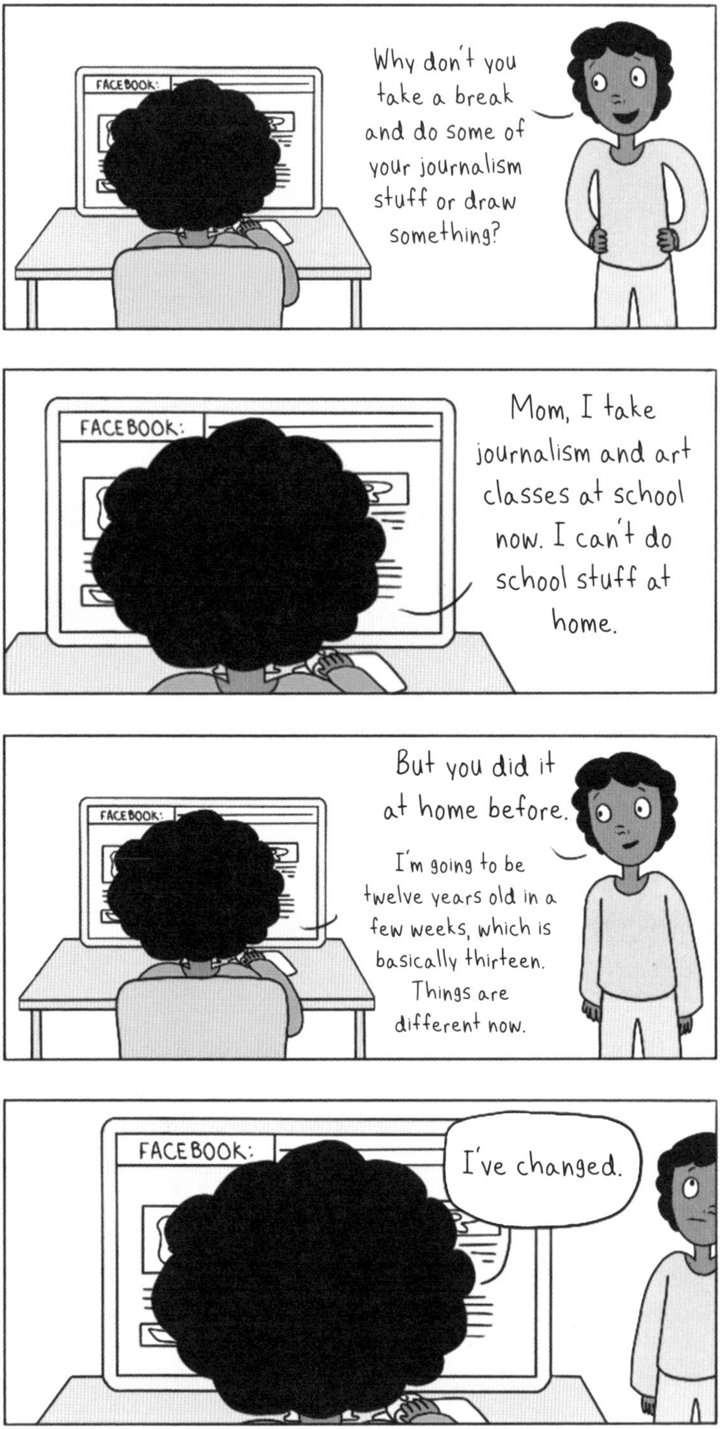
FACEBOOK:
Why don't you take a break and do some of your journalism stuff or draw something?
FACEBOOK:
Mom, I take journalism and art classes at school now. I can't do school stuff at home.
FACEBOOK:
But you did it at home before.
I'm going to be twelve years old in a few weeks, which is basically thirteen. Things are different now.
FACEBOOK:
I've changed.

A lot of things changed in 2008.

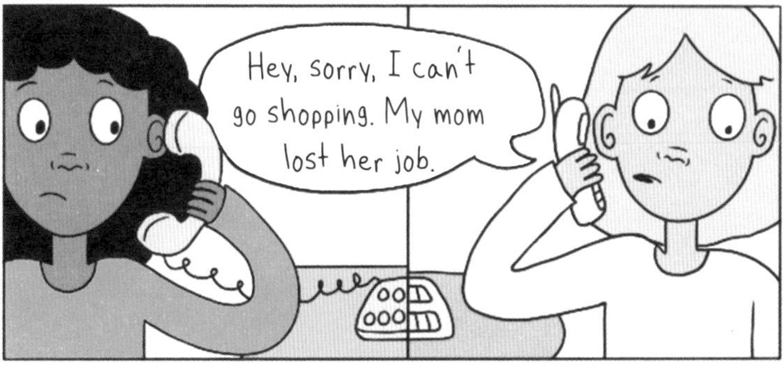
Hey, sorry, I can't go shopping. My mom lost her job.

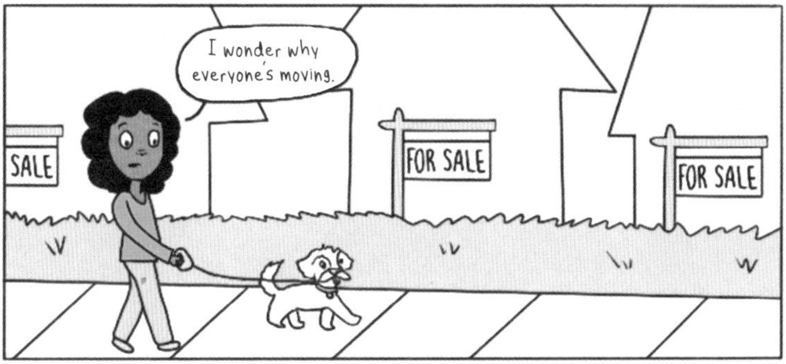
I wonder why everyone's moving.
SALE
FOR SALE
FOR SALE

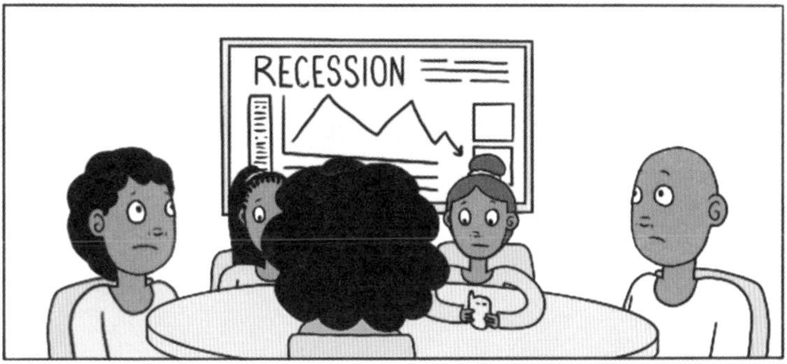
RECESSION

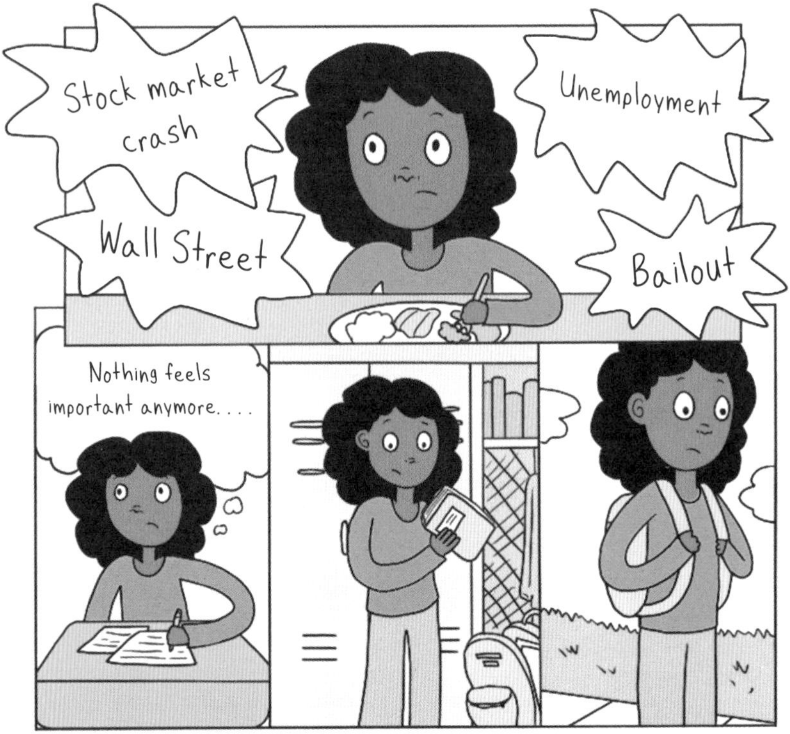
Stock market crash
Wall Street
Unemployment
Bailout
Nothing feels important anymore. . . .

Sixth grade felt small.

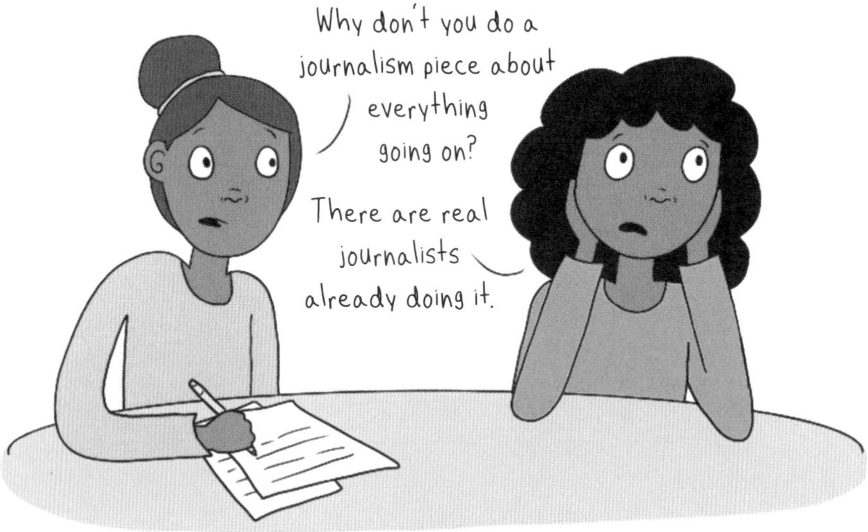
Why don't you do a journalism piece about everything going on?
There are real journalists already doing it.

The school year rolled to a stop like a marble on flat ground.

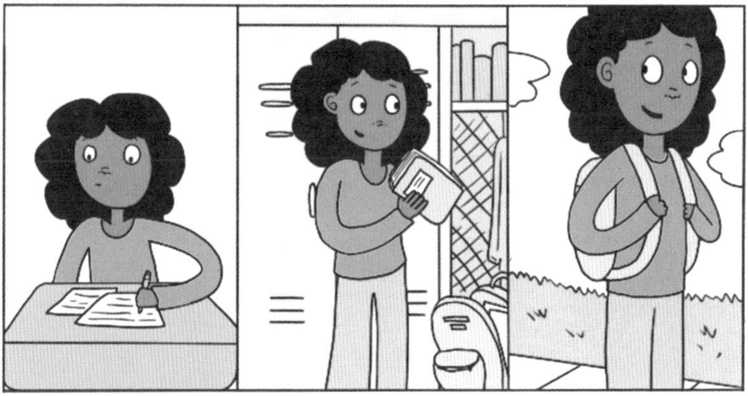

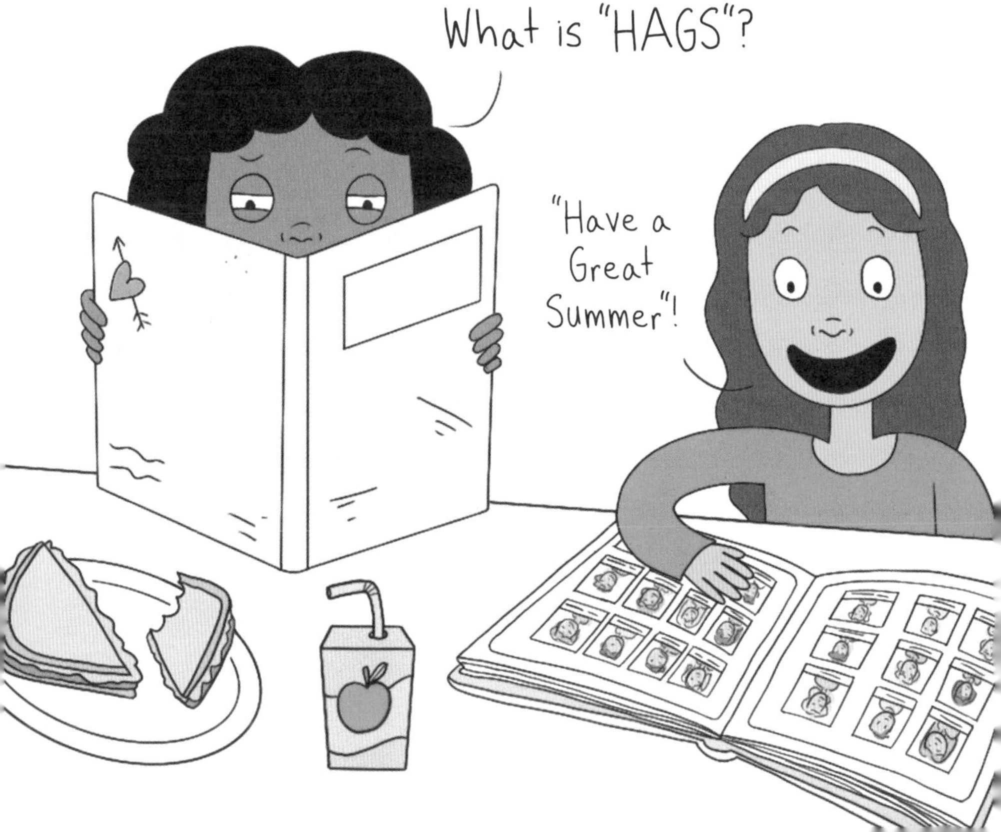
What is "HAGS"?
"Have a Great Summer"!

Summer started with Rachel leaving.

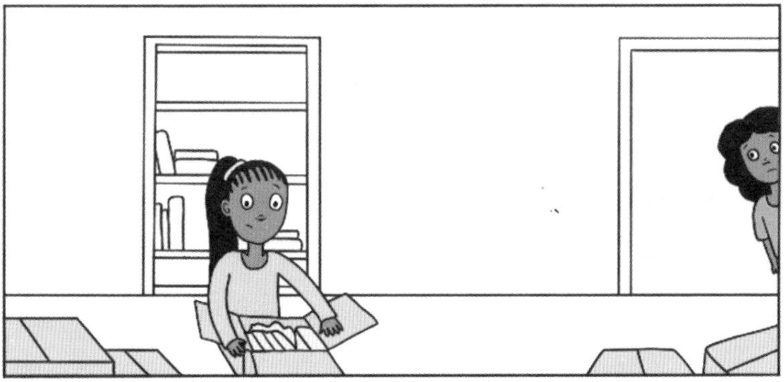

She got an athletic scholarship for school, and practice was beginning right away.

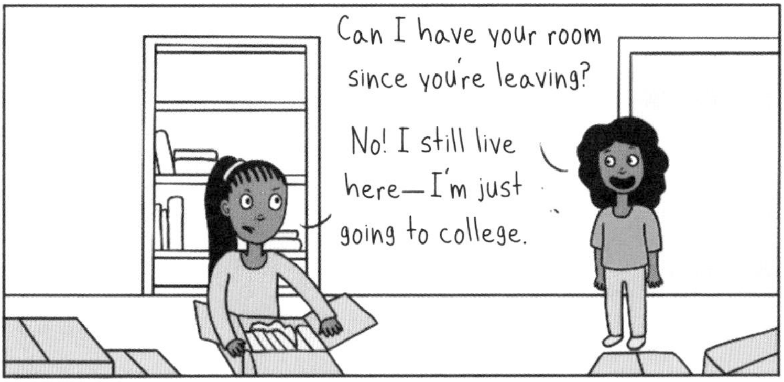
Can I have your room since you're leaving?
No! I still live here—I'm just going to college.

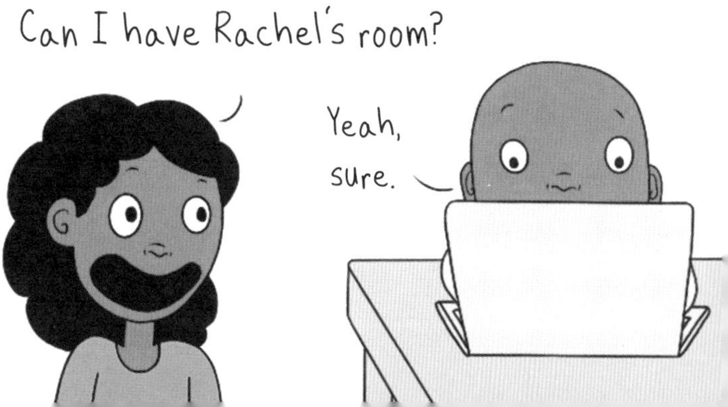
Can I have Rachel's room?
Yeah, sure.

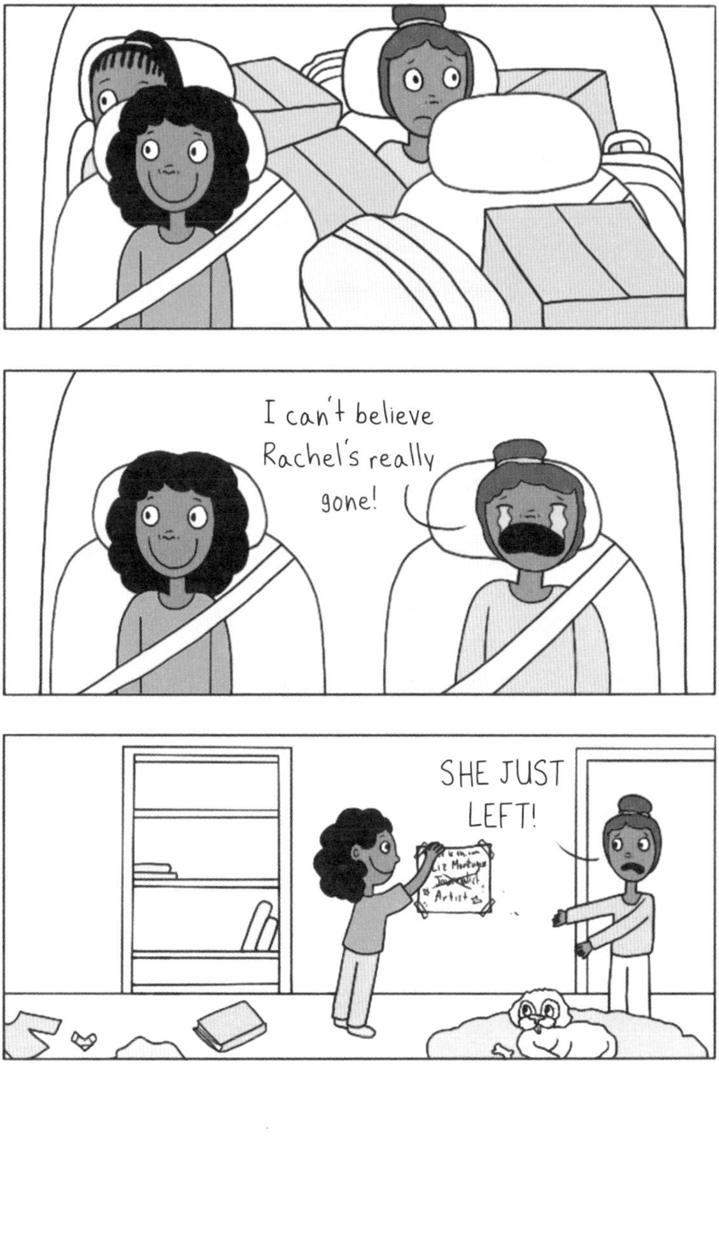
I can't believe Rachel's really gone!
SHE JUST LEFT!

Summer always starts fun and gets boring really quickly. I decided to ask Olivia to get me a job.

You steal Rachel's room on the day she moves out, and now I'm supposed to do **you** a favor?

Yeah.

She worked at a farm up the road a few hours a week. She got free doughnuts and could afford to go to the movies with her friends.

A few weeks later, I started my new job.

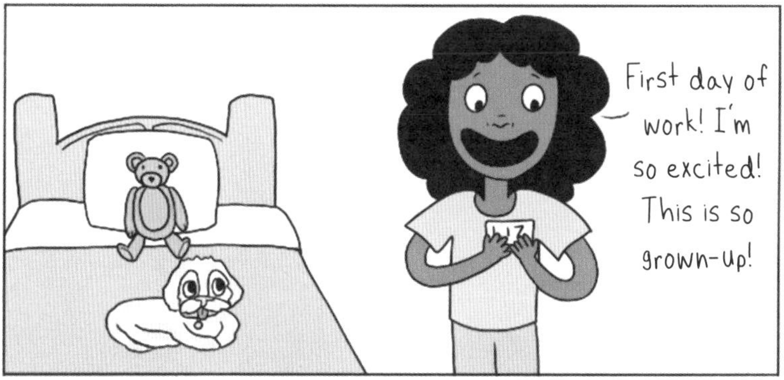
First day of work! I'm so excited! This is so grown-up!
LIZ

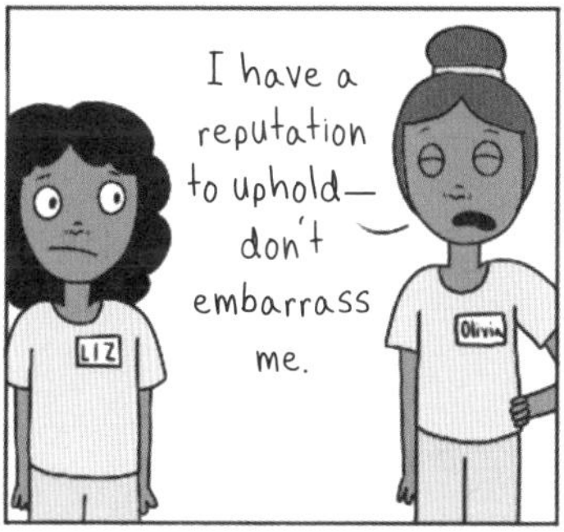
I have a reputation to uphold— don't embarrass me.
LIZ
Olivia

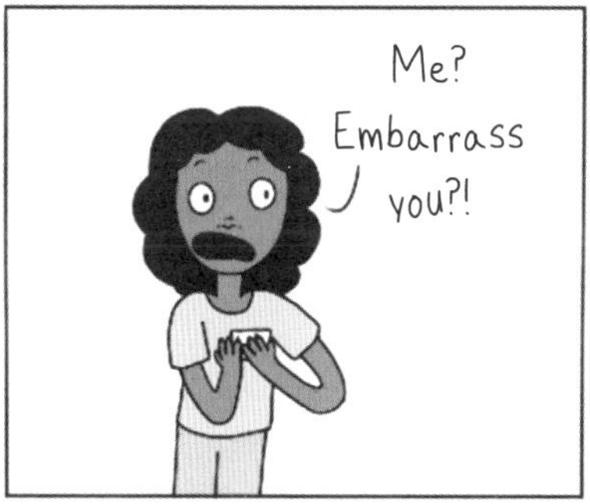
Me? Embarrass you?!

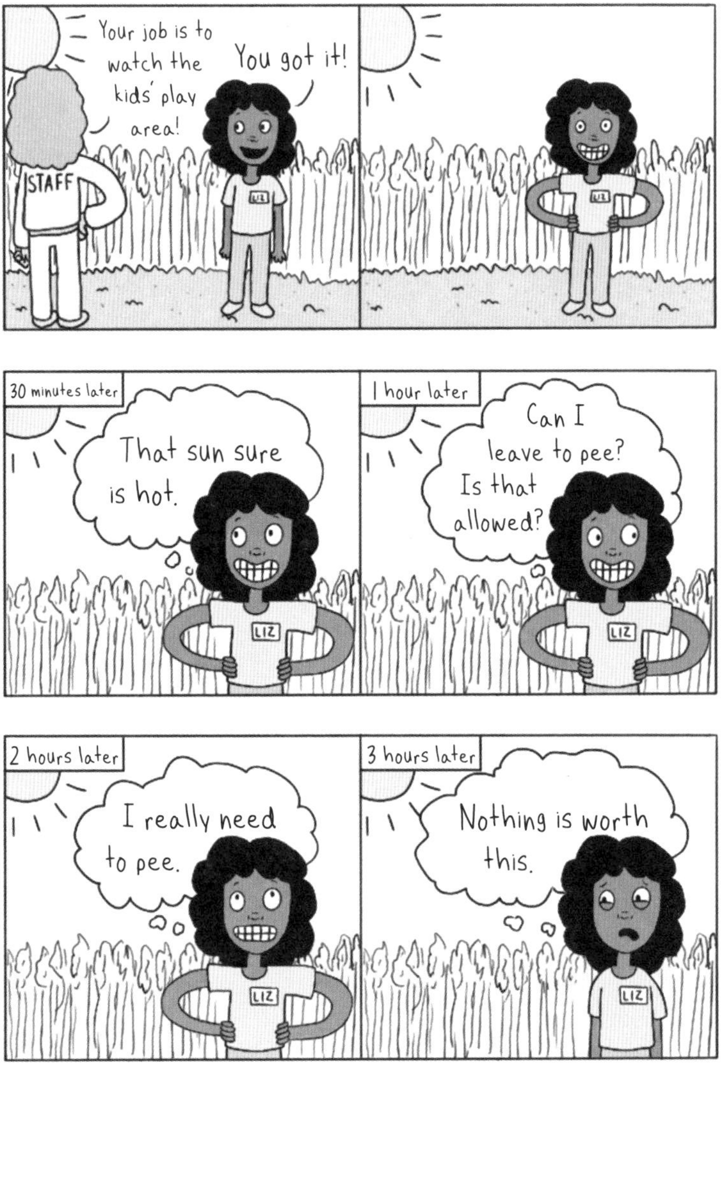

Your job is to watch the kids' play area!
You got it!
STAFF
LIZ
LIZ
30 minutes later
That sun sure is hot.
LIZ
1 hour later
Can I leave to pee? Is that allowed?
LIZ
2 hours later
I really need to pee.
LIZ
3 hours later
Nothing is worth this.
LIZ

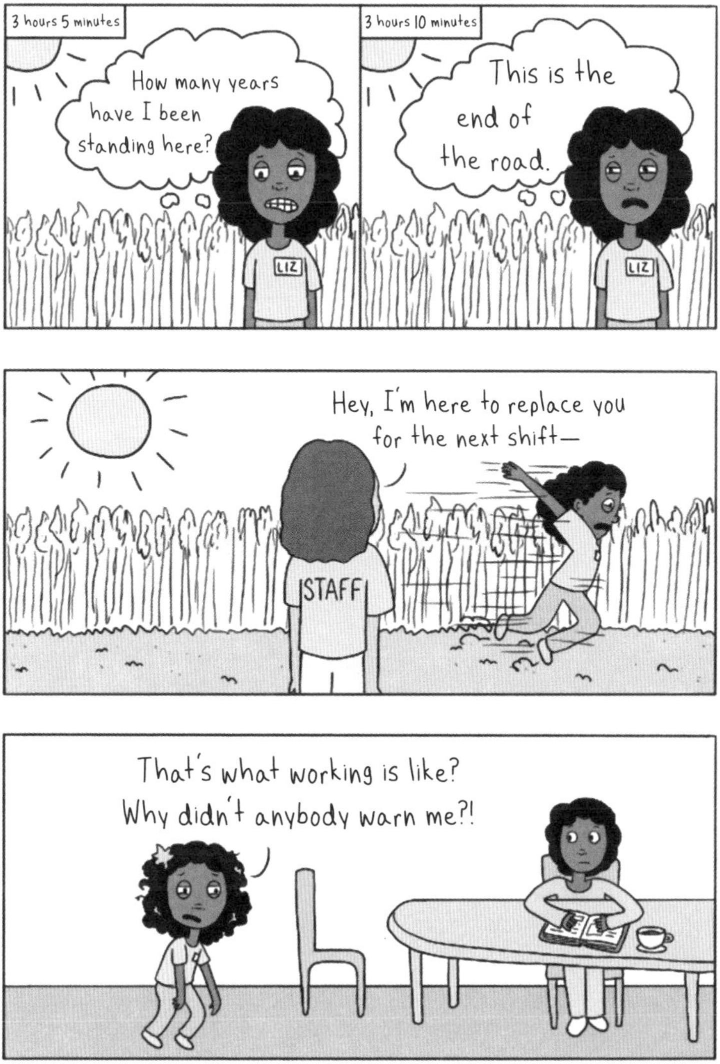
3 hours 5 minutes
How many years have I been standing here?
LIZ
3 hours 10 minutes
This is the end of the road.
LIZ
Hey, I'm here to replace you for the next shift—
STAFF
That's what working is like? Why didn't anybody warn me?!

How was your first day?
I will never stand again.
There's a leaf in your hair.
Hello, comrade. We did it.
We made it.

I advocated for myself during my next shift later that week.

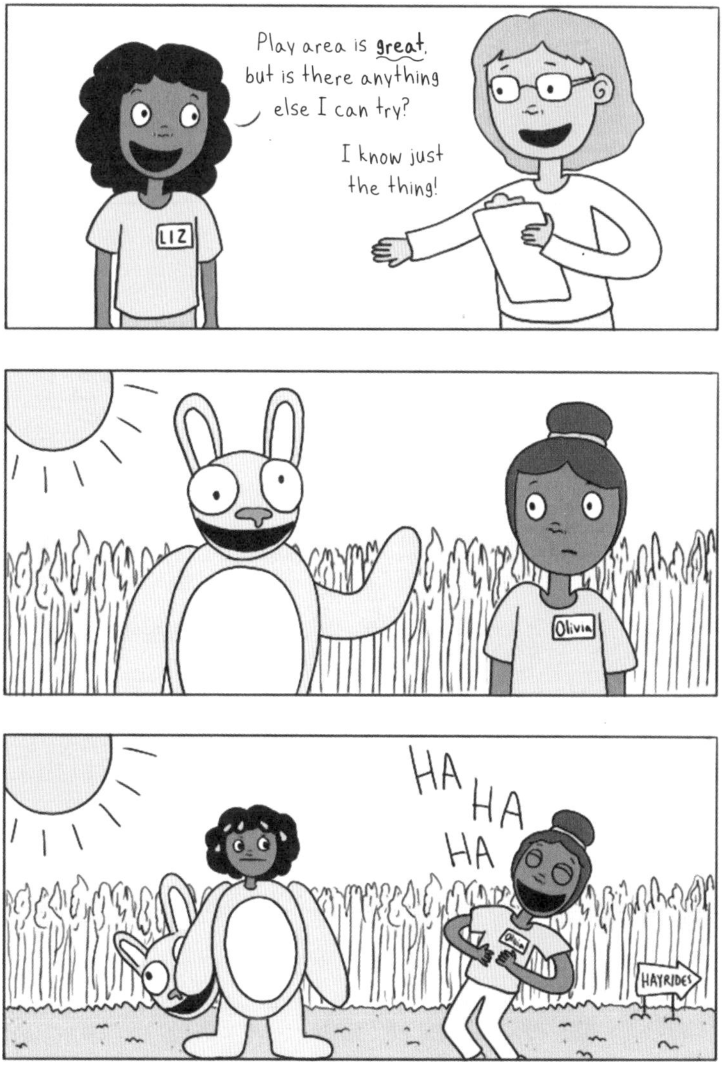
Play area is great, but is there anything else I can try?
I know just the thing!
LIZ
Olivia
HA HA HA
Olivia
HAYRIDES

Toward the end of summer, my luck started to change.

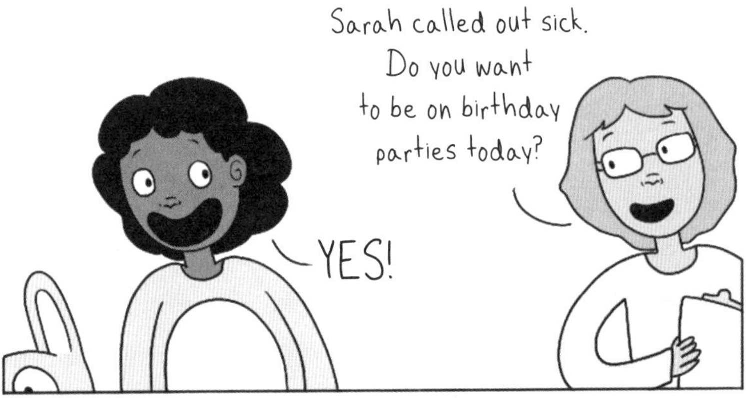
Sarah called out sick. Do you want to be on birthday parties today?
YES!

Birthday parties were the big leagues. Our job was mostly to just help set up and watch the kids, but afterward we usually got cake or pizza if there were any leftovers.

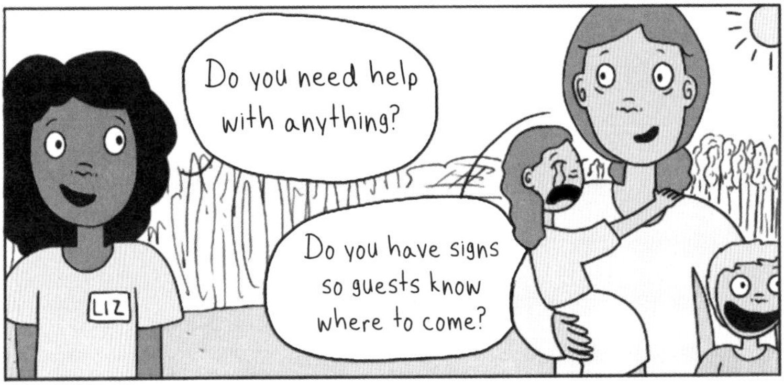
Do you need help with anything?
Do you have signs so guests know where to come?
LIZ

Happy Birthday
This is amazing! You're a very gifted artist.
20

Summer flew by after that, and seventh grade started with a bang.

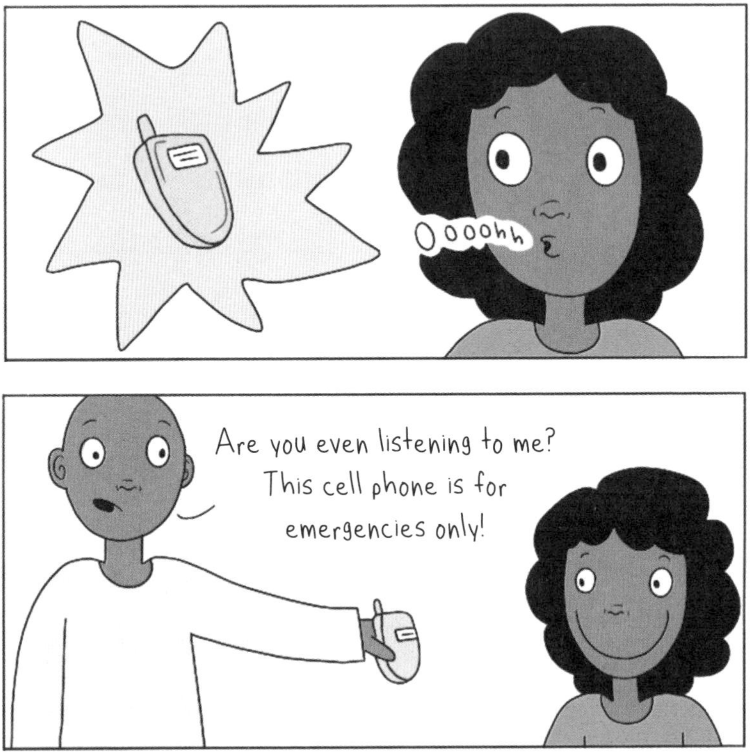
Oooohh
Are you even listening to me? This cell phone is for emergencies only!

Having a cell phone officially cemented my place in middle school society. I was on the edge of thirteen with a job to go to (only on the weekends) and friends to text. A boy to text too.

A boy named Patrick. He went by Pat, just like how I went by Liz instead of Elizabeth. We had so much in common.

> **Patrezio38:** hey
>
> **Trackgurlxoxo:** hey
>
> **Patrezio38:** wats up
>
> **Trackgurlxoxo:** nmu?
>
> **Patrezio38:** nm
>
> **Trackgurlxoxo:** cool
>
> **Patrezio38:** cool

We were in the same grade, so I saw him around a lot, but I was much better onscreen than I was in person.

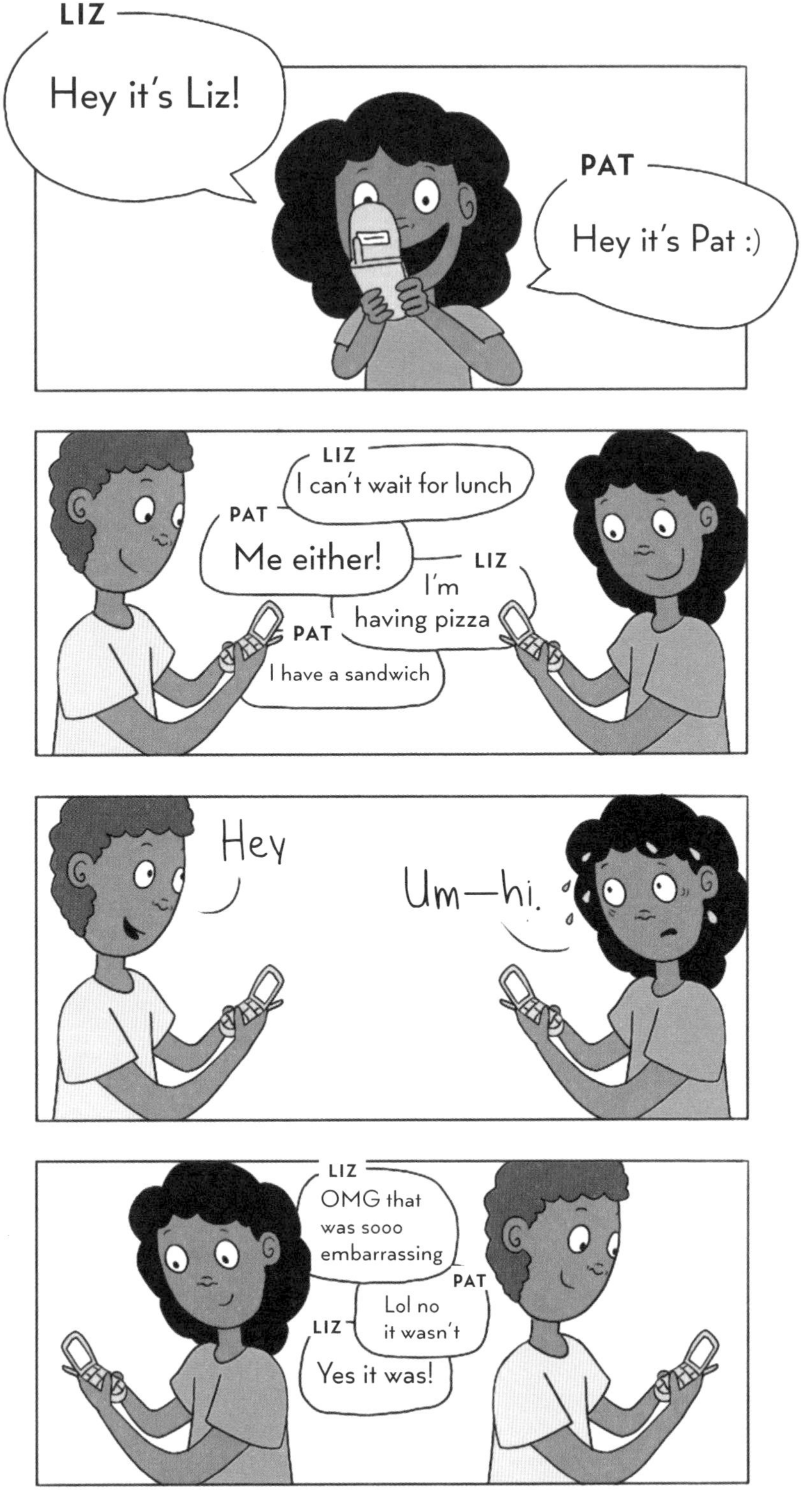
LIZ
Hey it's Liz!
PAT
Hey it's Pat :)
LIZ
I can't wait for lunch
PAT
Me either!
LIZ
I'm having pizza
PAT
I have a sandwich
Hey
Um—hi.
LIZ
OMG that was sooo embarrassing
PAT
Lol no it wasn't
LIZ
Yes it was!

We definitely liked each other, but it was complicated.

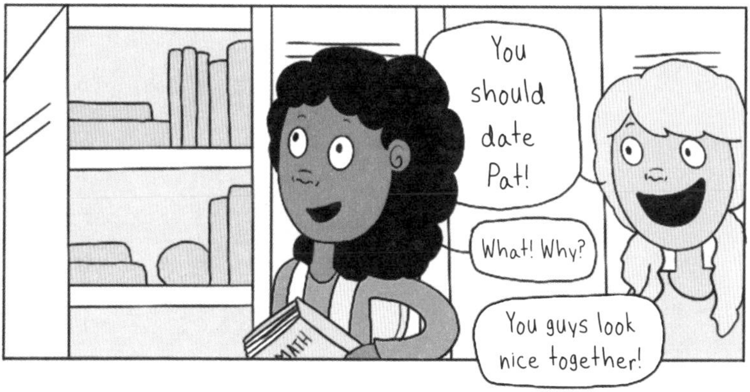
You should date Pat!
What! Why?
You guys look nice together!
MATH

You guys look nice together translated to The only two Black kids in school must be soul mates.

The annoying part was maybe we **were** soul mates,

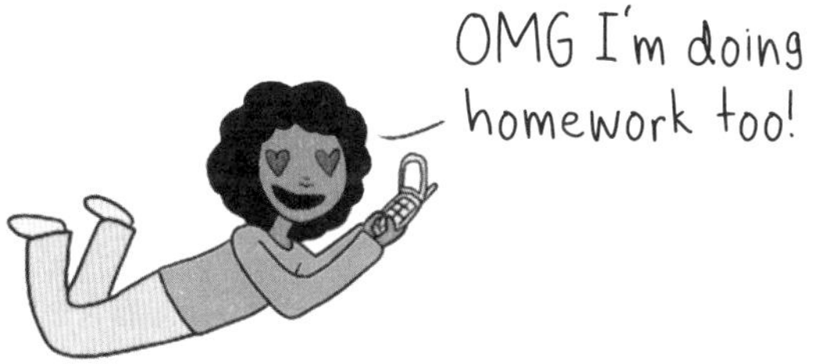
OMG I'm doing homework too!

but I didn't want everyone thinking we were soul mates just because we were both Black.

My town was not a hub of diversity.

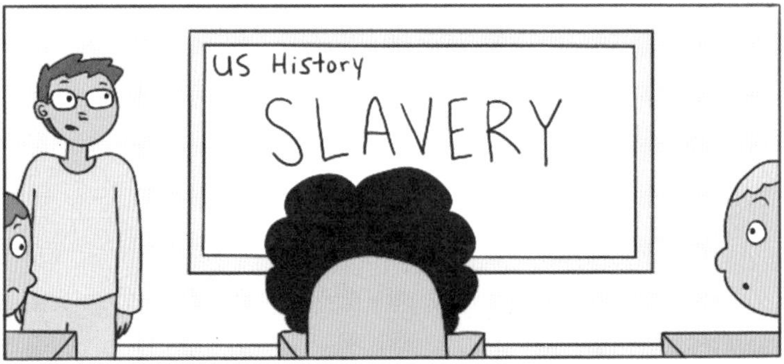
US History
SLAVERY

With the exception of the first two weeks of any US history class, I usually felt invisible. My classmates did the same choreography every time:

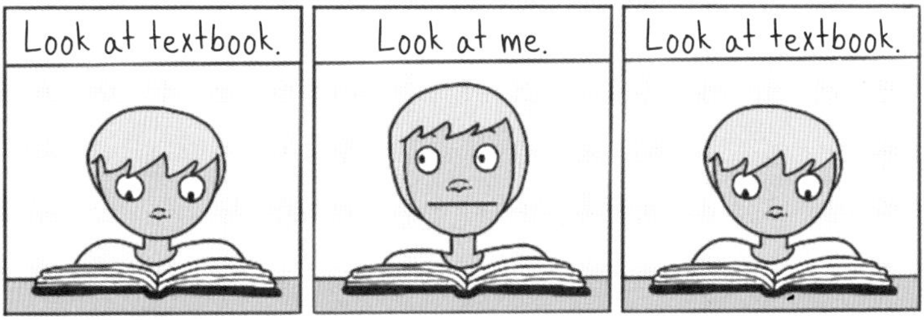
Look at textbook.
Look at me.
Look at textbook.

But others had it worse than me, and not just during the slavery talk, but all the time. I guess if I had to choose, I'd rather be invisible than be called a terrorist.

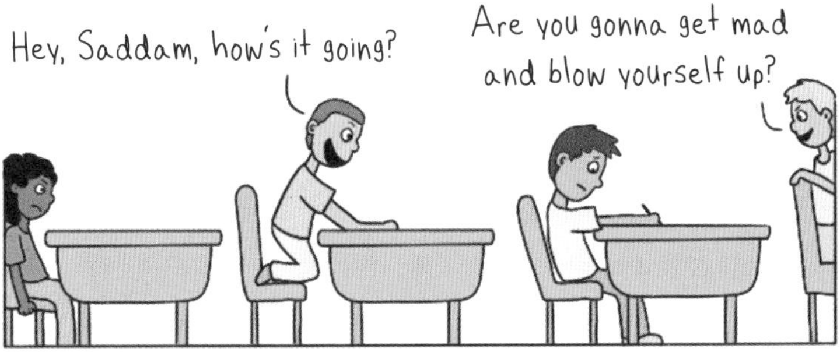
Hey, Saddam, how's it going?
Are you gonna get mad and blow yourself up?

But I was angry that I had to choose. I felt like my white classmates (especially the boys) were allowed to be ignorant, but I wasn't.

LIZ
Does it ever bother you?

PAT
What?

LIZ
That white kids can do and say whatever they want and we can't.

PAT
You could if you wanted. I do.

LIZ
It's not the same, and you know it!

PAT
You're overthinking this.

I had no desire to bully people or be mean, but being so aware was exhausting.

I talked to my sister about it when I got home from school.

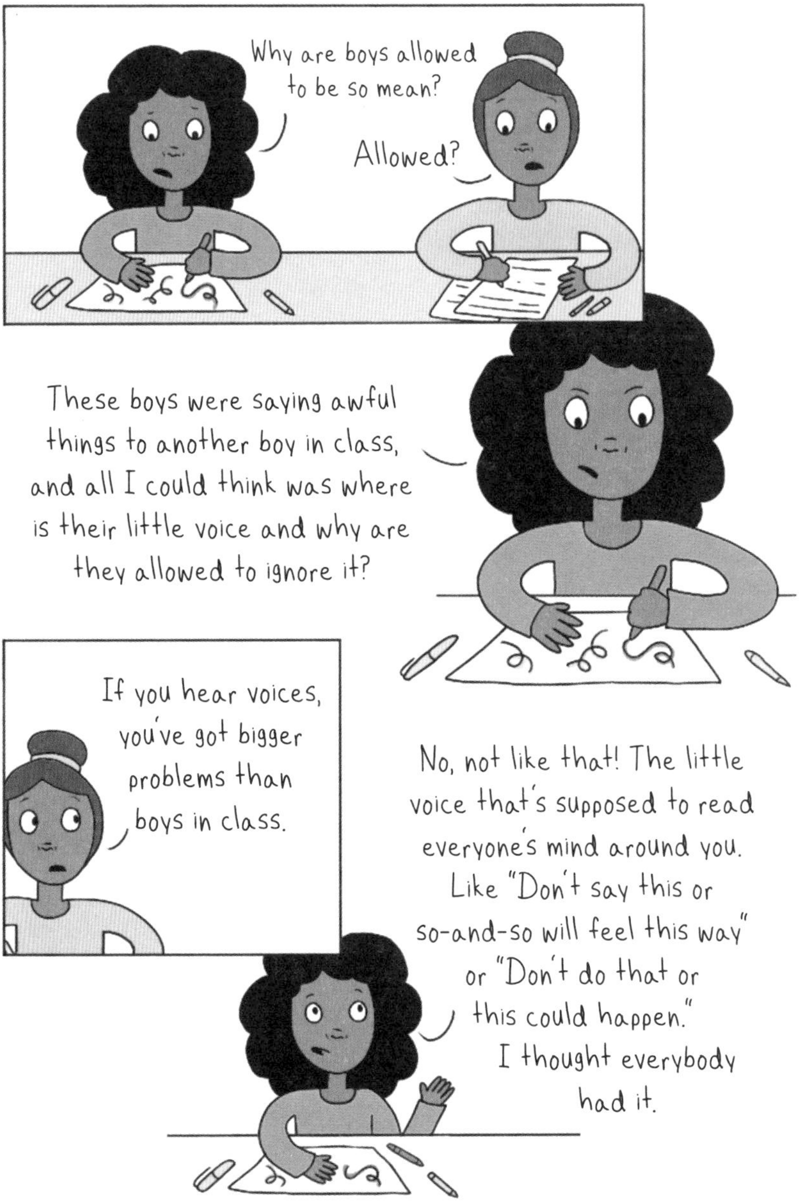
Why are boys allowed to be so mean?
Allowed?
These boys were saying awful things to another boy in class, and all I could think was where is their little voice and why are they allowed to ignore it?
If you hear voices, you've got bigger problems than boys in class.
No, not like that! The little voice that's supposed to read everyone's mind around you. Like "Don't say this or so-and-so will feel this way" or "Don't do that or this could happen." I thought everybody had it.

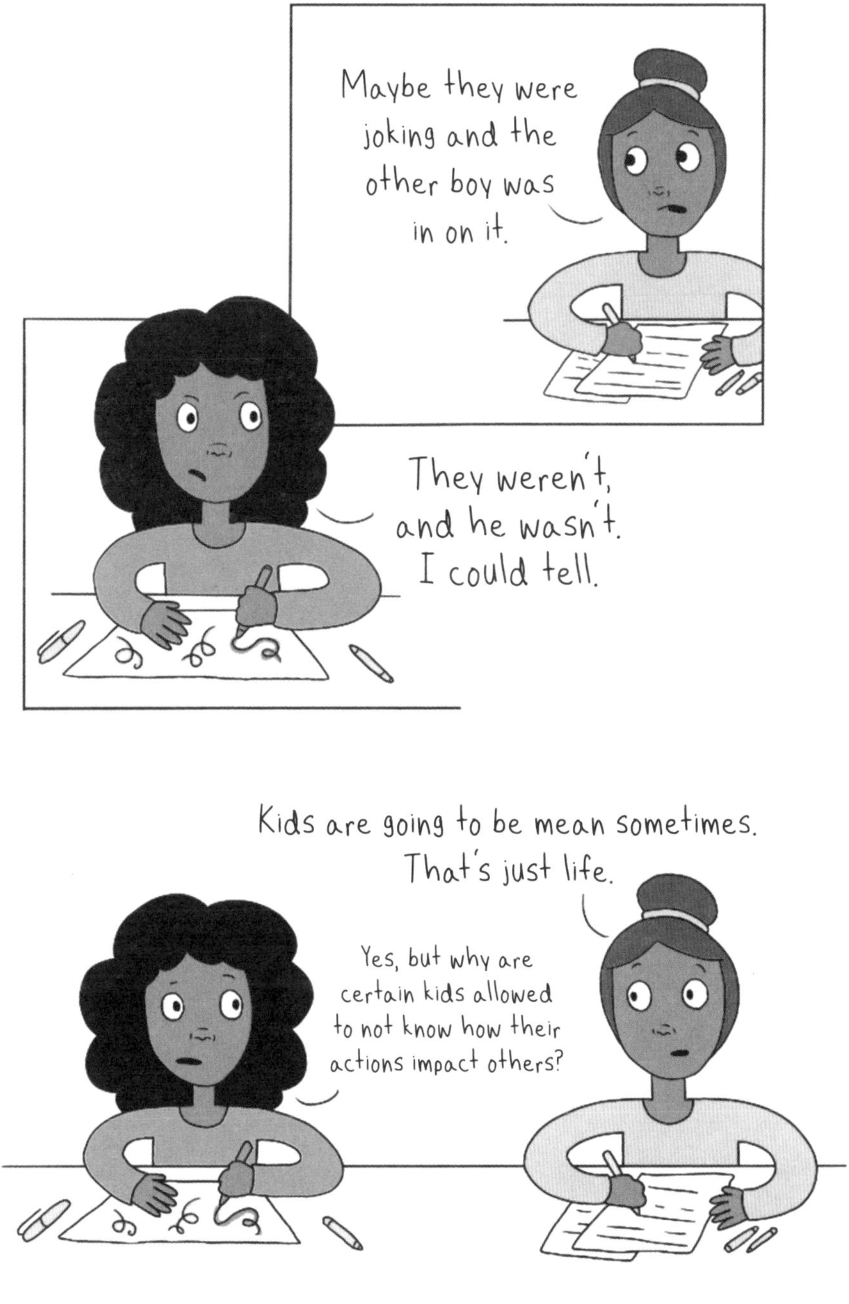

Maybe they were joking and the other boy was in on it.
They weren't, and he wasn't. I could tell.
Kids are going to be mean sometimes. That's just life.
Yes, but why are certain kids allowed to not know how their actions impact others?

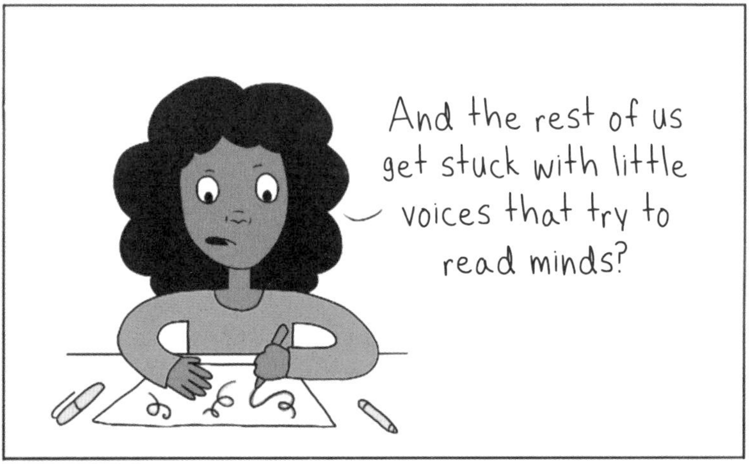
And the rest of us get stuck with little voices that try to read minds?

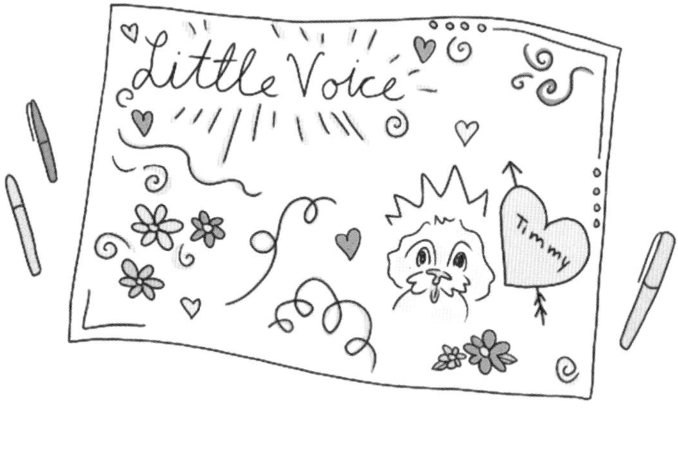
Little Voice
Timmy

I didn't mean to draw anything while we talked. I was just doodling on what was supposed to be homework.

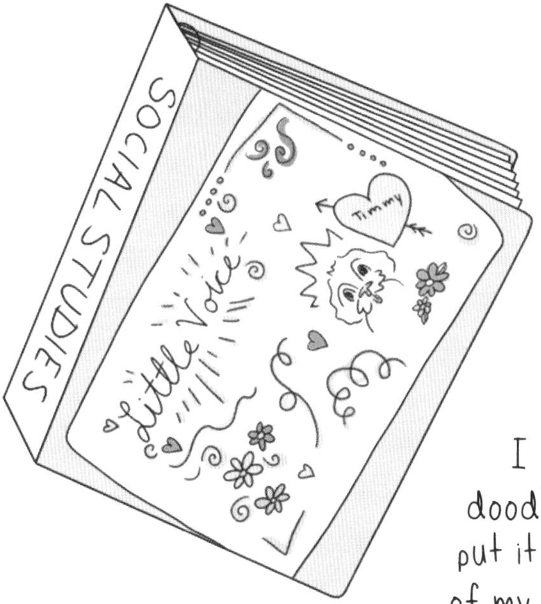
SOCIAL STUDIES
Little Voice
Timmy

I liked the doodle enough to put it in the cover of my school binder the next day.

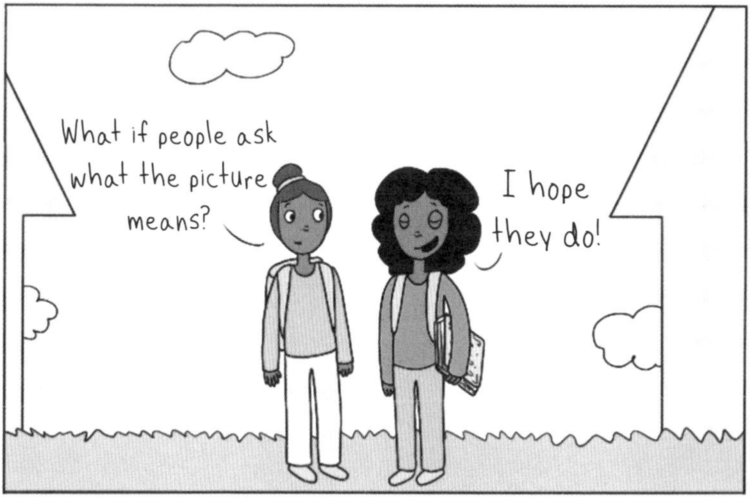
What if people ask what the picture means?
I hope they do!

And the more I thought about it, the more I realized doodling really helped me think.

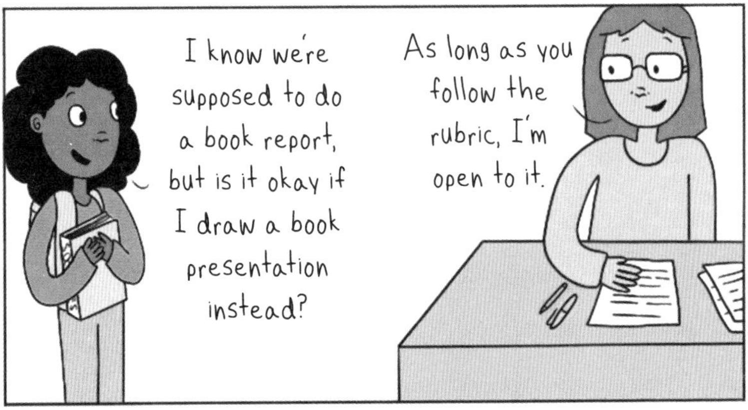
I know we're supposed to do a book report, but is it okay if I draw a book presentation instead?
As long as you follow the rubric, I'm open to it.

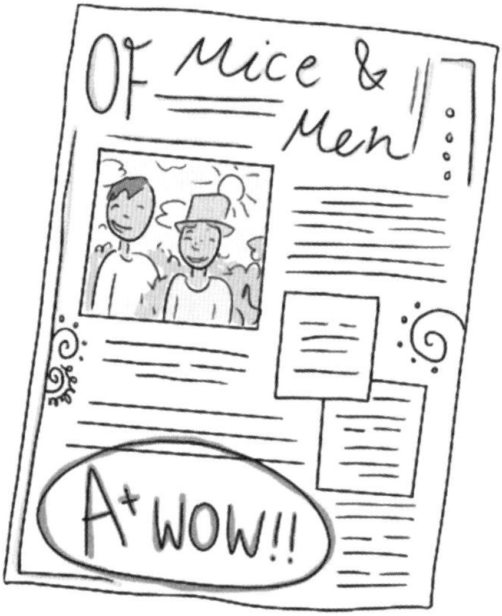
Of Mice & Men
A+ WOW!!

After that, I drew every assignment I could.

My classes were becoming much more manageable, but extracurriculars were becoming more and more important to my future. I'd done sports my entire life.

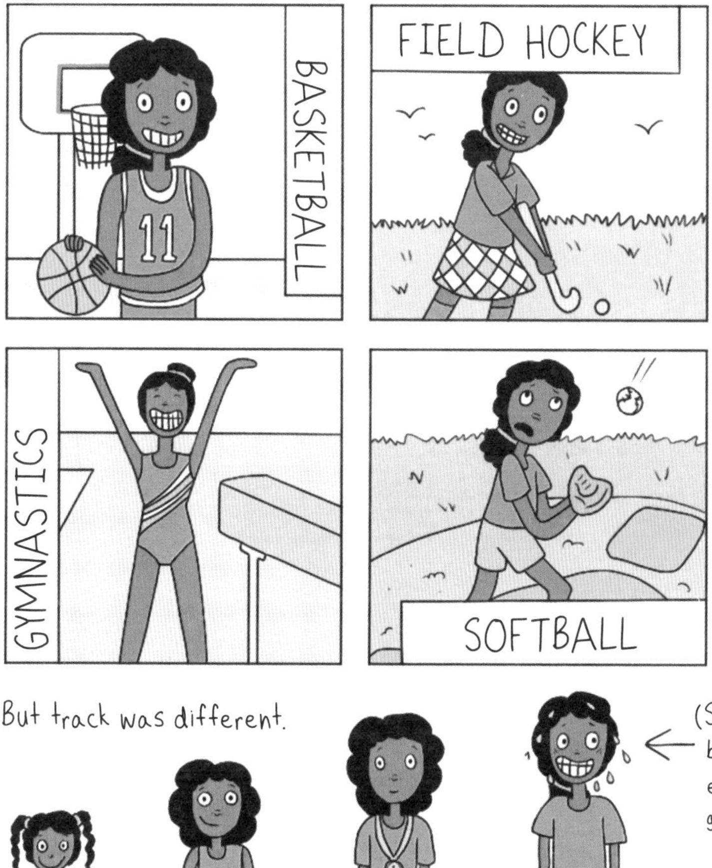
BASKETBALL
11
FIELD HOCKEY
GYMNASTICS
SOFTBALL

But track was different.

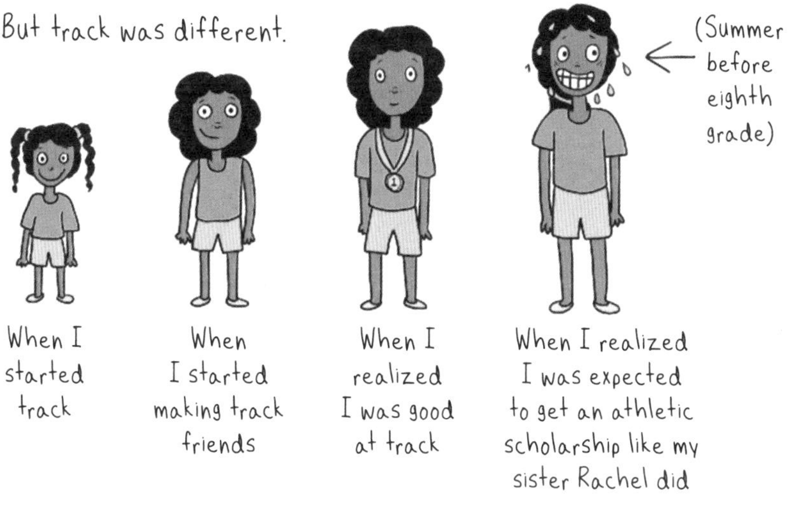
(Summer before eighth grade)
When I started track
When I started making track friends
When I realized I was good at track
When I realized I was expected to get an athletic scholarship like my sister Rachel did

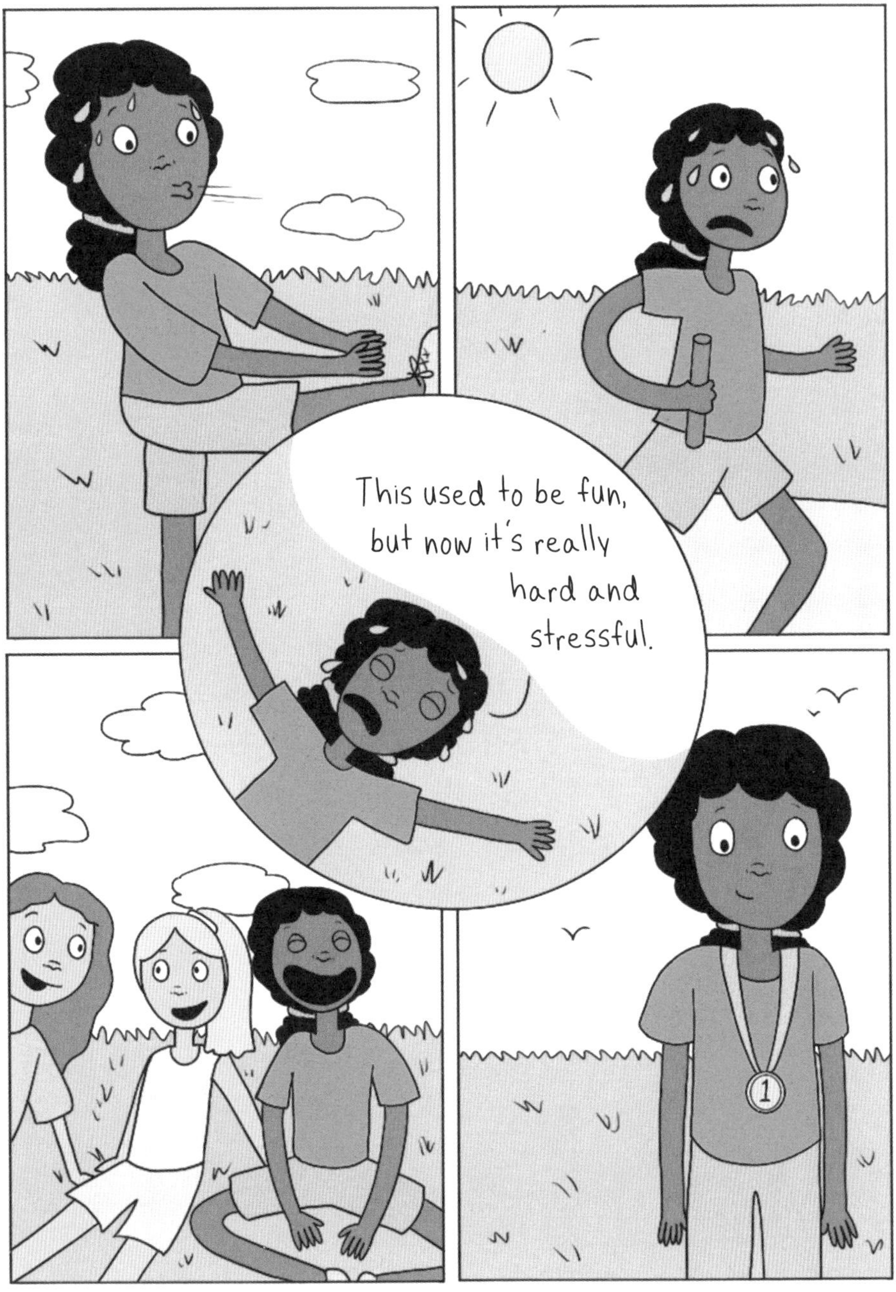
This used to be fun, but now it's really hard and stressful.

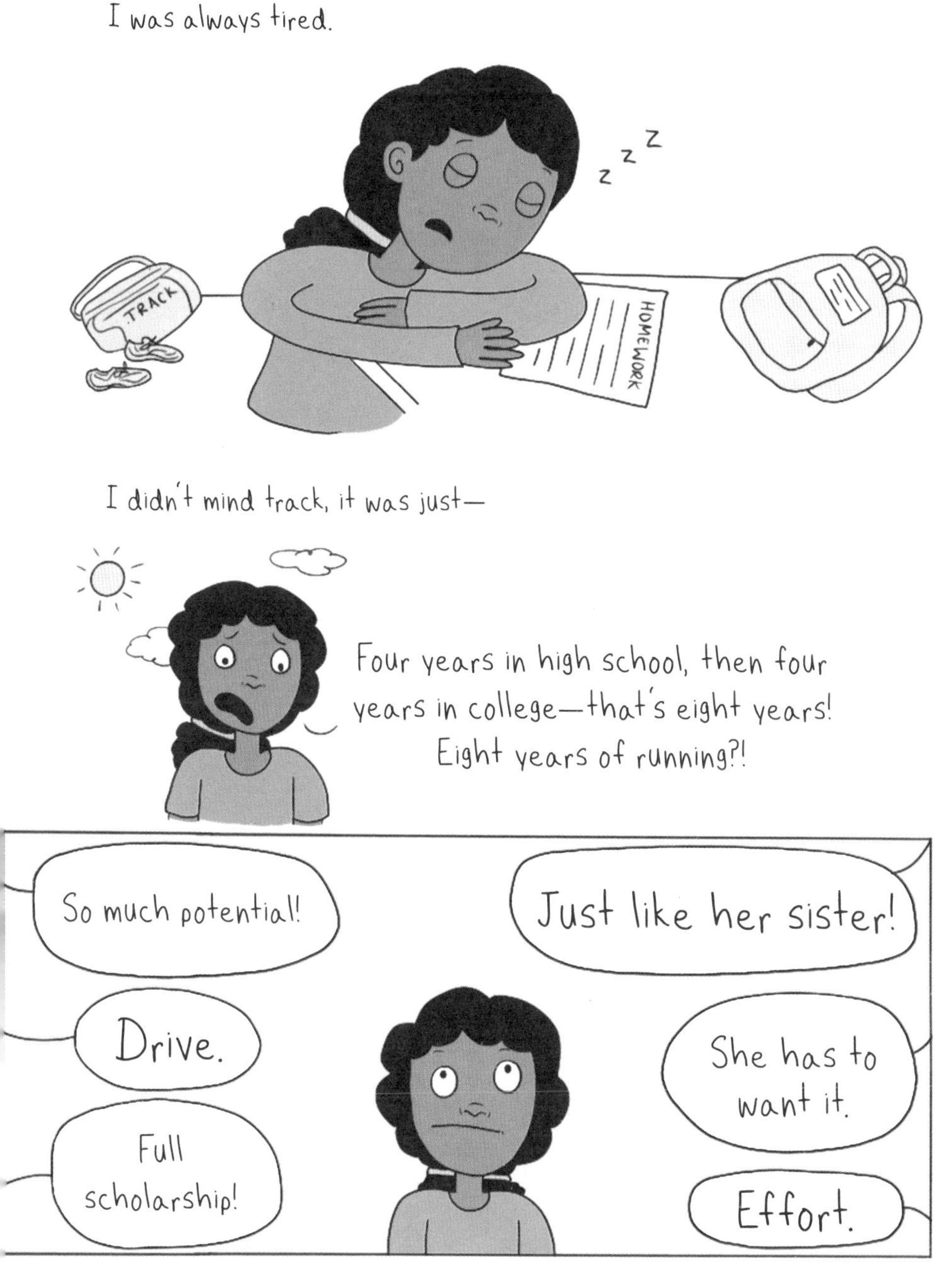
I was always tired.
TRACK
HOMEWORK
z z Z
I didn't mind track, it was just—
Four years in high school, then four years in college—that's eight years! Eight years of running?!
So much potential!
Just like her sister!
Drive.
She has to want it.
Full scholarship!
Effort.

For eighth grade superlatives, I was voted Most Athletic.

MOST ATHLETIC

Which was cool, I guess.

MOST CREATIVE

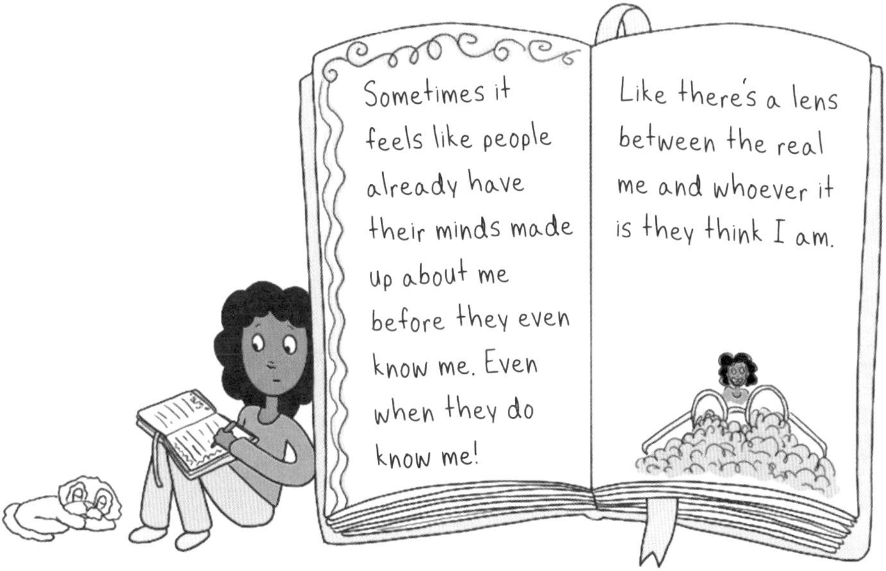
Sometimes it feels like people already have their minds made up about me before they even know me. Even when they do know me!
Like there's a lens between the real me and whoever it is they think I am.

I thought a lot about how people saw me versus how I saw myself.

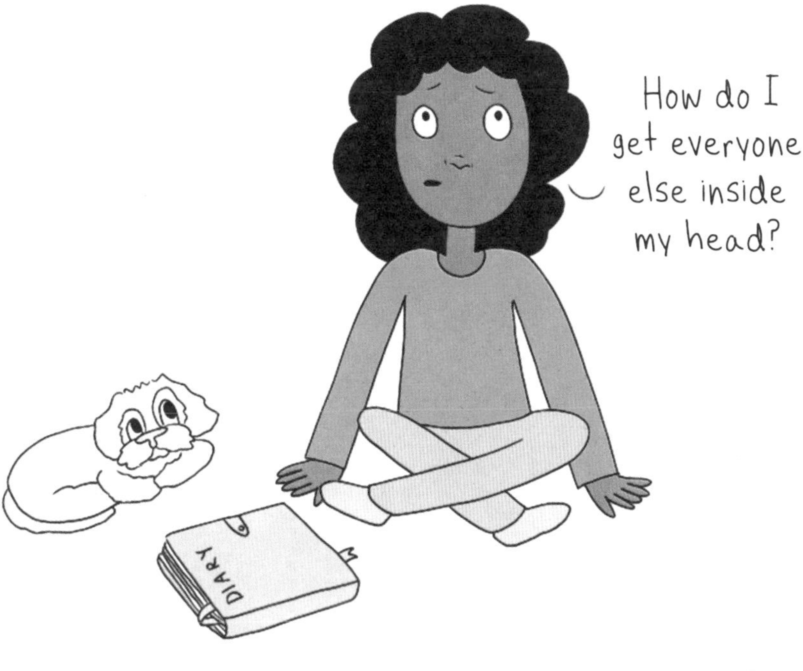
How do I get everyone else inside my head?
DIARY

Or should I make my own little world and keep everyone else out?

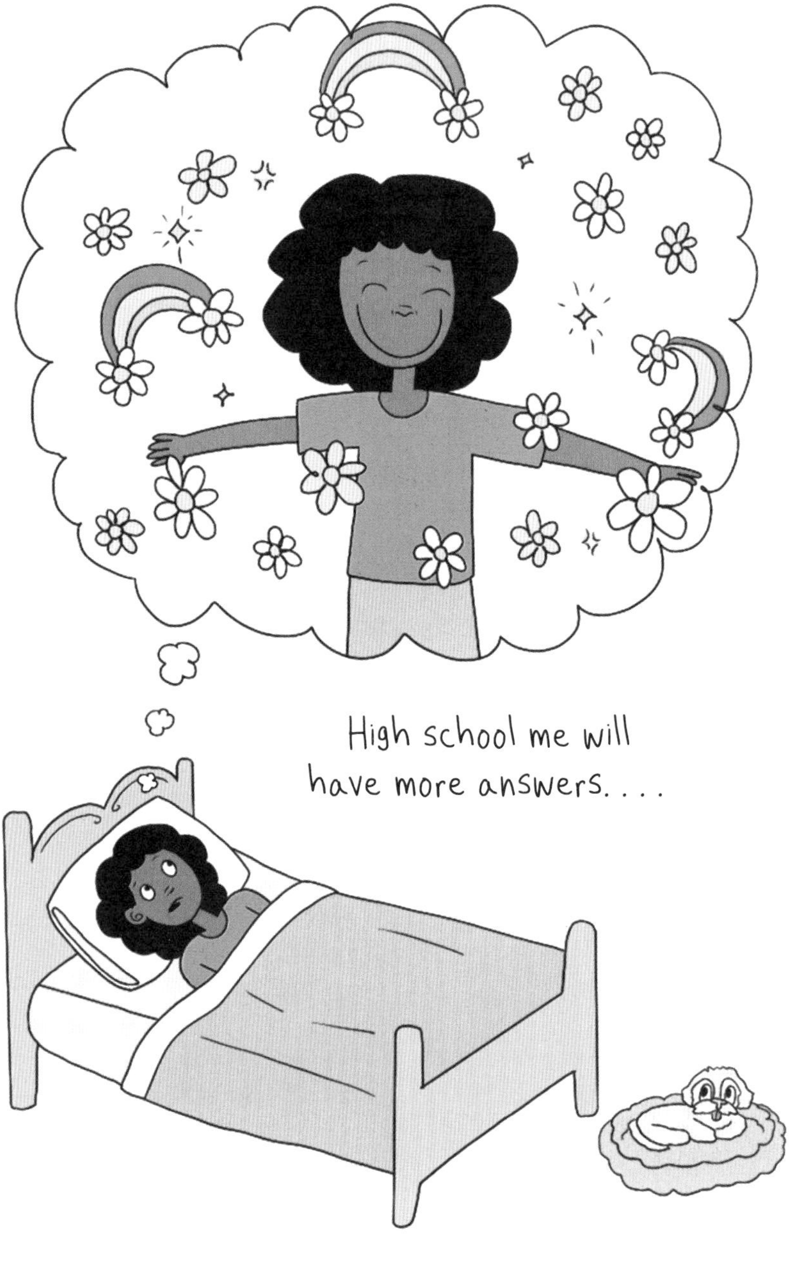
High school me will
have more answers. . . .

I hope.

GREEN RIVER HIGH SCHOOL

MARLTON, NEW JERSEY
2010-2014

My first few weeks of ninth grade, something strange began to happen.

I knew my quest,

You are here!
High School
Track Scholarship
College
TOTAL FREEDOM

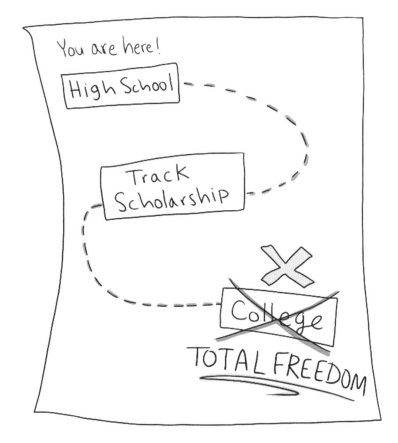

but I didn't know I'd become invisible along the way.

And I don't think anybody noticed that I was becoming invisible.

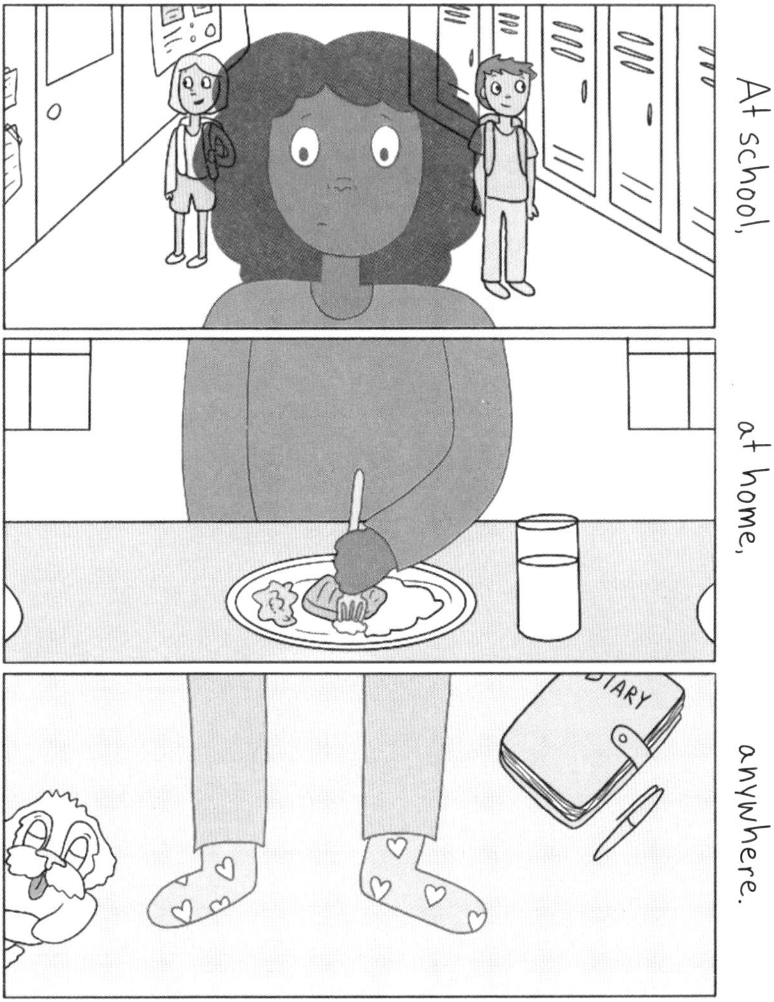

At school,
at home,
DIARY
anywhere.

Green River High had over 4,000 students, five times as many as Hurston Middle.

LIZ

I didn't think things would be this different.

LIZ

Even girls I went to Goldfinch Elementary with seem like total strangers.

LIZ

Hello?

LIZ

Pat?

LIZ

. . .

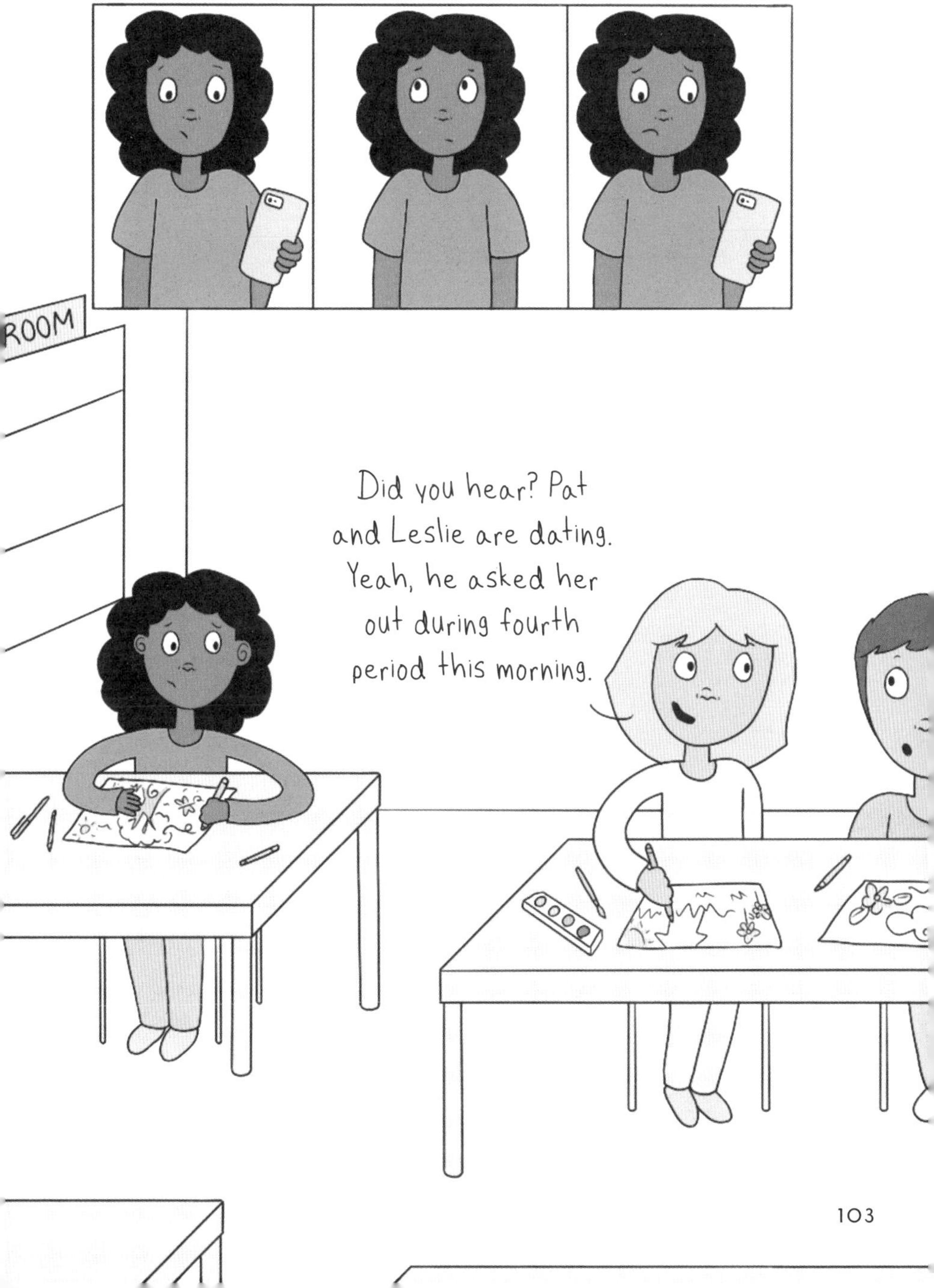
ROOM
Did you hear? Pat and Leslie are dating. Yeah, he asked her out during fourth period this morning.

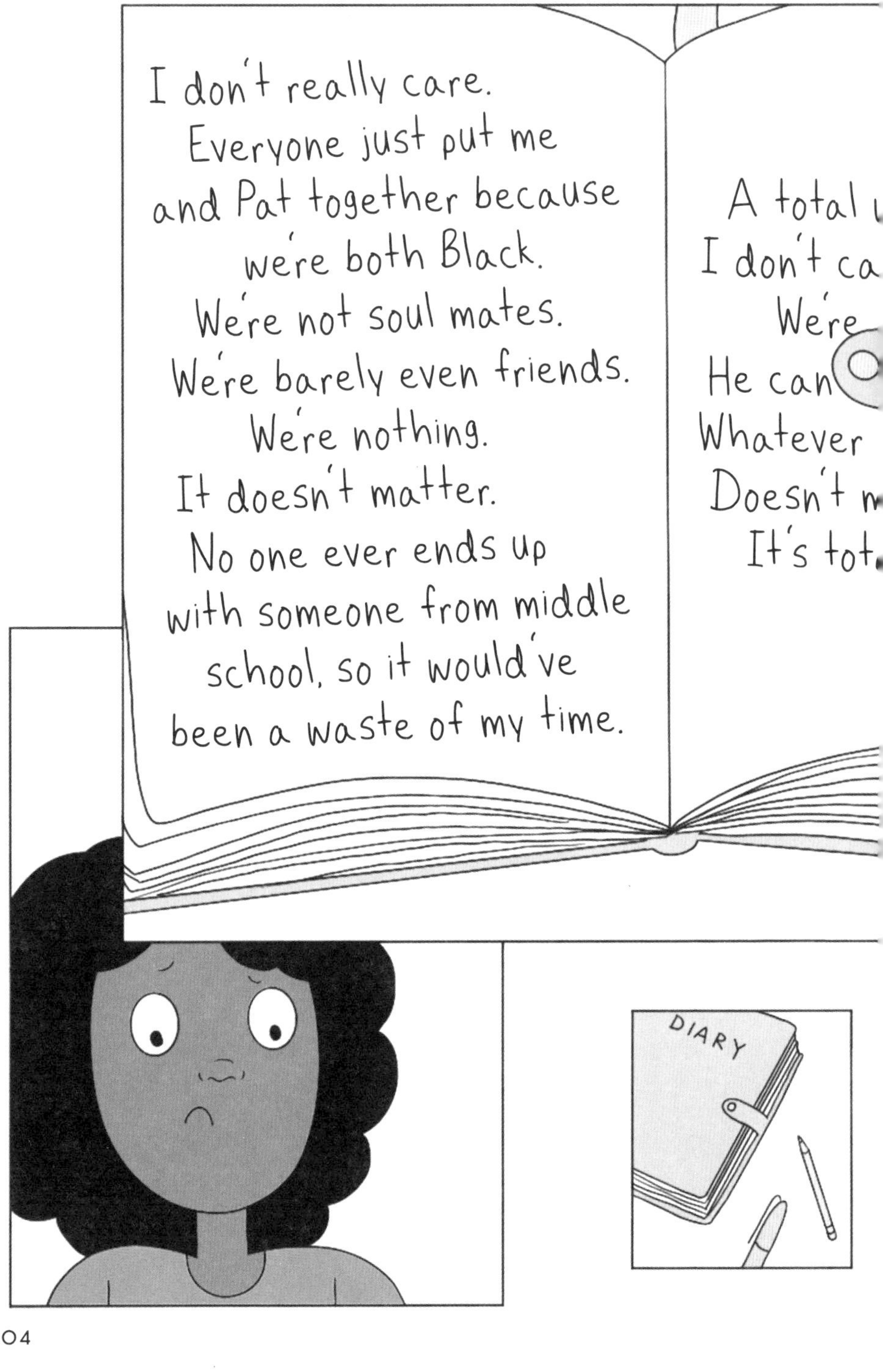
I don't really care.
Everyone just put me
and Pat together because
we're both Black.
We're not soul mates.
We're barely even friends.
We're nothing.
It doesn't matter.
No one ever ends up
with someone from middle
school, so it would've
been a waste of my time.
A total
I don't
We're
He can
Whatever
Doesn't
It's
DIARY

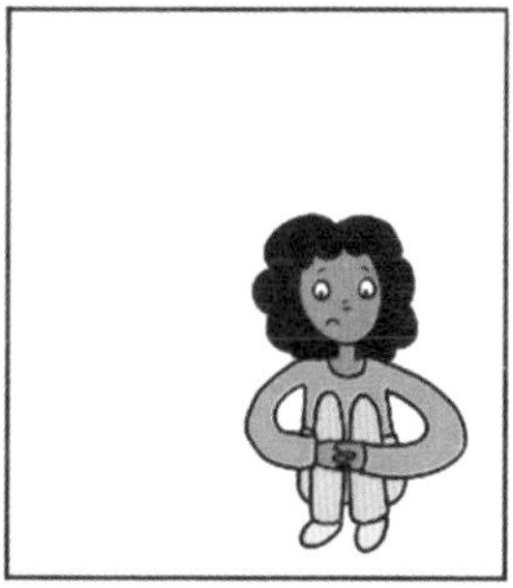

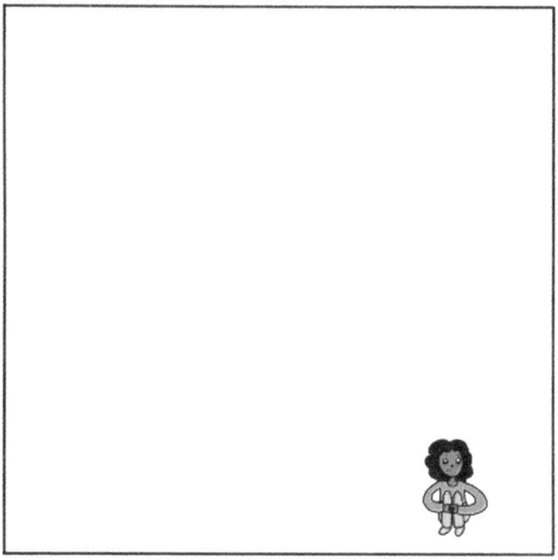

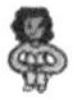

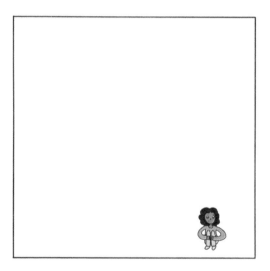

It turns out invisible people move faster through time.

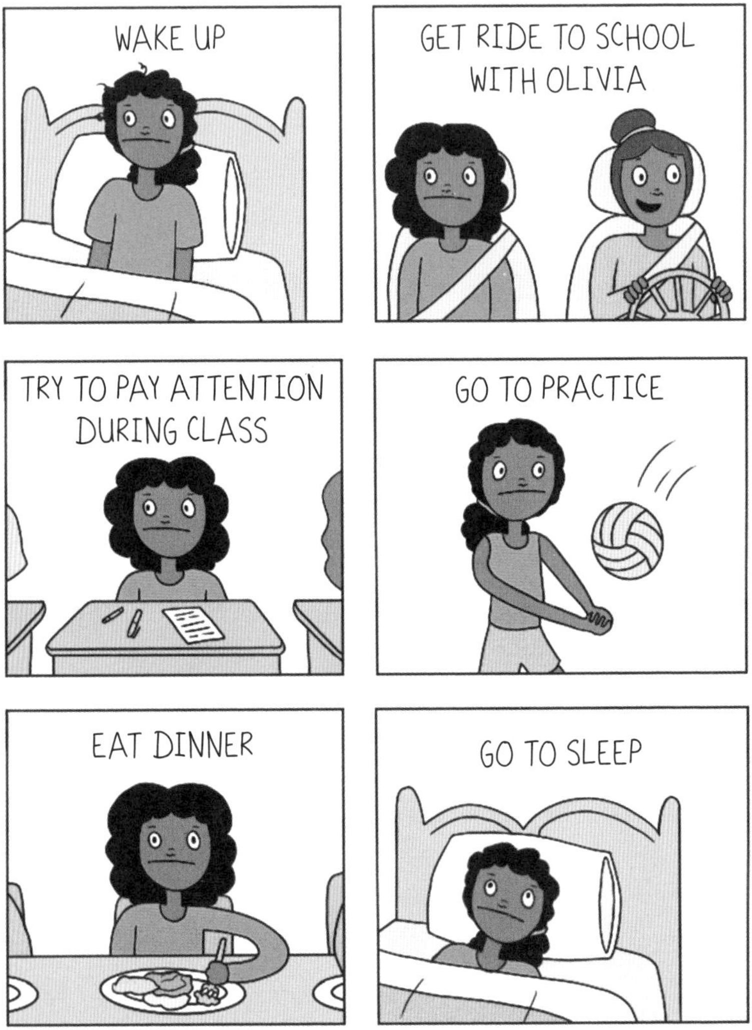
WAKE UP
GET RIDE TO SCHOOL WITH OLIVIA
TRY TO PAY ATTENTION DURING CLASS
GO TO PRACTICE
EAT DINNER
GO TO SLEEP

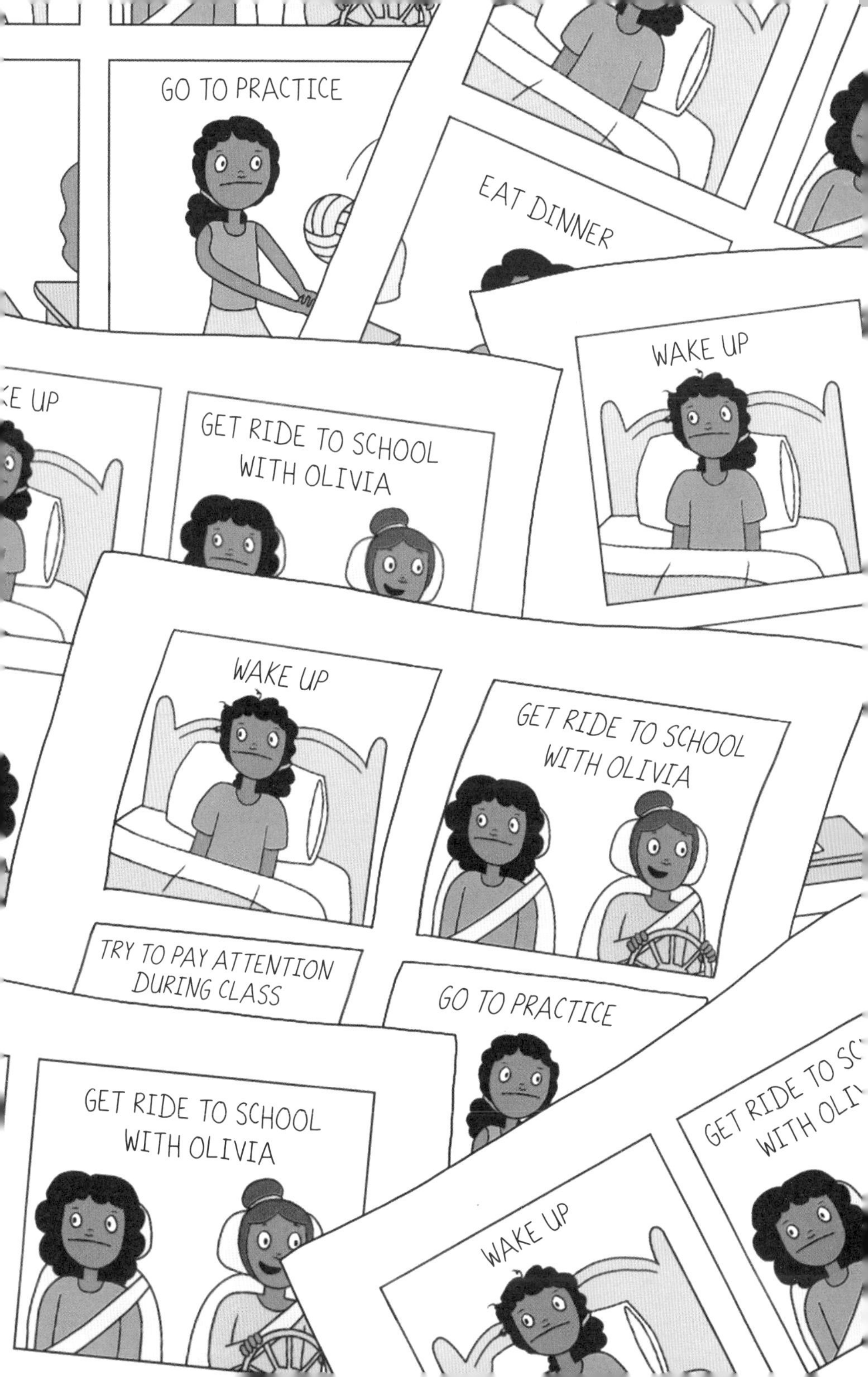
GO TO PRACTICE
EAT DINNER
WAKE UP
GET RIDE TO SCHOOL WITH OLIVIA
WAKE UP
GET RIDE TO SCHOOL WITH OLIVIA
TRY TO PAY ATTENTION DURING CLASS
GO TO PRACTICE
GET RIDE TO SCHOOL WITH OLIVIA
WAKE UP

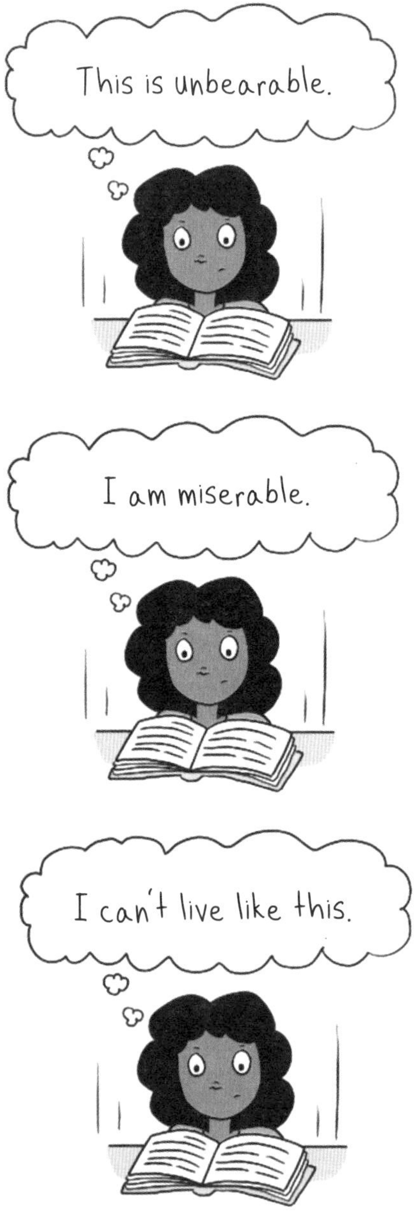
This is unbearable.
I am miserable.
I can't live like this.

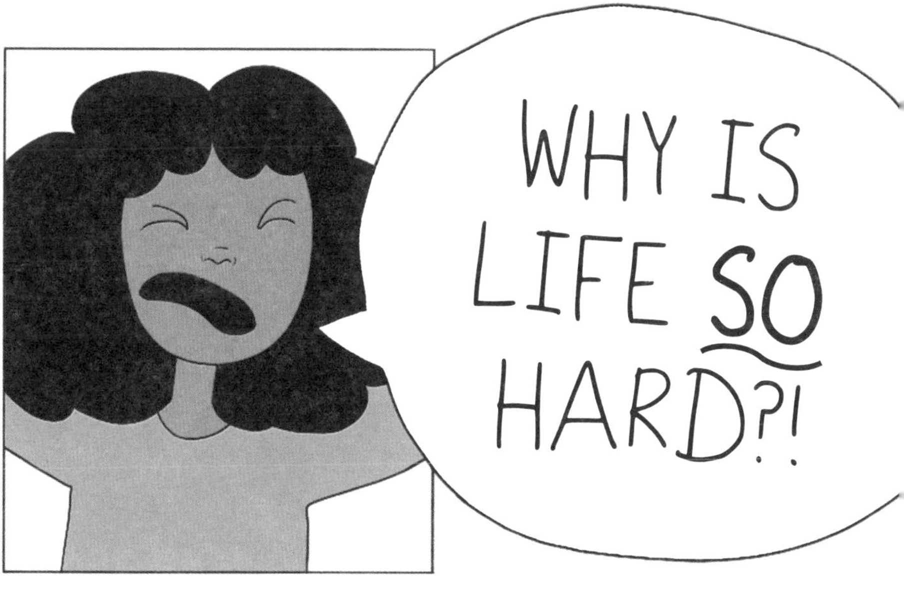
WHY IS LIFE SO HARD?!

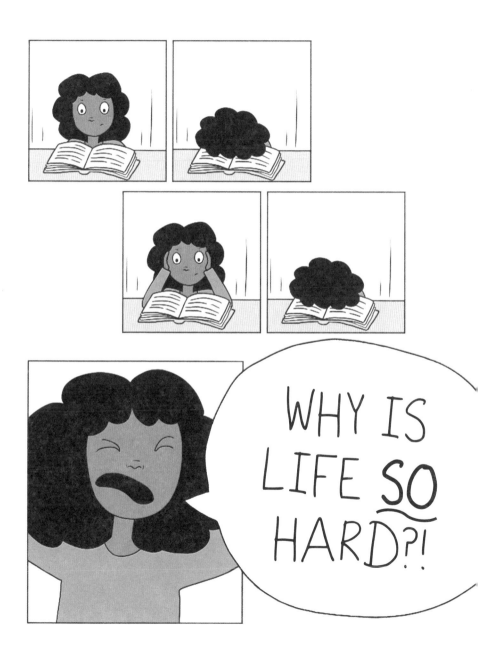

How are we supposed to read 400 pages in two days and go to six-hour practices. Like for what?!

It's so unnecessary and we just do it like it makes sense, but none of it makes sense!

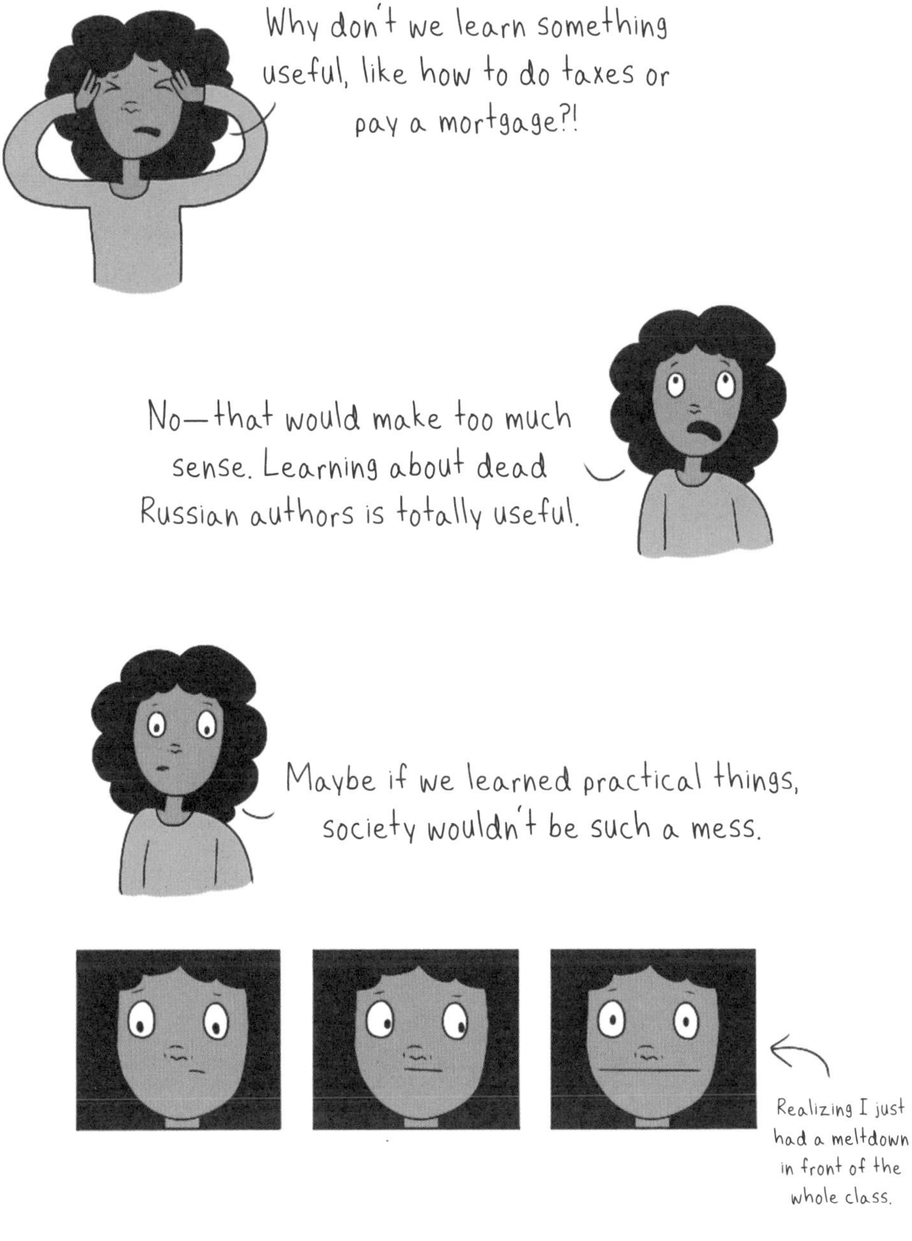
Why don't we learn something useful, like how to do taxes or pay a mortgage?!
No—that would make too much sense. Learning about dead Russian authors is totally useful.
Maybe if we learned practical things, society wouldn't be such a mess.
Realizing I just had a meltdown in front of the whole class.

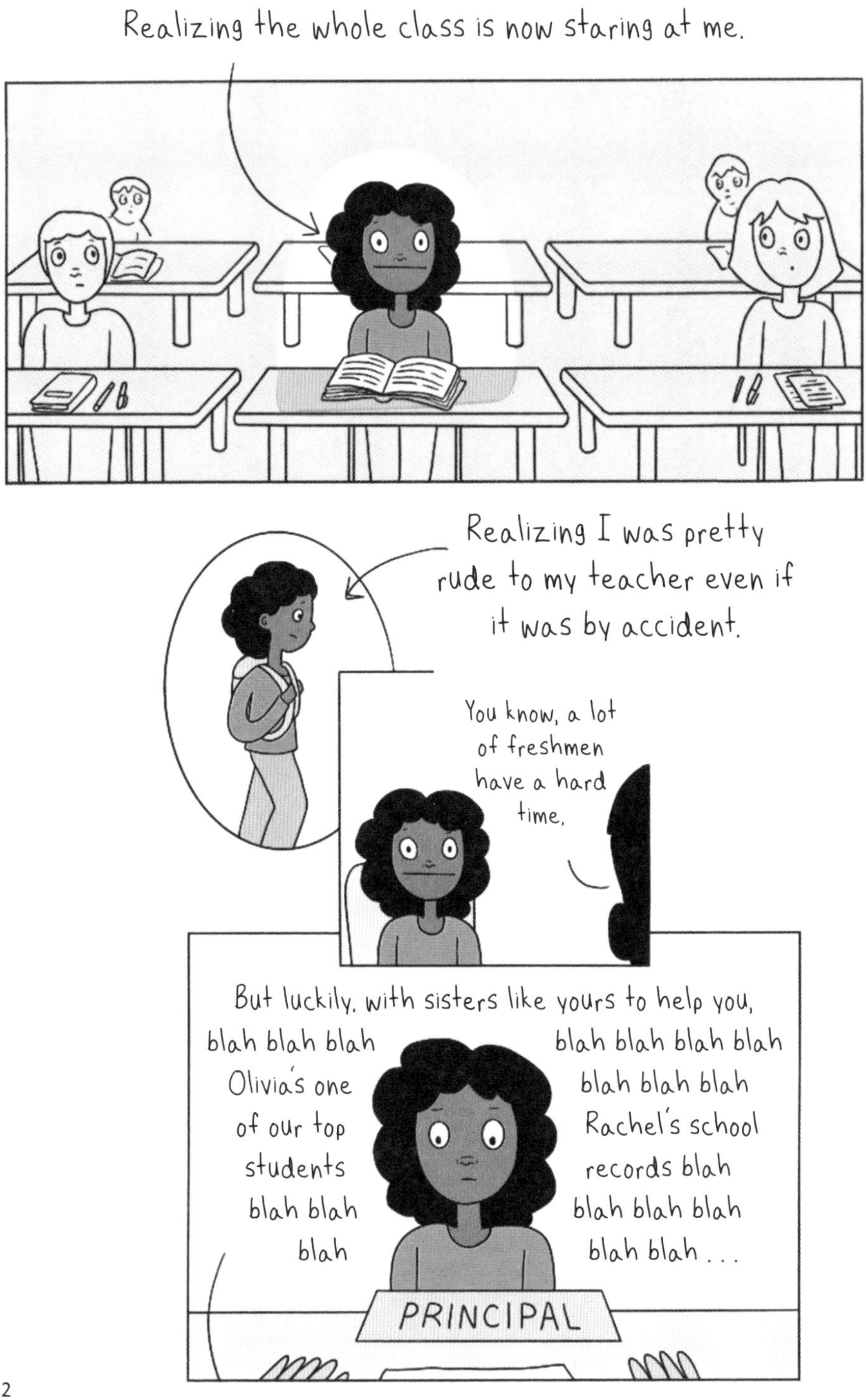

Realizing the whole class is now staring at me.
Realizing I was pretty rude to my teacher even if it was by accident.
You know, a lot of freshmen have a hard time.
But luckily, with sisters like yours to help you,
blah blah blah
Olivia's one of our top students
blah blah blah
blah blah blah blah
blah blah blah
Rachel's school records blah
blah blah blah
blah blah . . .
PRINCIPAL

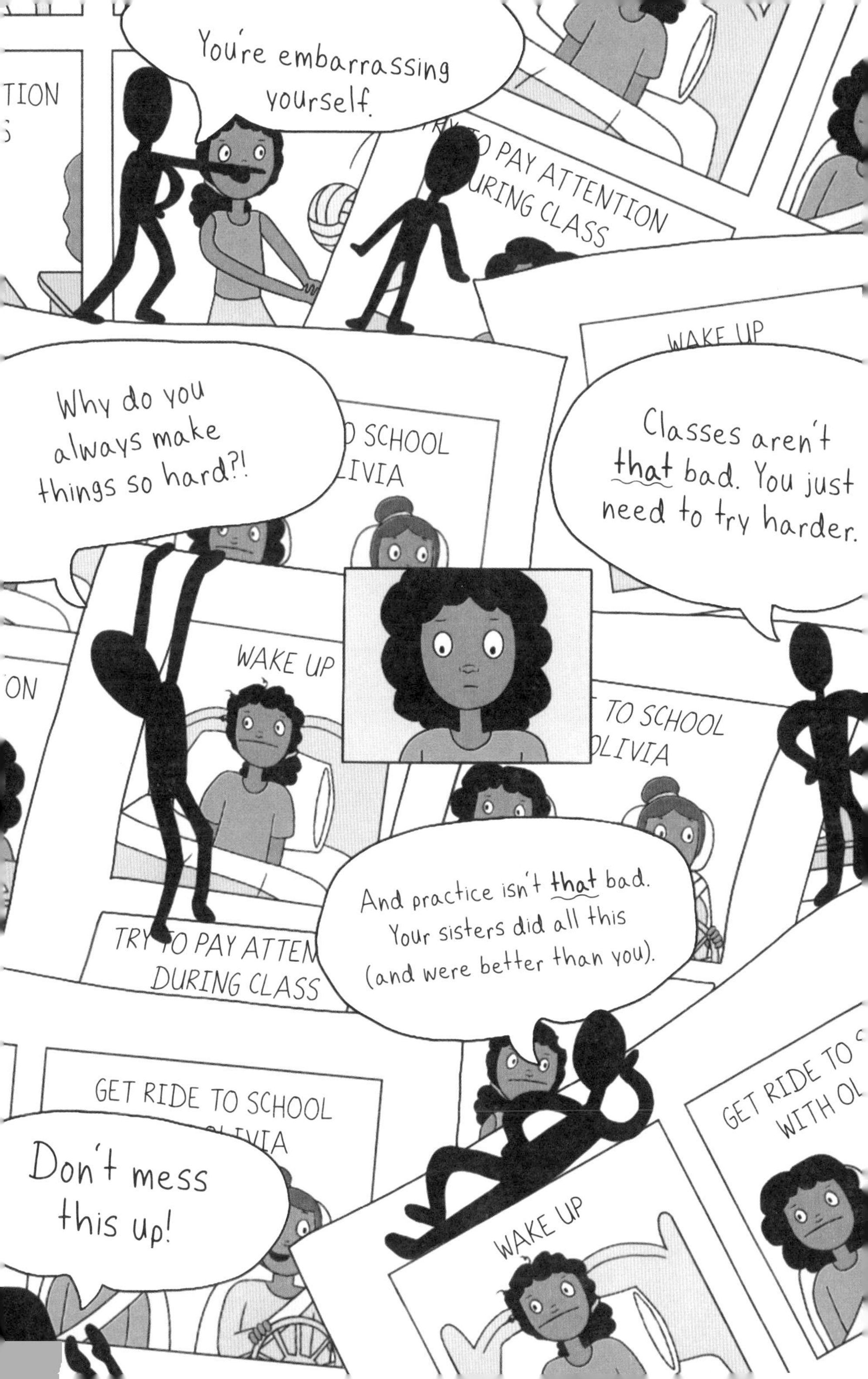
You're embarrassing yourself.
TRY TO PAY ATTENTION DURING CLASS
WAKE UP
Why do you always make things so hard?!
Classes aren't that bad. You just need to try harder.
WAKE UP
TO SCHOOL
OLIVIA
And practice isn't that bad. Your sisters did all this (and were better than you).
TRY TO PAY ATTEN
DURING CLASS
GET RIDE TO SCHOOL
Don't mess this up!
GET RIDE TO
WITH OL
WAKE UP

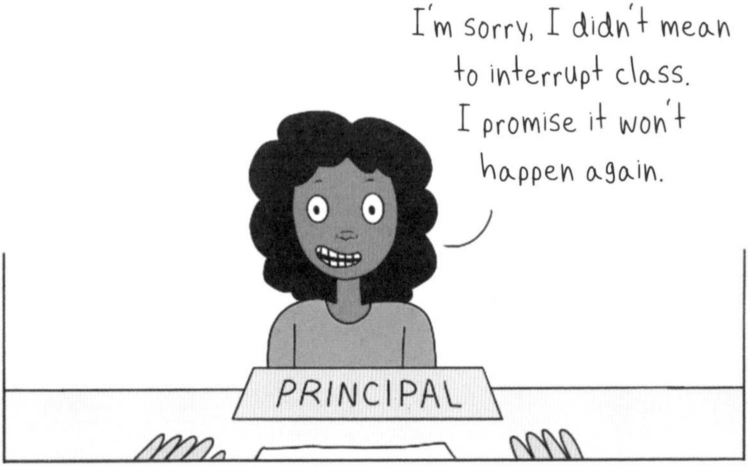
I'm sorry, I didn't mean to interrupt class. I promise it won't happen again.
PRINCIPAL

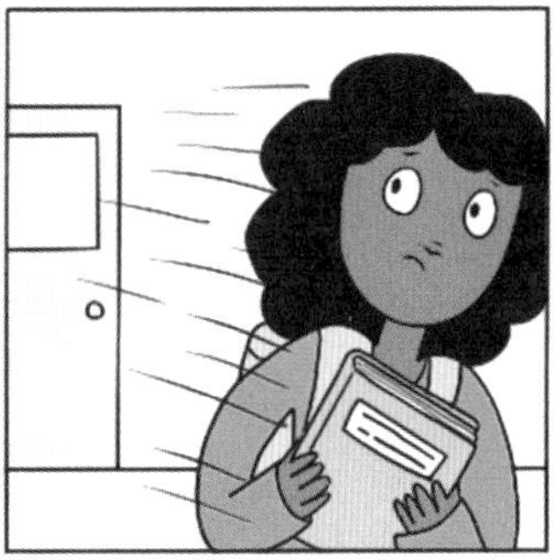

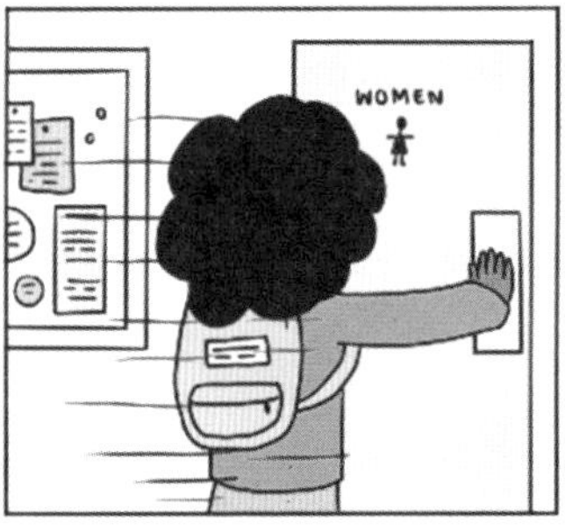
WOMEN

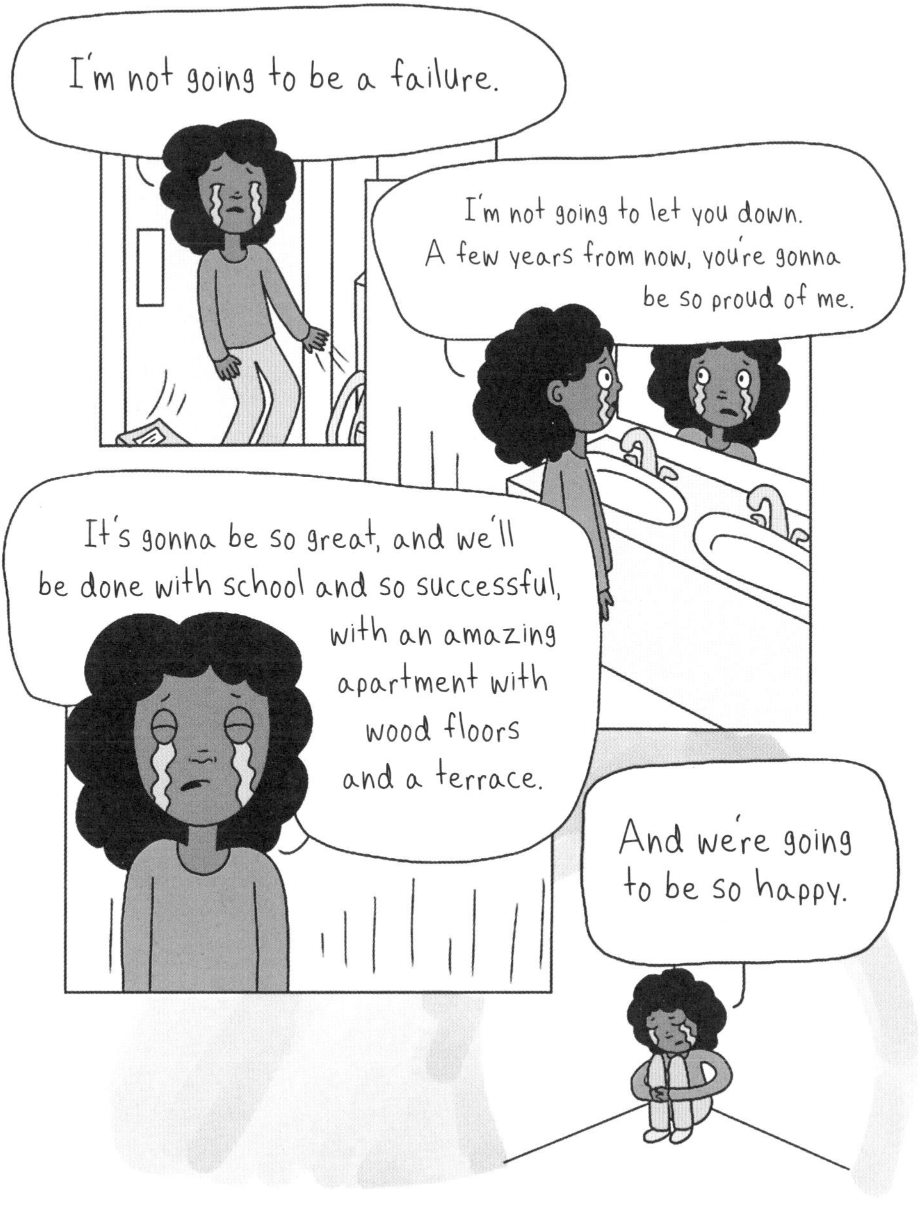
I'm not going to be a failure.
I'm not going to let you down. A few years from now, you're gonna be so proud of me.
It's gonna be so great, and we'll be done with school and so successful, with an amazing apartment with wood floors and a terrace.
And we're going to be so happy.

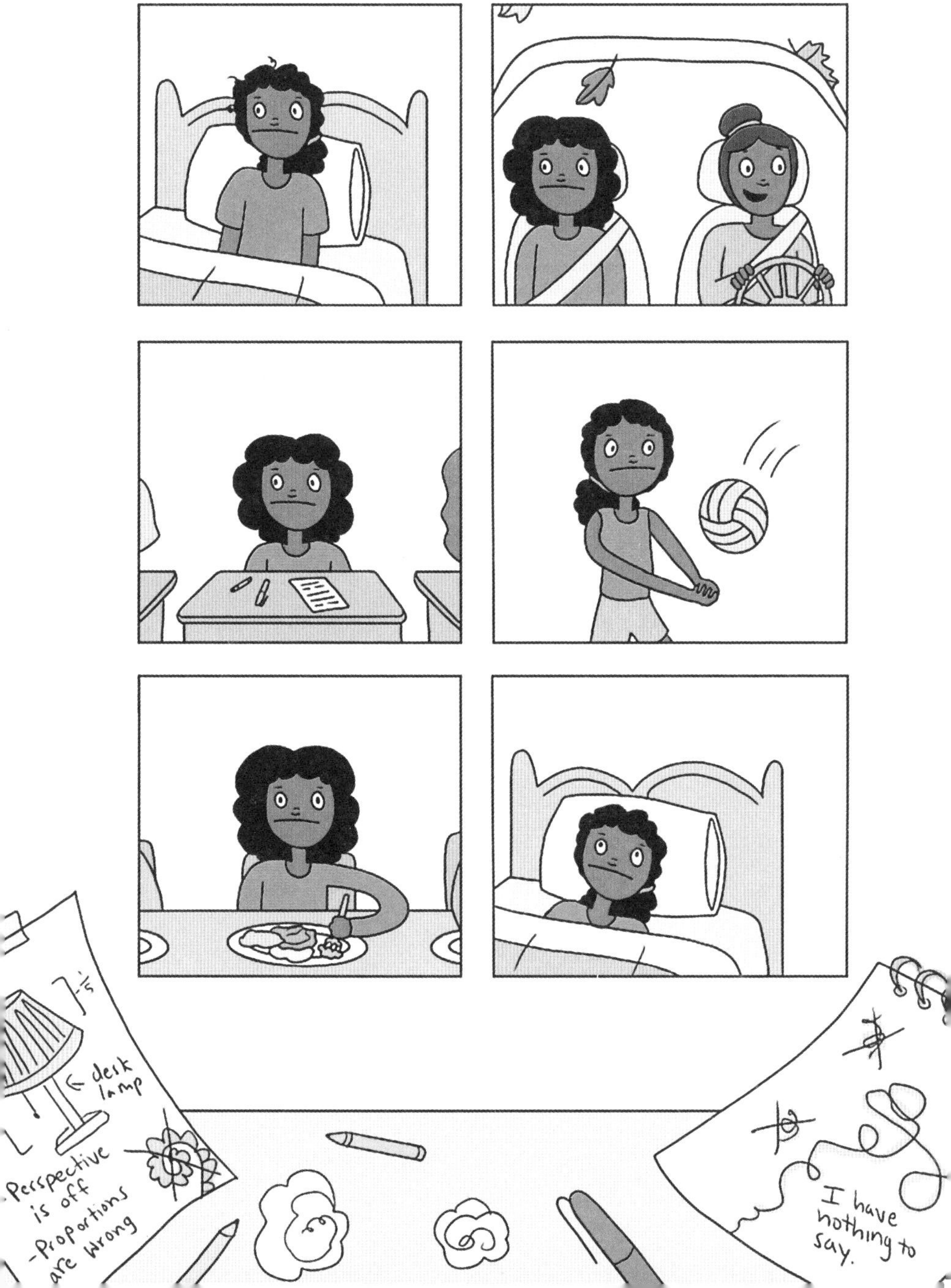
desk lamp
Perspective is off
-Proportions are wrong
I have nothing to say.

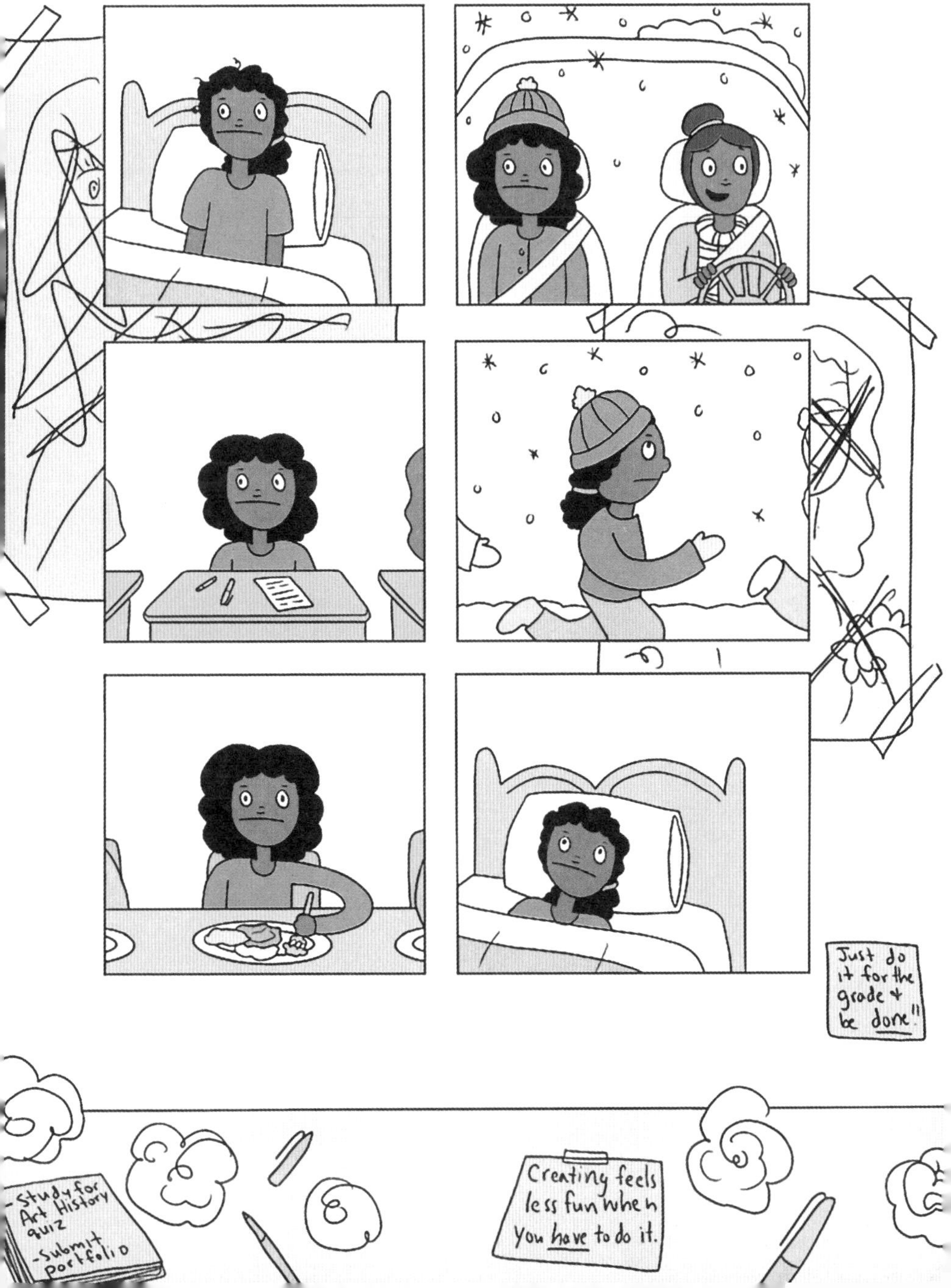
Just do it for the grade + be done!!
-Study for Art History quiz
-Submit portfolio
Creating feels less fun when you have to do it.

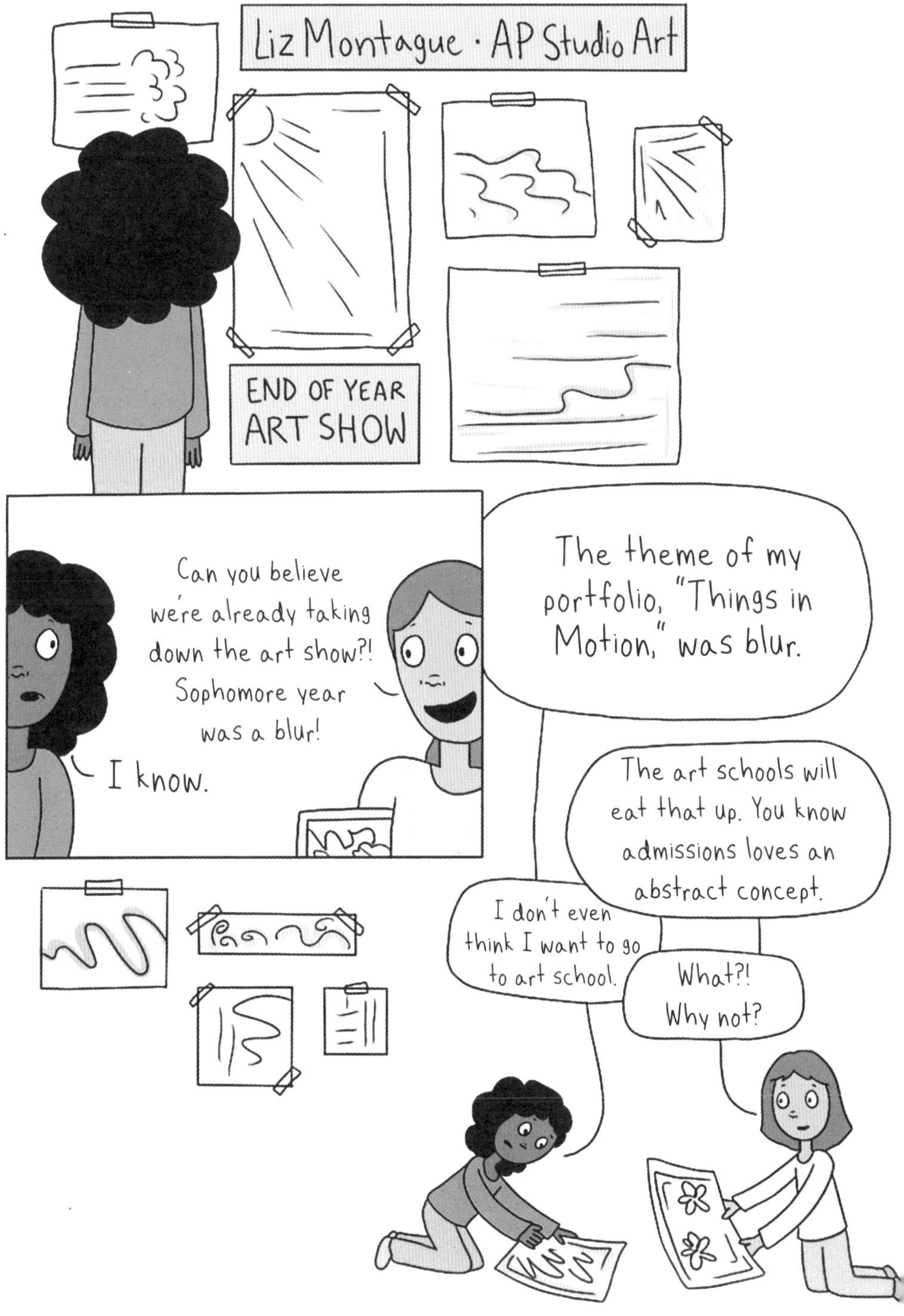

Liz Montague · AP Studio Art
END OF YEAR ART SHOW
Can you believe we're already taking down the art show?! Sophomore year was a blur!
I know.
The theme of my portfolio, "Things in Motion," was blur.
The art schools will eat that up. You know admissions loves an abstract concept.
I don't even think I want to go to art school.
What?! Why not?

I need to get an athletic scholarship, and art schools don't have good enough sports programs to give decent money.

And I don't know . . .

I didn't even really like this "blur-motion" idea. I just picked it because I had to pick something, and then I wasted a year making work I don't even like.

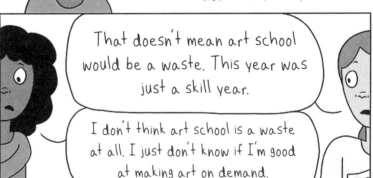

That doesn't mean art school would be a waste. This year was just a skill year.

I don't think art school is a waste at all. I just don't know if I'm good at making art on demand.

But what I didn't say was that I wasn't just unsure about art school—I was unsure about college as a whole.

I felt like I wasn't good at doing anything on demand.
I couldn't understand how everyone already knew what they wanted to do with their life.

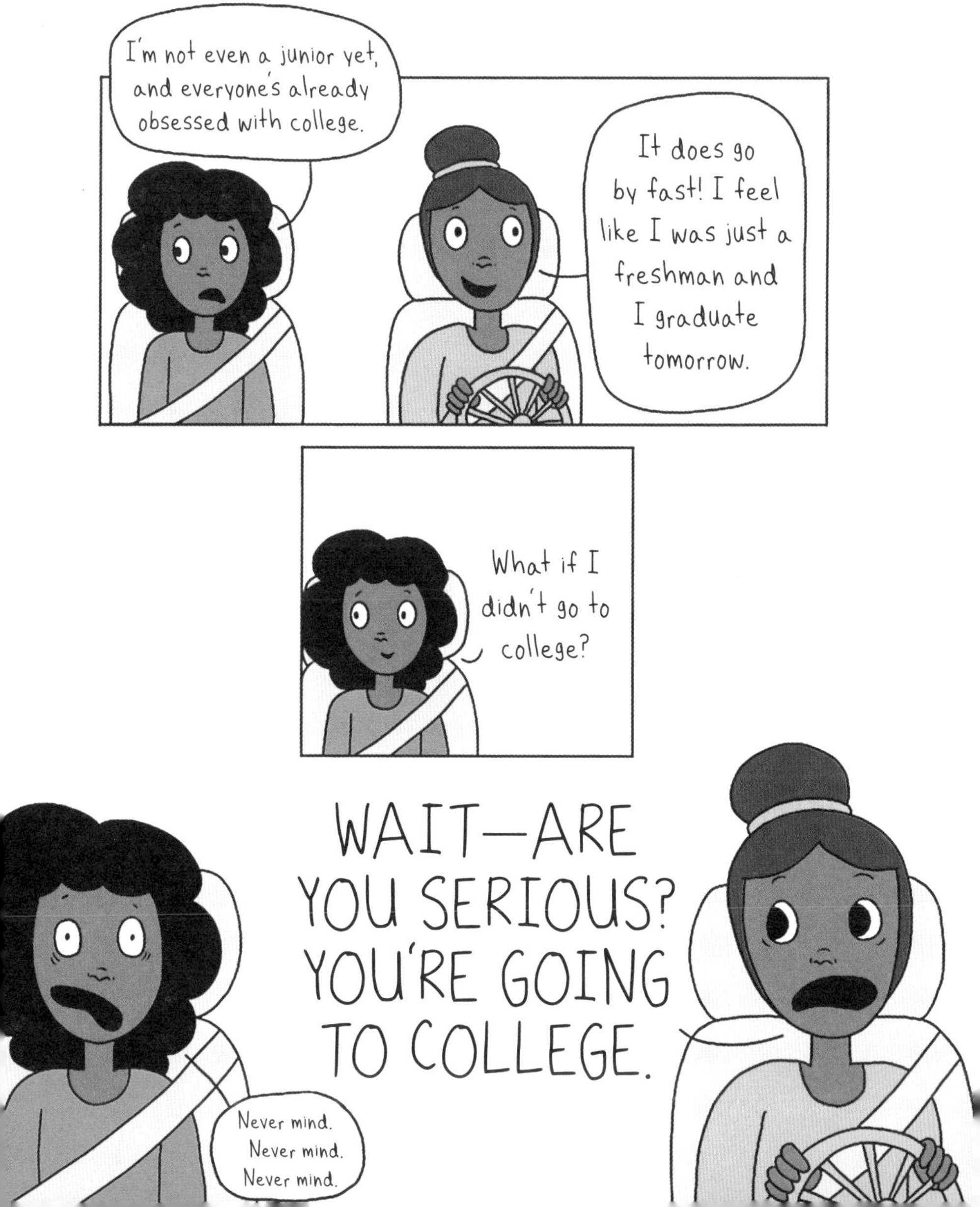
I'm not even a junior yet, and everyone's already obsessed with college.
It does go by fast! I feel like I was just a freshman and I graduate tomorrow.
What if I didn't go to college?
WAIT—ARE YOU SERIOUS? YOU'RE GOING TO COLLEGE.
Never mind. Never mind. Never mind.

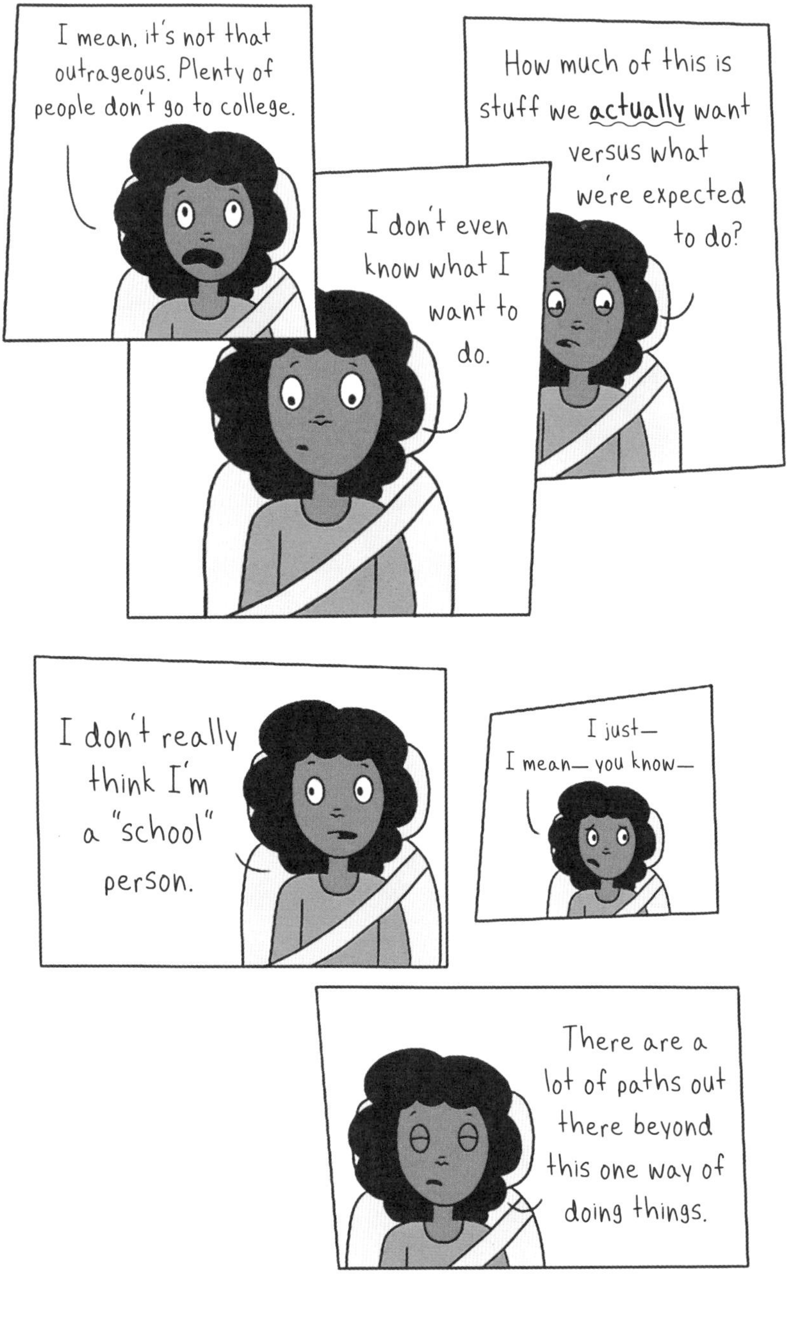
I mean, it's not that outrageous. Plenty of people don't go to college.
I don't even know what I want to do.
How much of this is stuff we **actually** want versus what we're expected to do?
I don't really think I'm a "school" person.
I just—
I mean— you know—
There are a lot of paths out there beyond this one way of doing things.

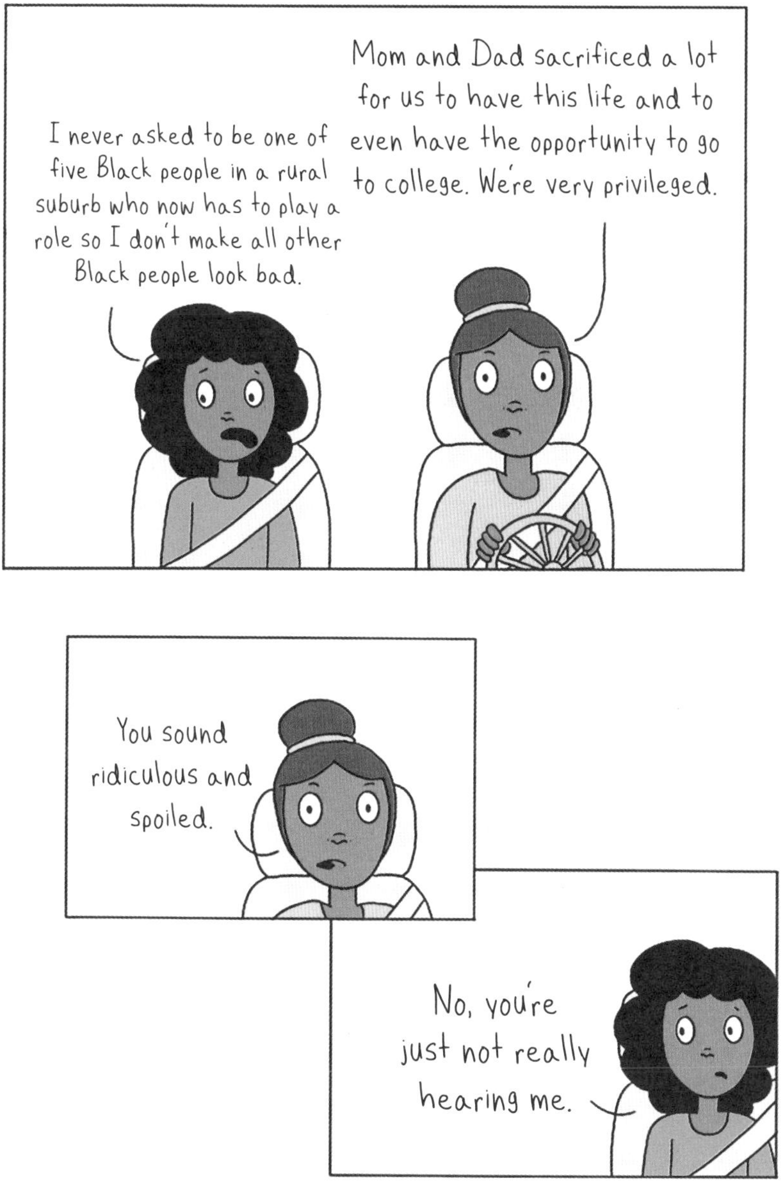
I never asked to be one of five Black people in a rural suburb who now has to play a role so I don't make all other Black people look bad.
Mom and Dad sacrificed a lot for us to have this life and to even have the opportunity to go to college. We're very privileged.
You sound ridiculous and spoiled.
No, you're just not really hearing me.

Don't tell Mom and Dad.

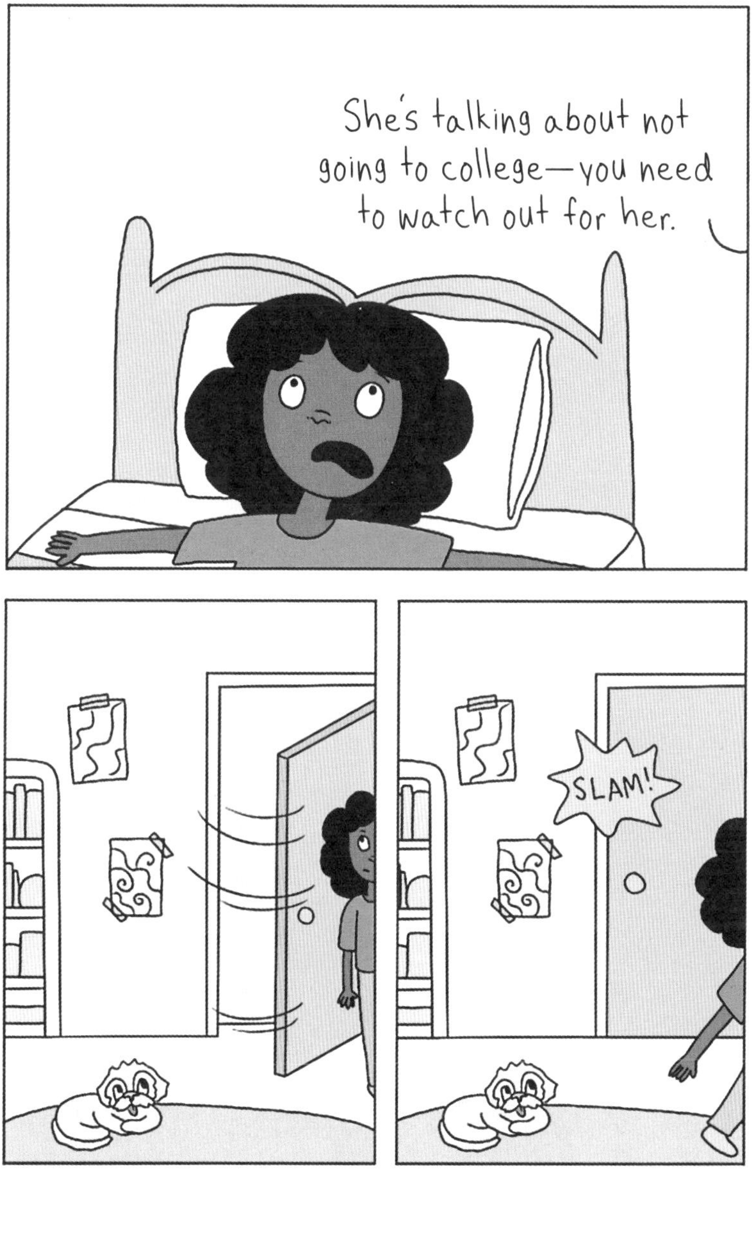
She's talking about not going to college—you need to watch out for her.
SLAM!

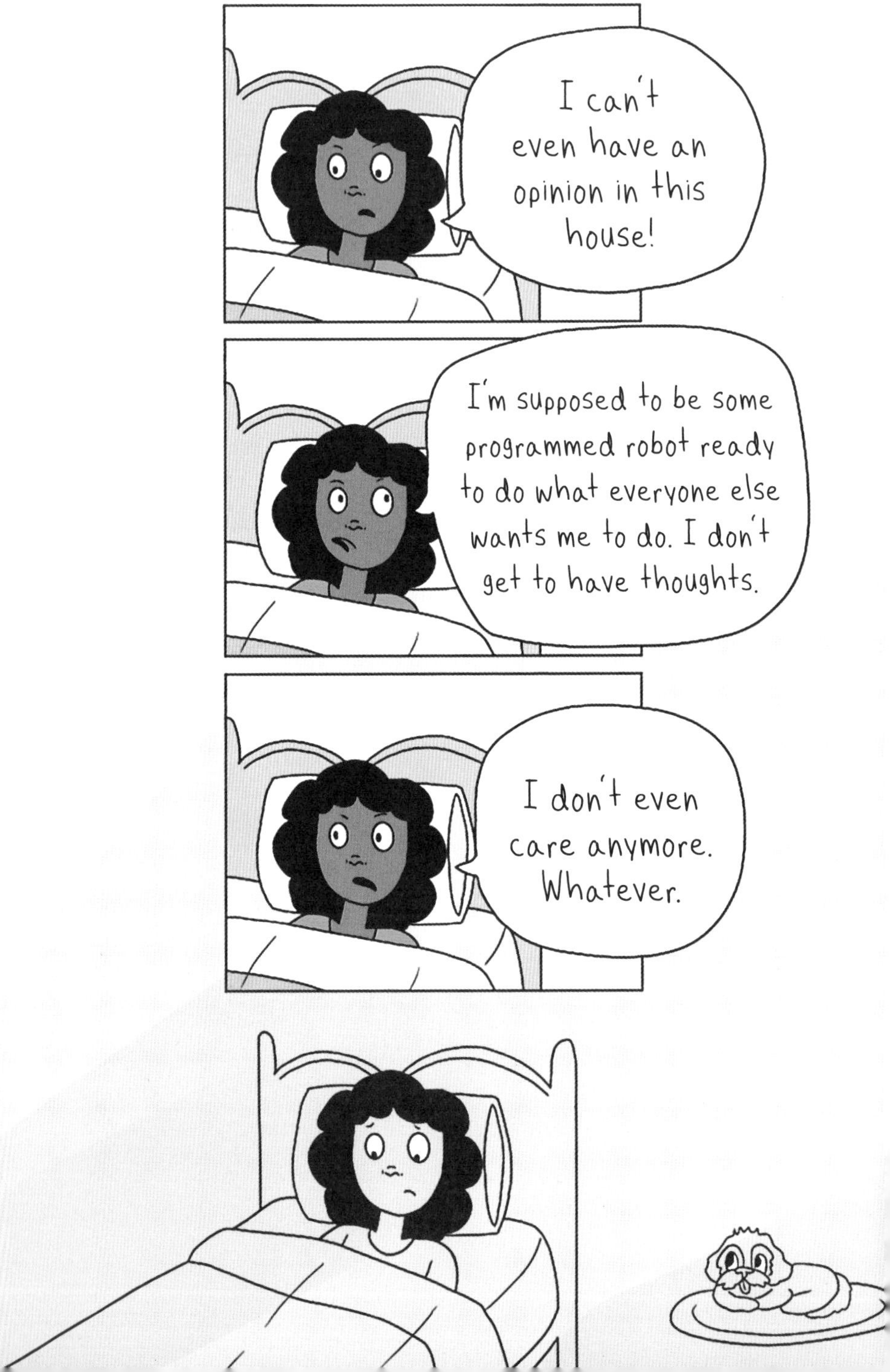
I can't even have an opinion in this house!
I'm supposed to be some programmed robot ready to do what everyone else wants me to do. I don't get to have thoughts.
I don't even care anymore. Whatever.

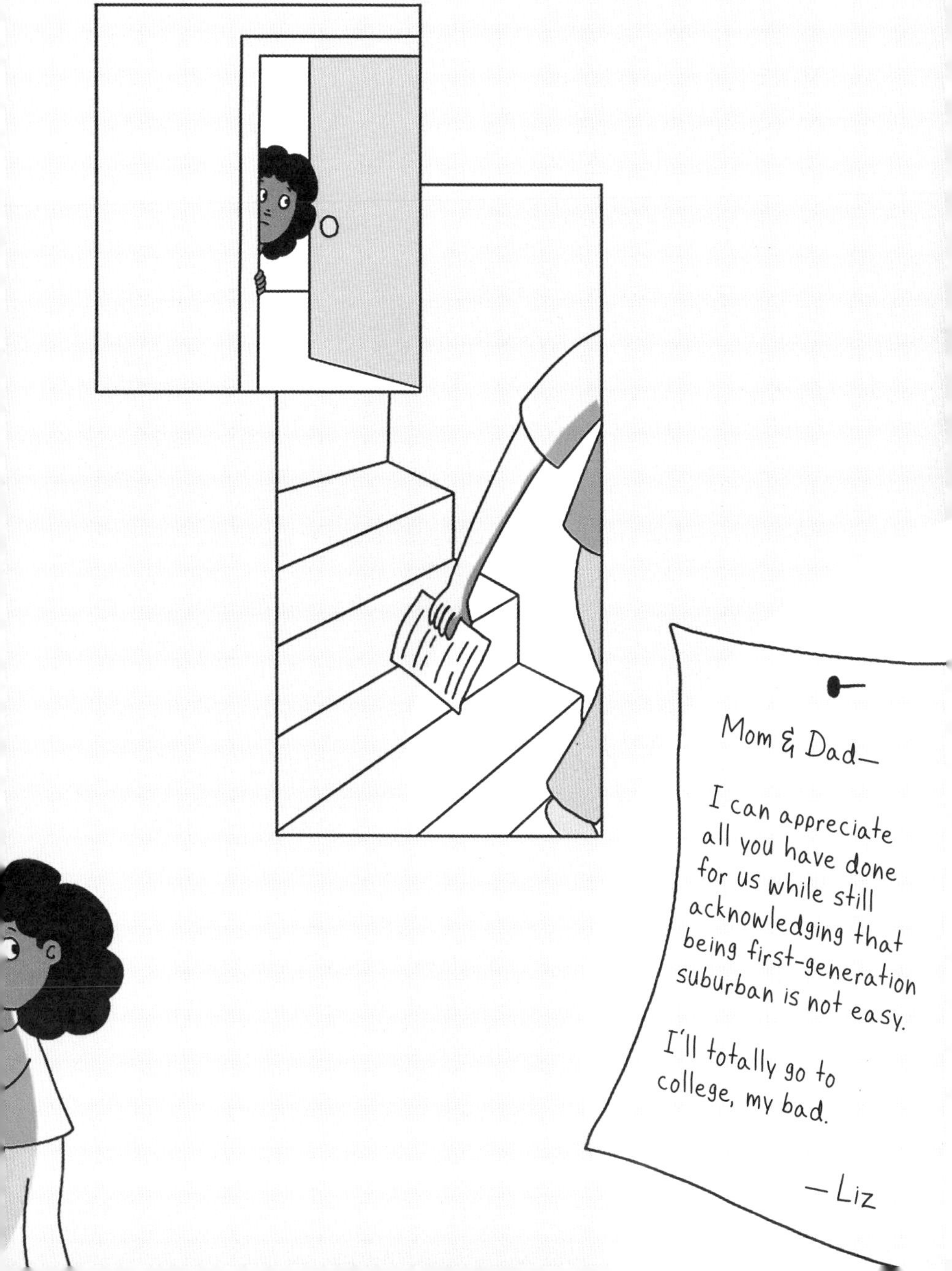
Mom & Dad—
I can appreciate all you have done for us while still acknowledging that being first-generation suburban is not easy.
I'll totally go to college, my bad.
—Liz

The older I got, the less I had a summer.

Instead I had practice and college visits and SAT prep.

LIZ
The house feels too quiet

OLIVIA
You can always come visit me and Rachel

LIZ
I will

OLIVIA
:)

By the end of junior year, I'd broken nearly all of Rachel's school records. I was getting heavily recruited, and with each recruiting letter I became more panicked.

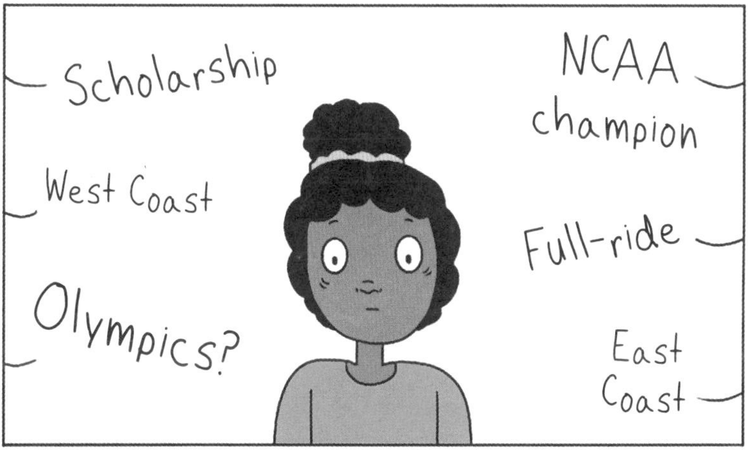
Scholarship
NCAA champion
West Coast
Full-ride
Olympics?
East Coast

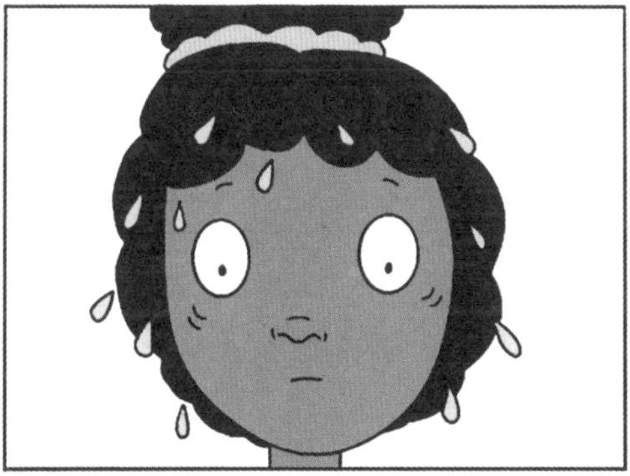

I didn't have a dream school or a major I was super passionate about. I just didn't want to let anyone down.

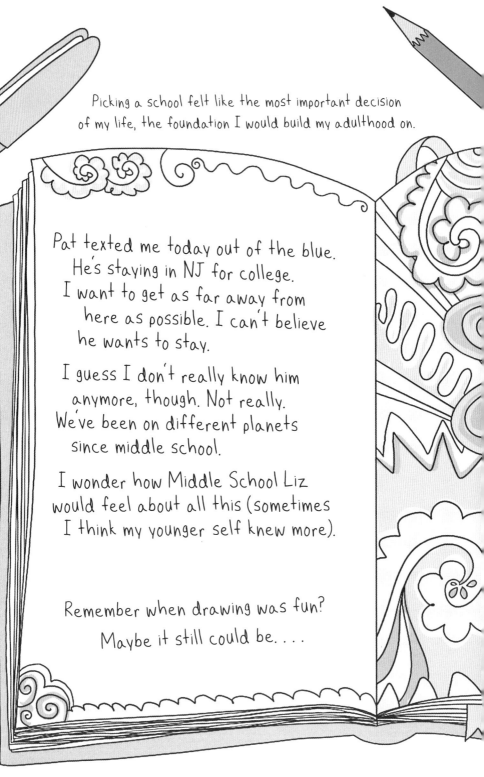

Picking a school felt like the most important decision of my life, the foundation I would build my adulthood on.

Pat texted me today out of the blue.
   He's staying in NJ for college.
I want to get as far away from
   here as possible. I can't believe
   he wants to stay.

I guess I don't really know him
   anymore, though. Not really.
We've been on different planets
   since middle school.

I wonder how Middle School Liz
would feel about all this (sometimes
   I think my younger self knew more).

Remember when drawing was fun?
   Maybe it still could be. . . .

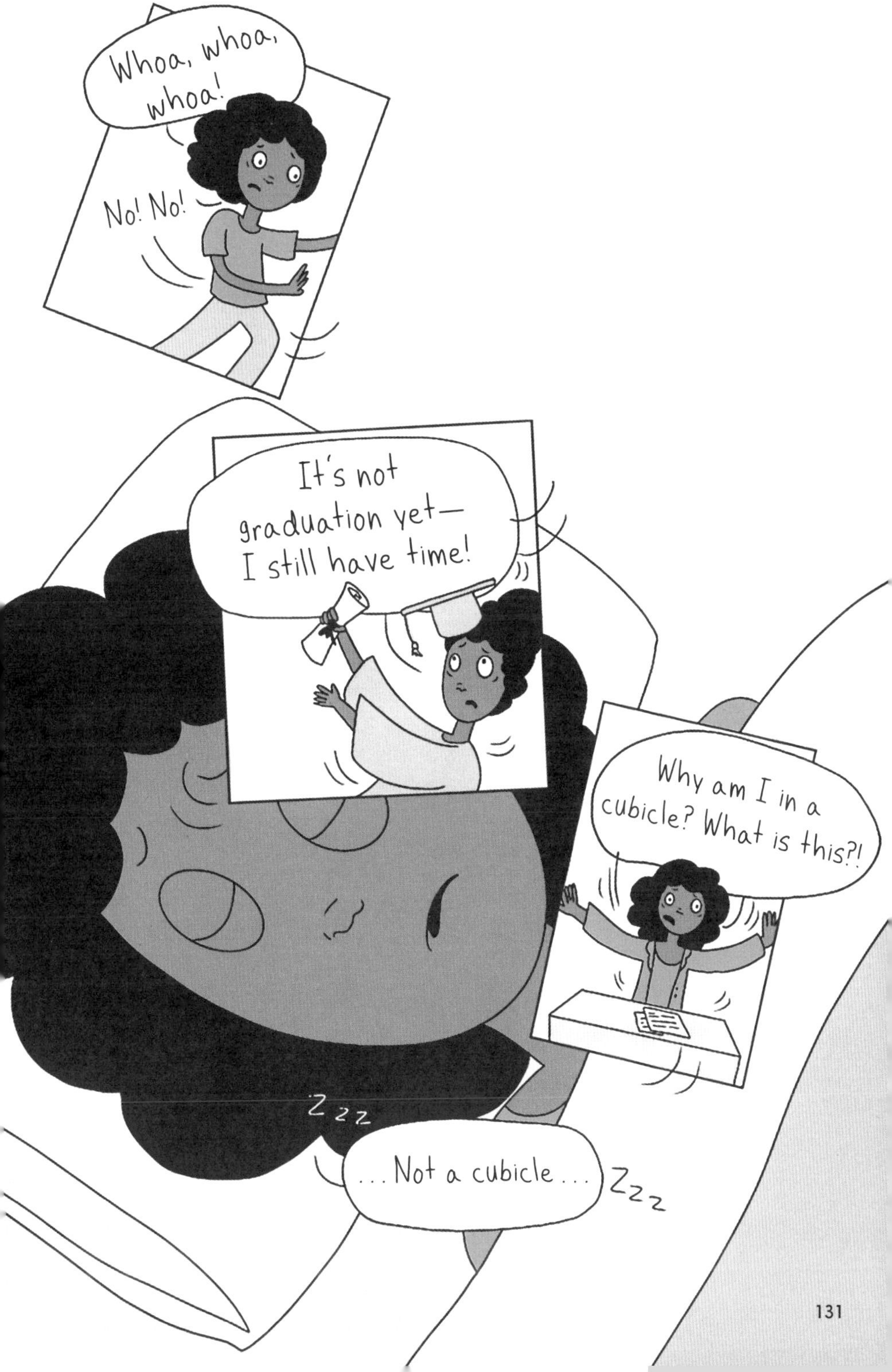
Whoa, whoa, whoa!
No! No!
It's not graduation yet—I still have time!
Why am I in a cubicle? What is this?!
Zzz
. . . Not a cubicle . . .
Zzz

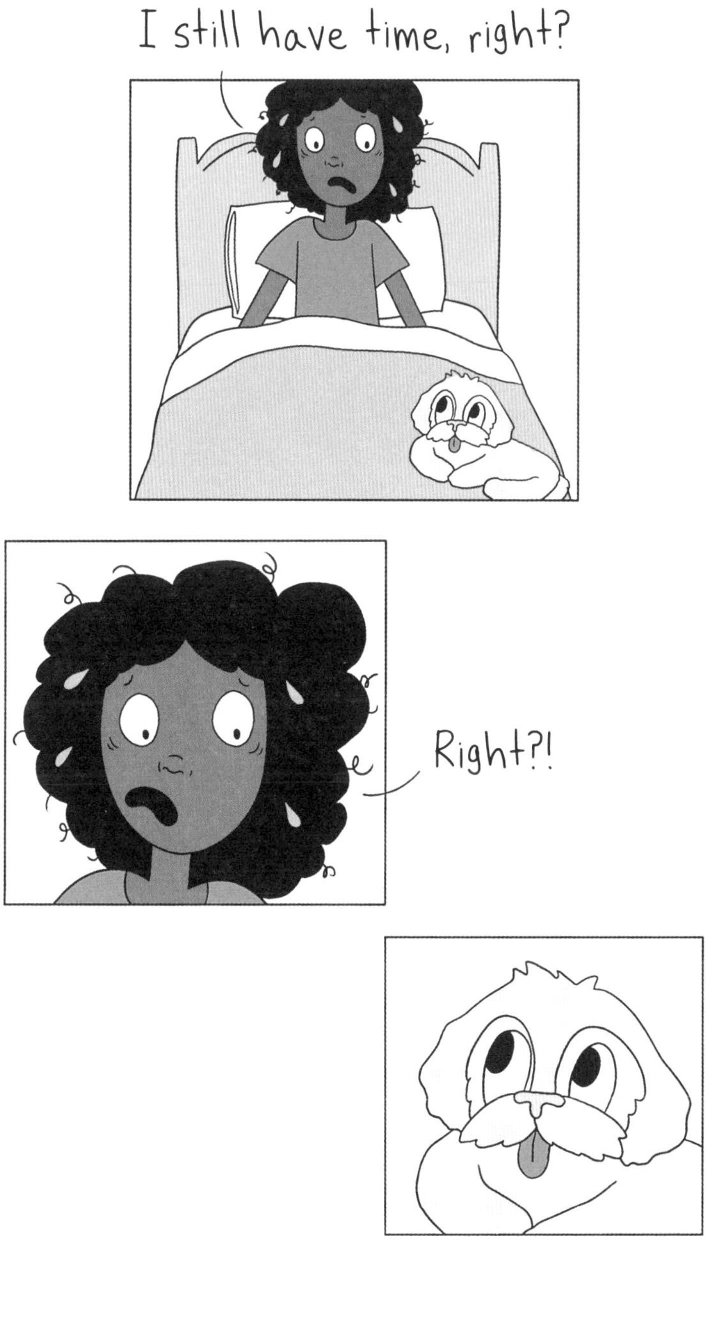
I still have time, right?
Right?!

3 ½ YEARS LATER

RICHMOND, VIRGINIA

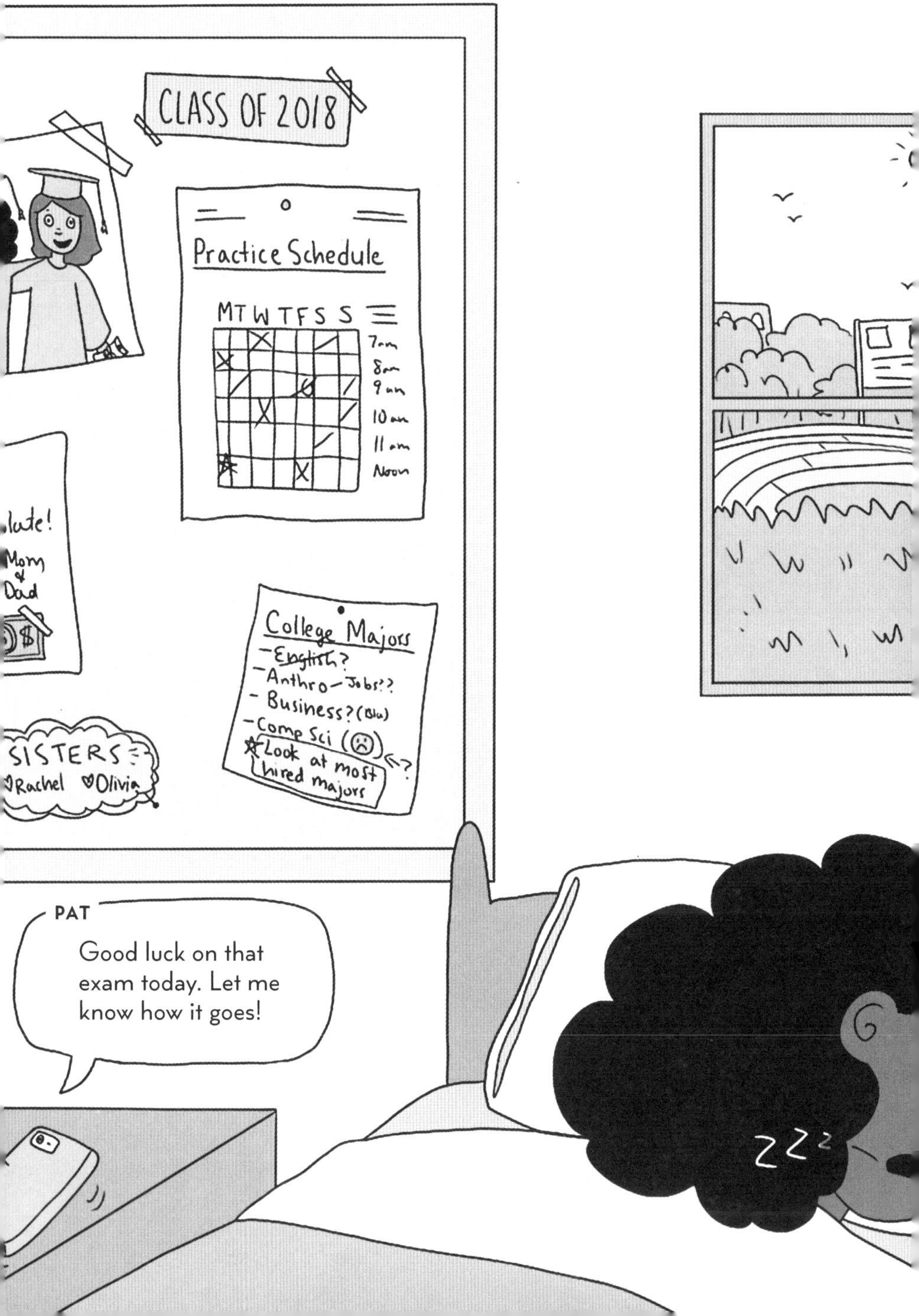
CLASS OF 2018
Practice Schedule
M T W T F S S
7am
8am
9am
10am
11am
Noon
College Majors
-English?
-Anthro-Jobs??
-Business? (Blu)
-Comp Sci
Look at most hired majors
SISTERS
Rachel Olivia
Mom & Dad
$
PAT
Good luck on that exam today. Let me know how it goes!
ZZZ

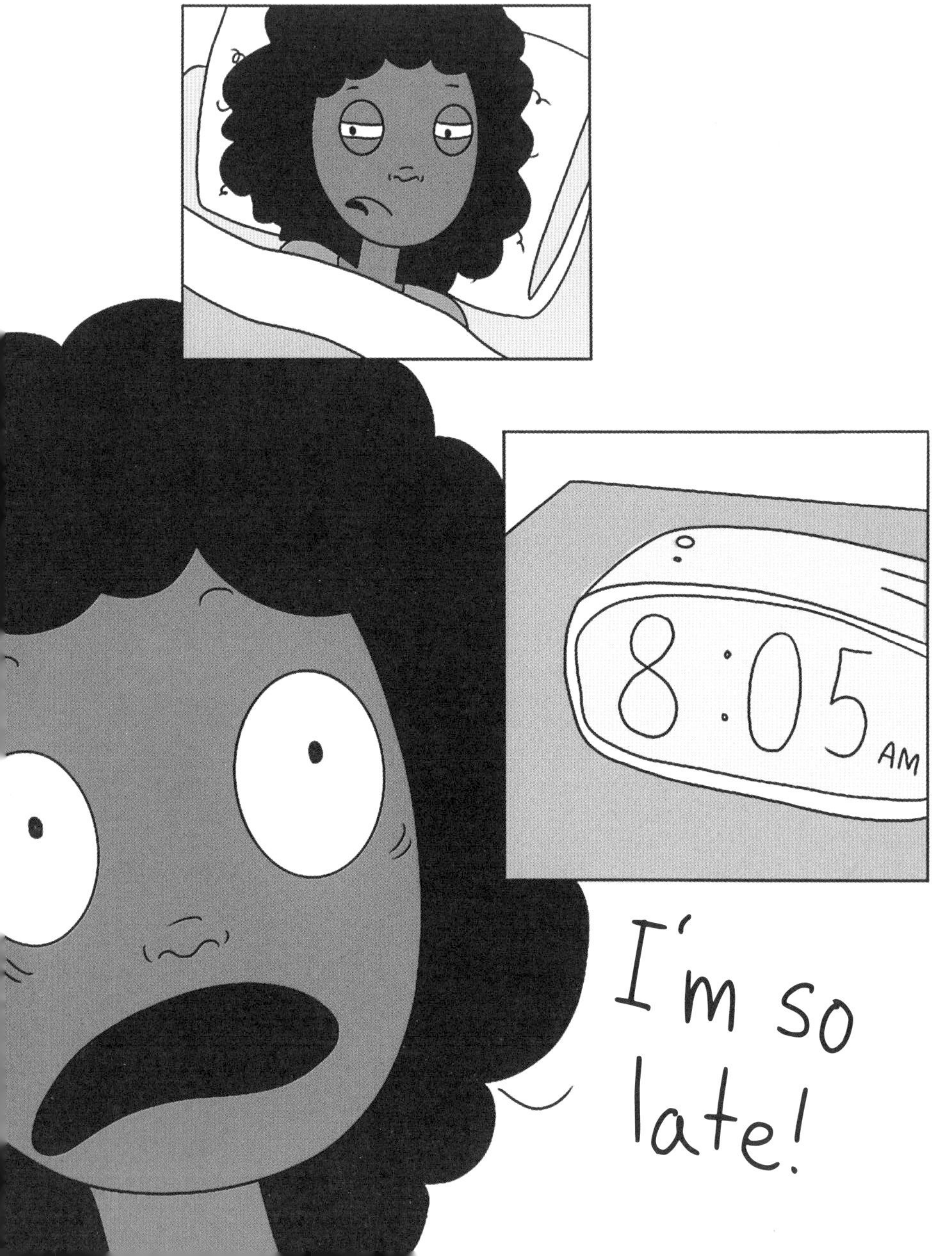
8:05 AM
I'm so late!

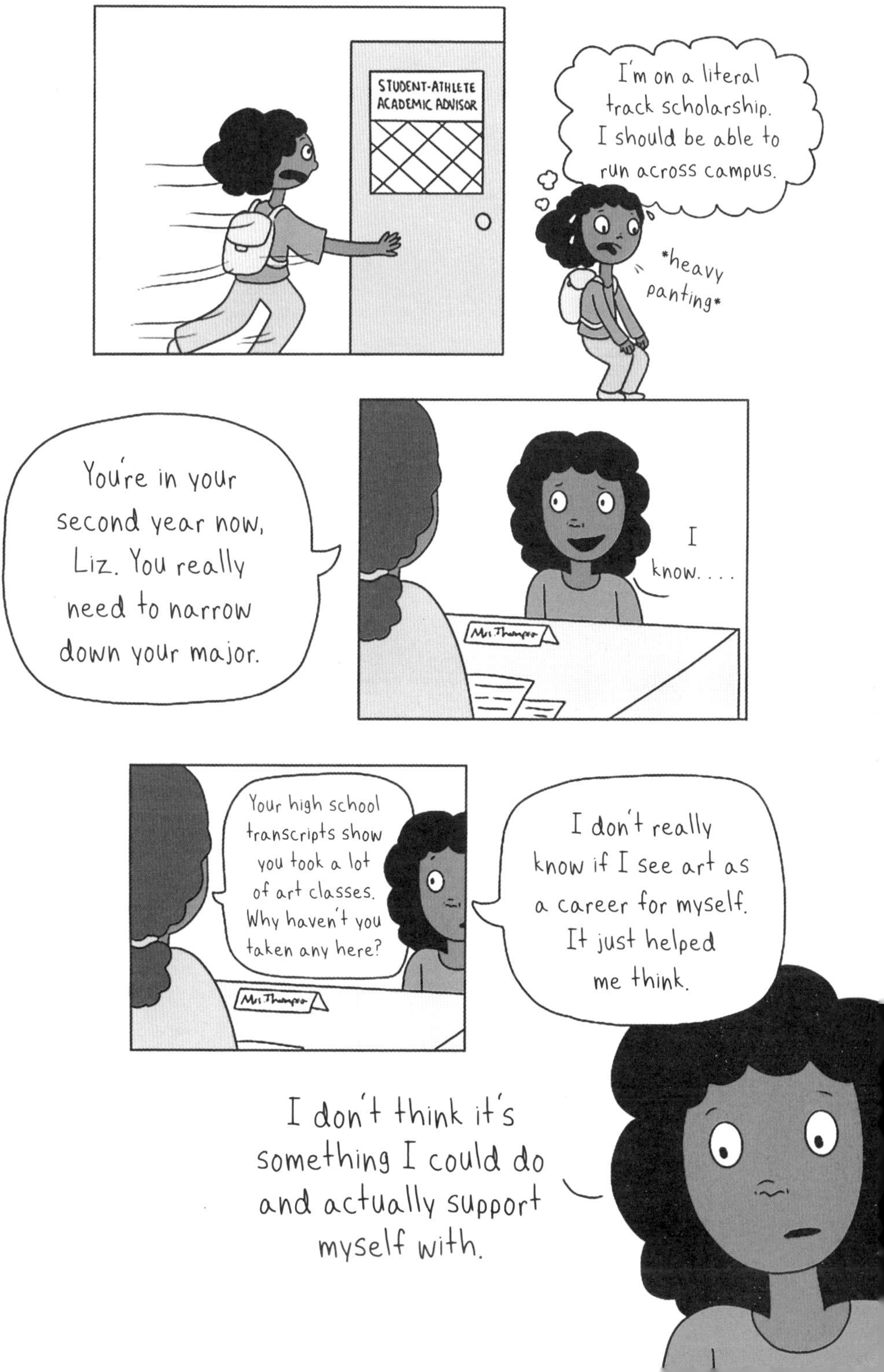
STUDENT-ATHLETE ACADEMIC ADVISOR
I'm on a literal track scholarship. I should be able to run across campus.
heavy panting
You're in your second year now, Liz. You really need to narrow down your major.
I know. . . .
Your high school transcripts show you took a lot of art classes. Why haven't you taken any here?
I don't really know if I see art as a career for myself. It just helped me think.
I don't think it's something I could do and actually support myself with.

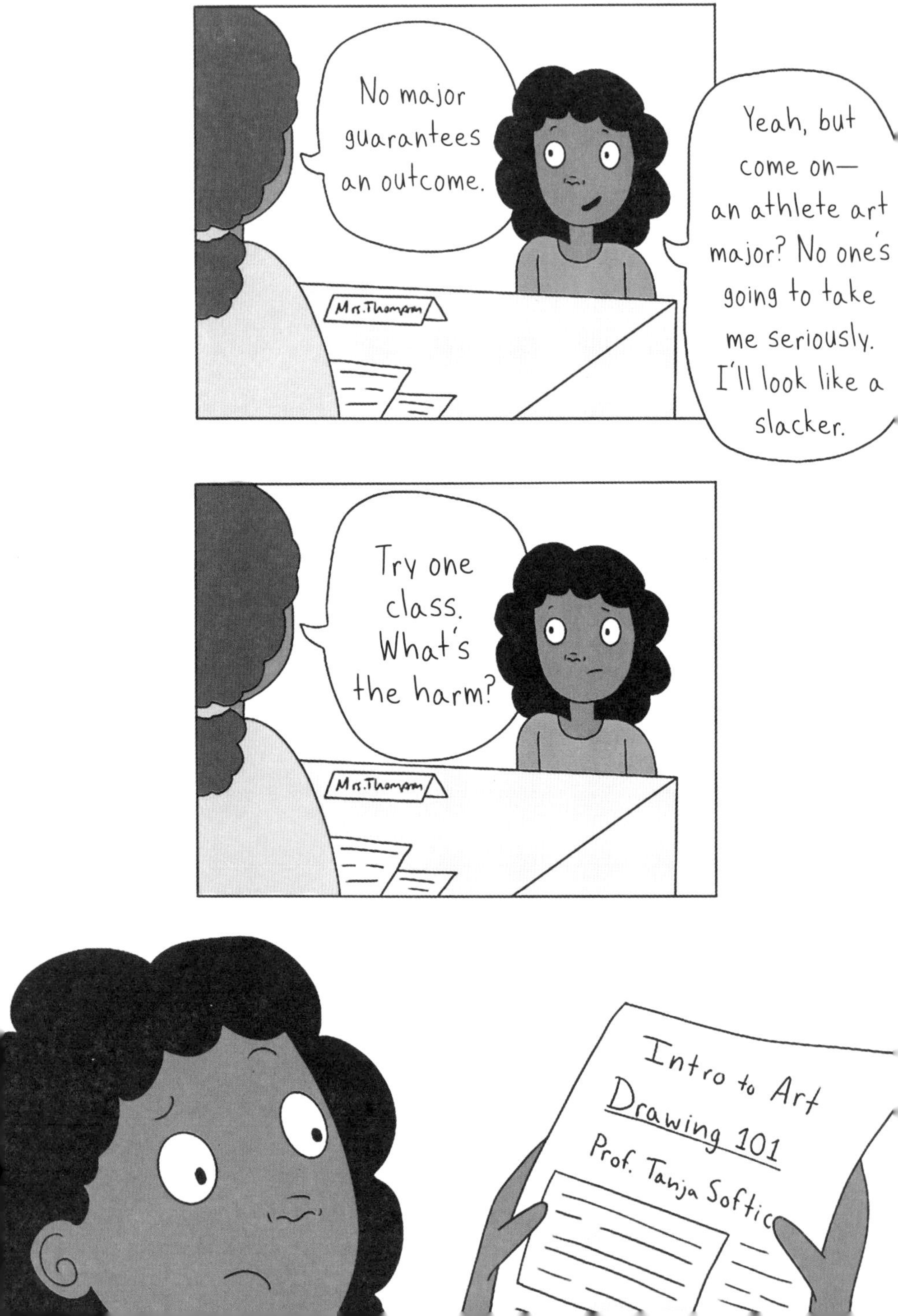
No major guarantees an outcome.
Yeah, but come on— an athlete art major? No one's going to take me seriously. I'll look like a slacker.
Mrs. Thompson
Try one class. What's the harm?
Mrs. Thompson
Intro to Art
Drawing 101
Prof. Tanja Softic

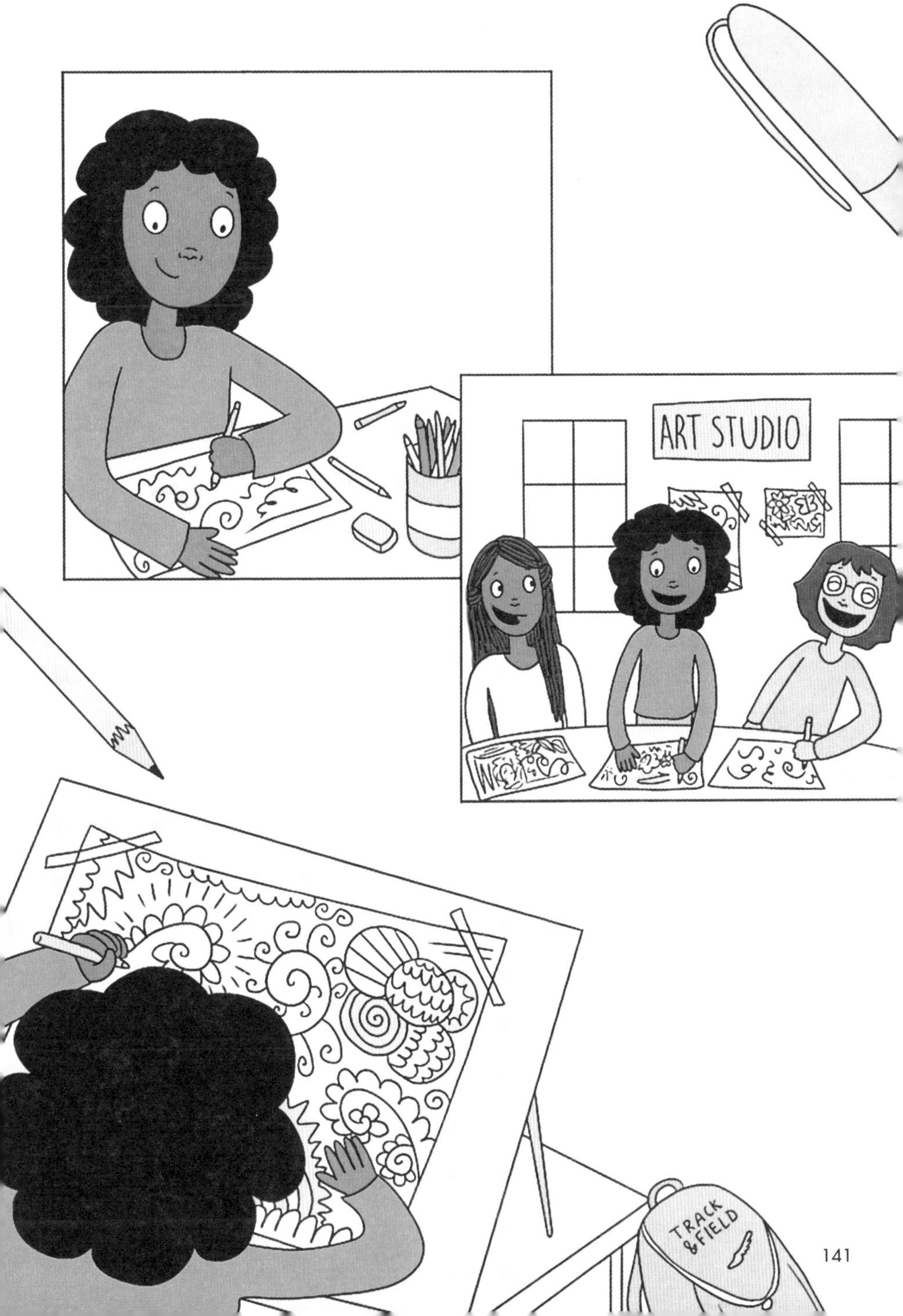
ART STUDIO
TRACK & FIELD

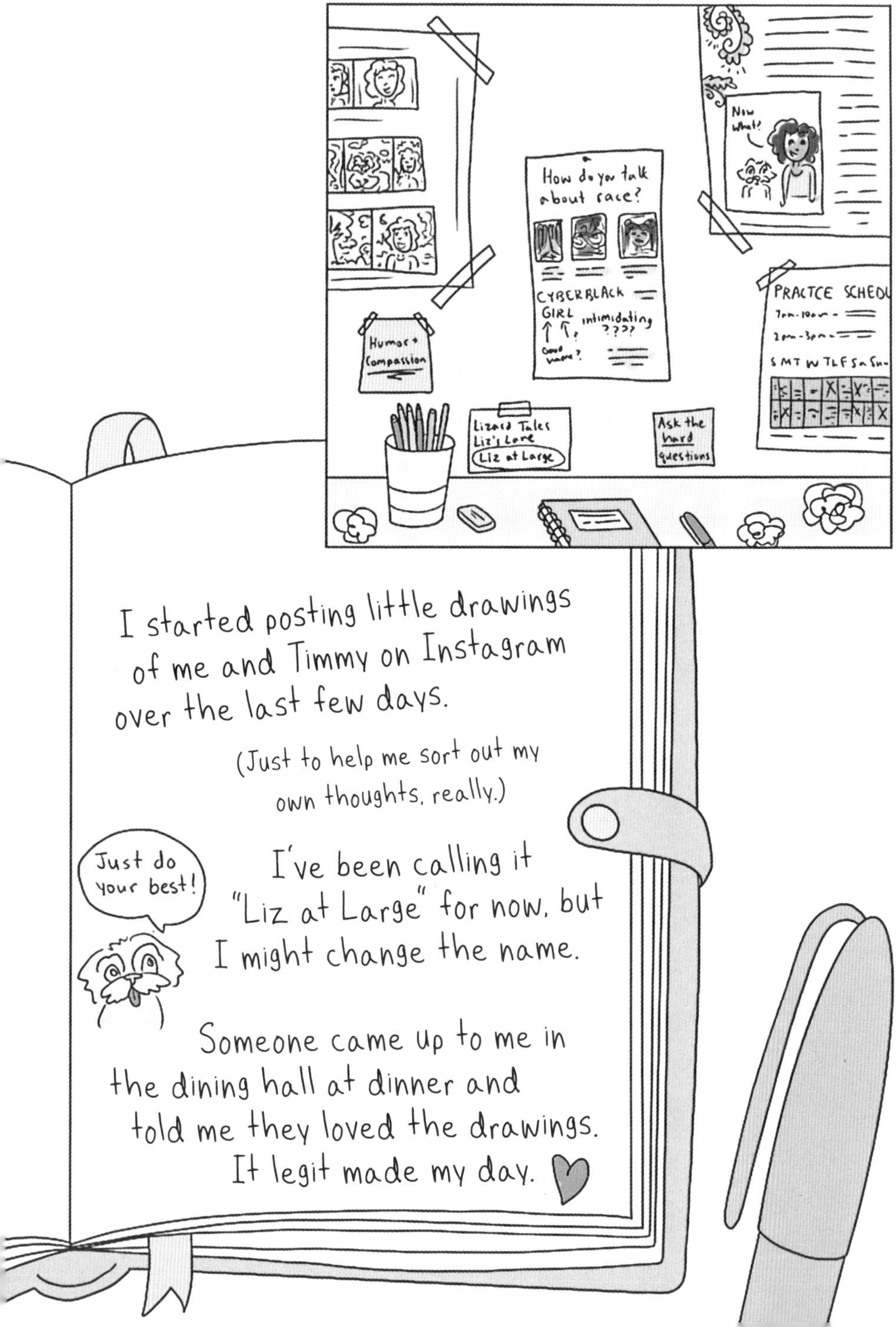
Now what?
How do you talk about race?
CYBERBLACK GIRL
intimidating ????
Good name?
PRACTCE SCHEDU
Humor + Compassion
Lizard Tales
Liz's Love
Liz at Large
Ask the hard questions
I started posting little drawings of me and Timmy on Instagram over the last few days.
(Just to help me sort out my own thoughts, really.)
Just do your best!
I've been calling it "Liz at Large" for now, but I might change the name.
Someone came up to me in the dining hall at dinner and told me they loved the drawings. It legit made my day.

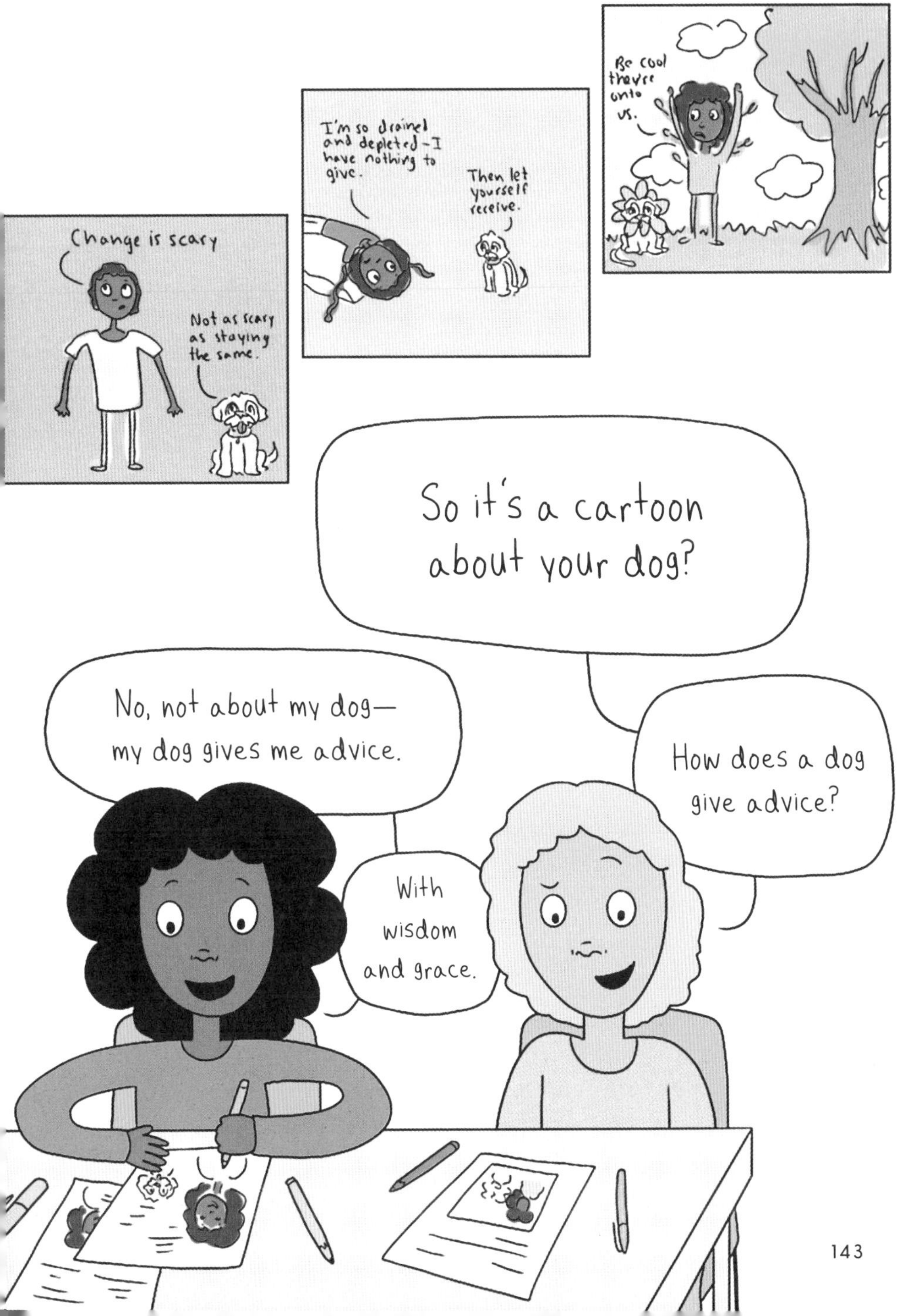
Change is scary
Not as scary as staying the same.
I'm so drained and depleted—I have nothing to give.
Then let yourself receive.
Be cool they're onto us.
So it's a cartoon about your dog?
No, not about my dog—my dog gives me advice.
How does a dog give advice?
With wisdom and grace.

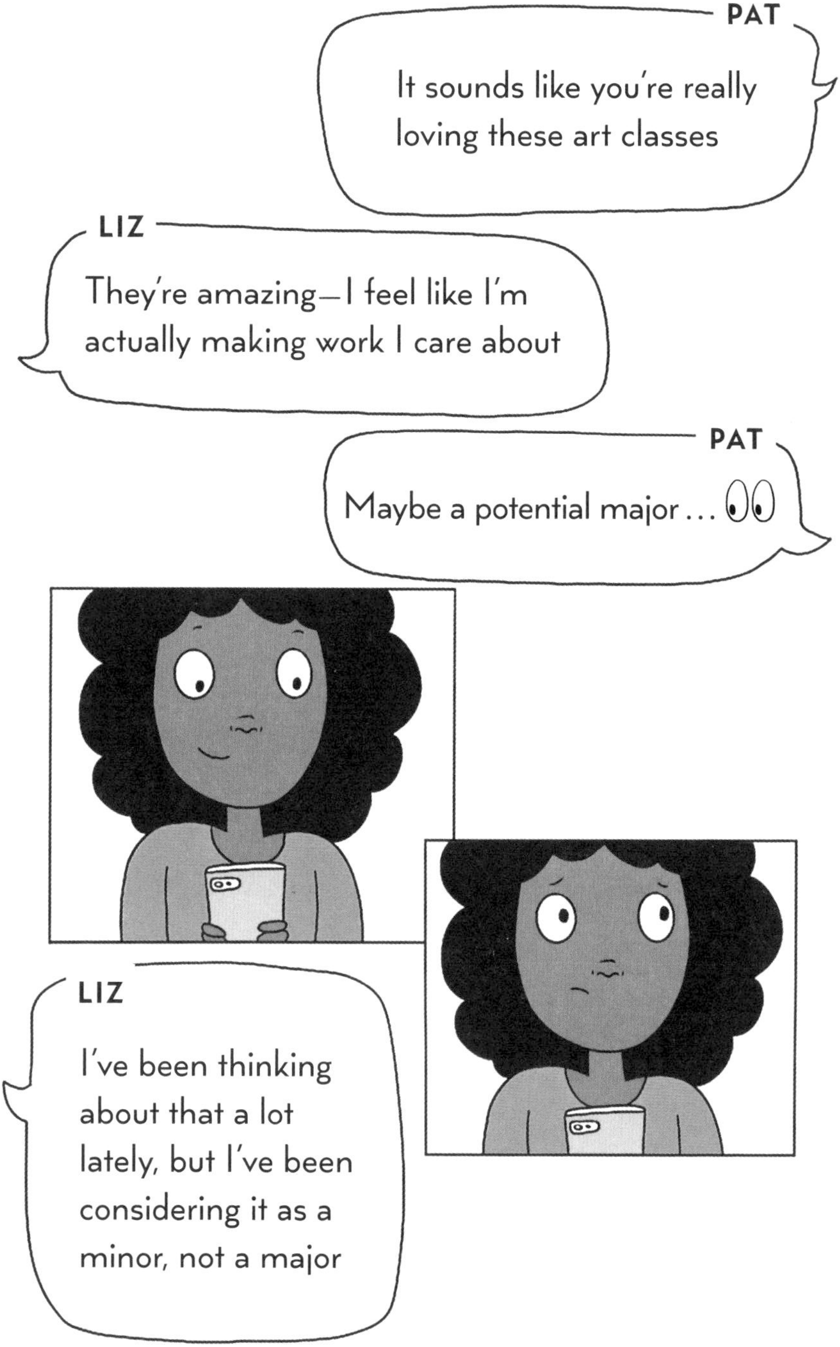
PAT
It sounds like you're really loving these art classes
LIZ
They're amazing—I feel like I'm actually making work I care about
PAT
Maybe a potential major . . .
LIZ
I've been thinking about that a lot lately, but I've been considering it as a minor, not a major

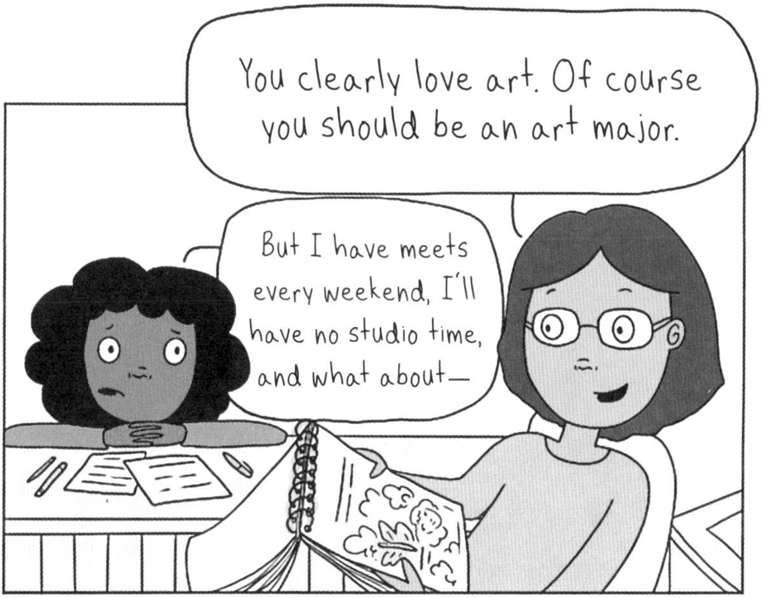
You clearly love art. Of course you should be an art major.
But I have meets every weekend, I'll have no studio time, and what about—

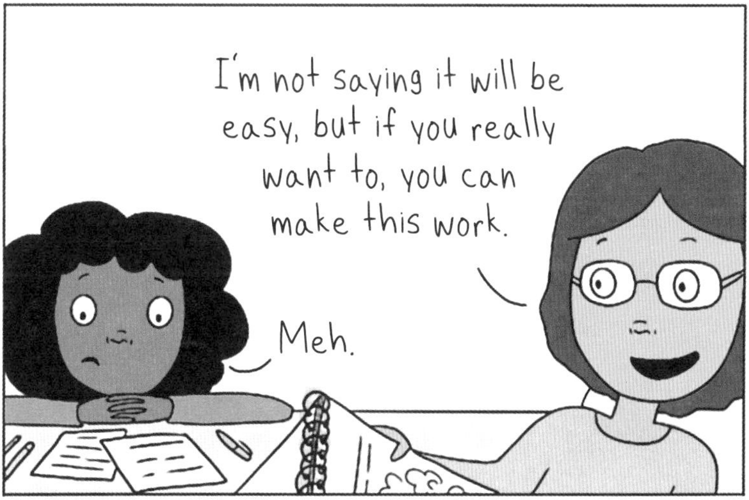
I'm not saying it will be easy, but if you really want to, you can make this work.
Meh.

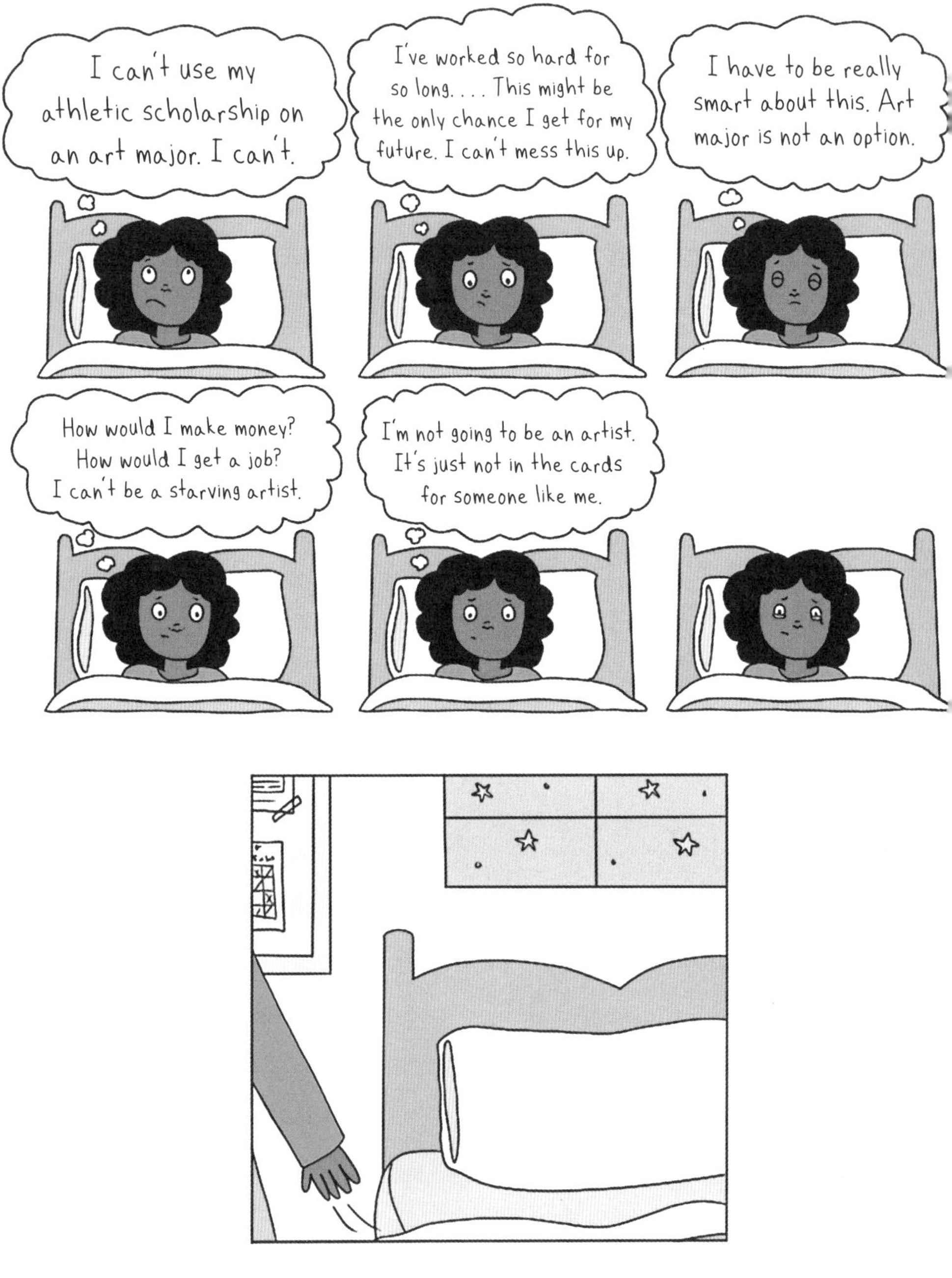
I can't use my athletic scholarship on an art major. I can't.
I've worked so hard for so long. . . . This might be the only chance I get for my future. I can't mess this up.
I have to be really smart about this. Art major is not an option.
How would I make money? How would I get a job? I can't be a starving artist.
I'm not going to be an artist. It's just not in the cards for someone like me.

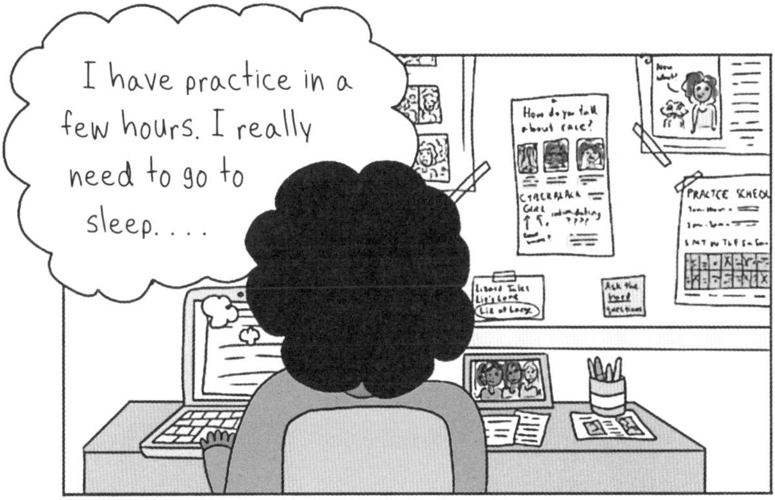
I have practice in a few hours. I really need to go to sleep. . . .

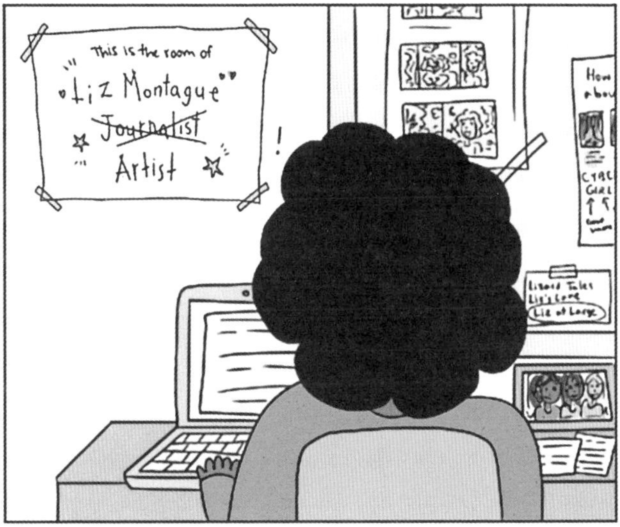
This is the room of
Liz Montague
Journalist
Artist
!

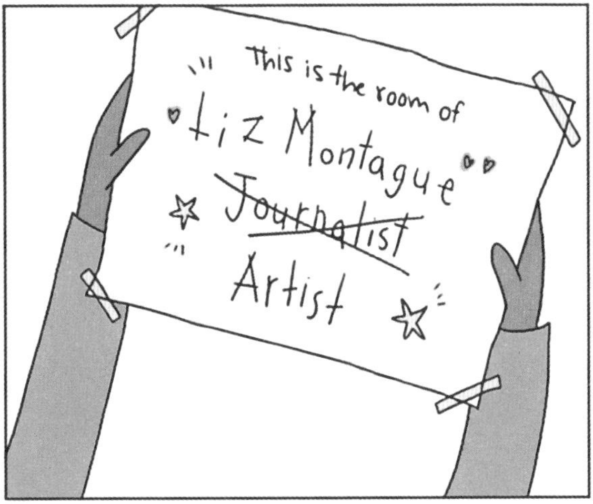
This is the room of
Liz Montague
~~Journalist~~
Artist

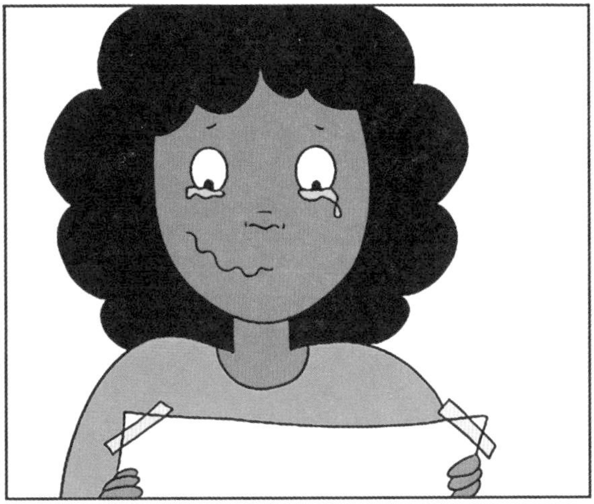

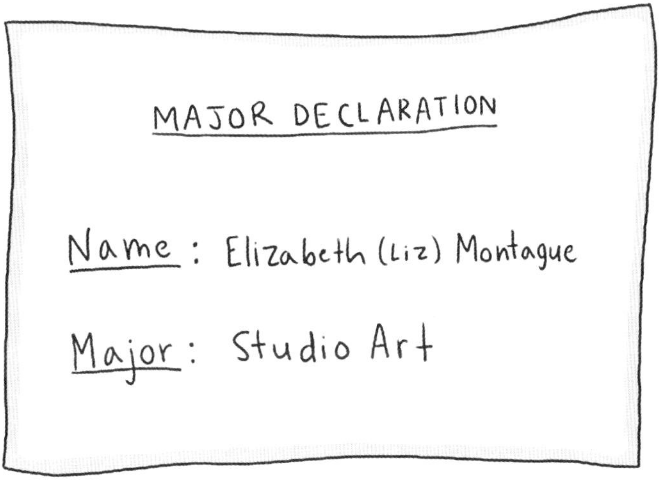
MAJOR DECLARATION
Name: Elizabeth (Liz) Montague
Major: Studio Art

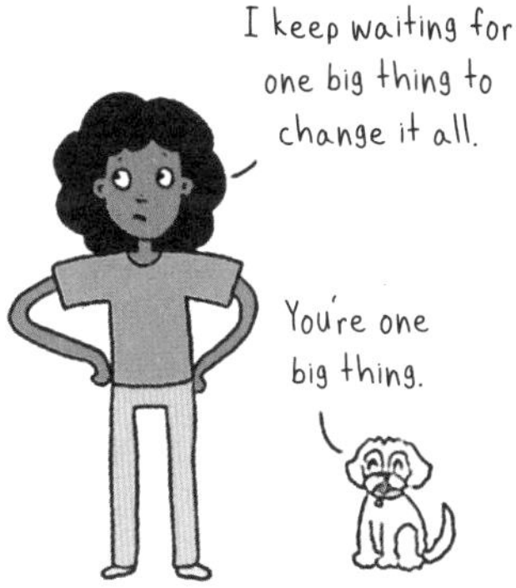
I keep waiting for one big thing to change it all.
You're one big thing.

~~AFTERWORD~~

ADULTING

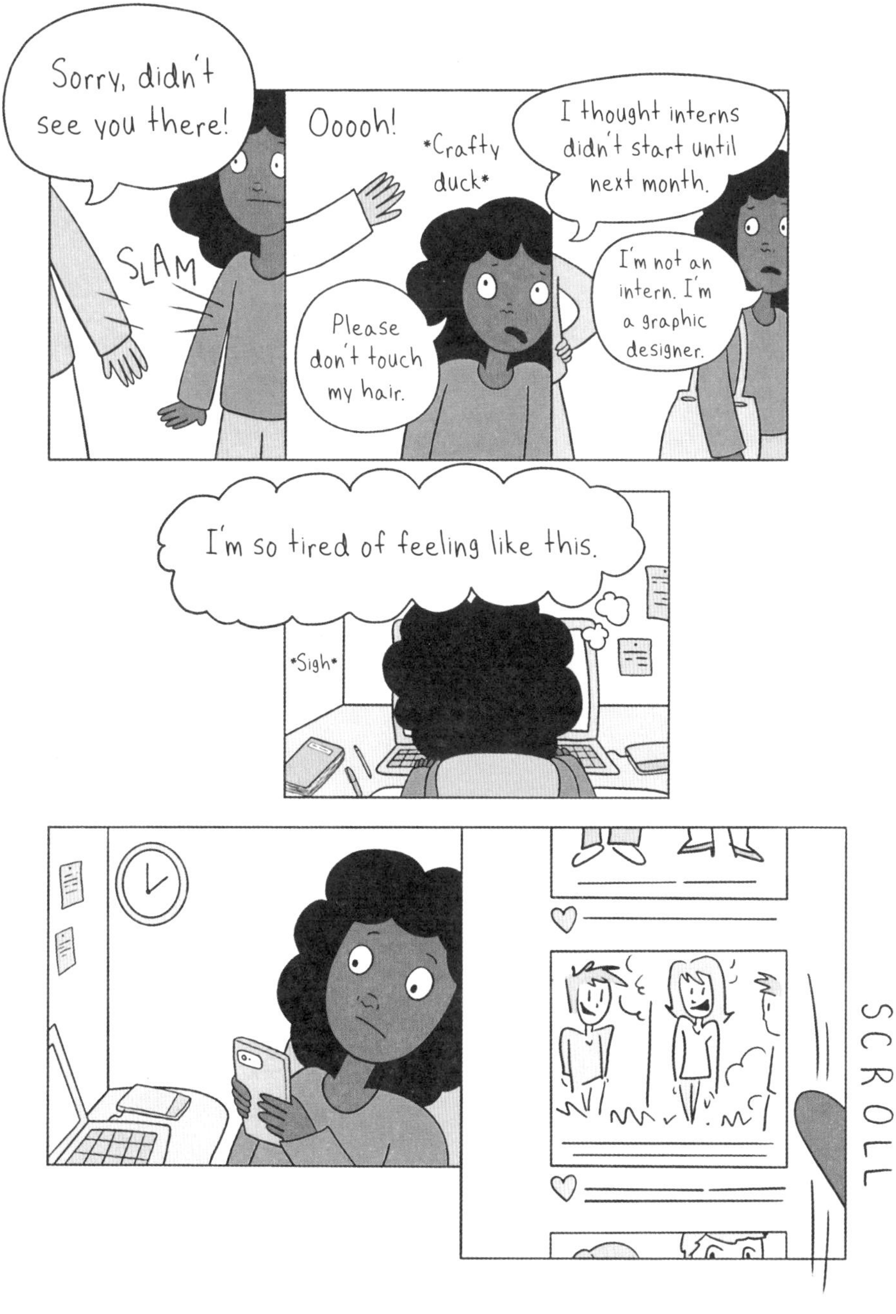
Sorry, didn't see you there!
SLAM
Ooooh!
Crafty duck
Please don't touch my hair.
I thought interns didn't start until next month.
I'm not an intern. I'm a graphic designer.
I'm so tired of feeling like this.
Sigh
SCROLL

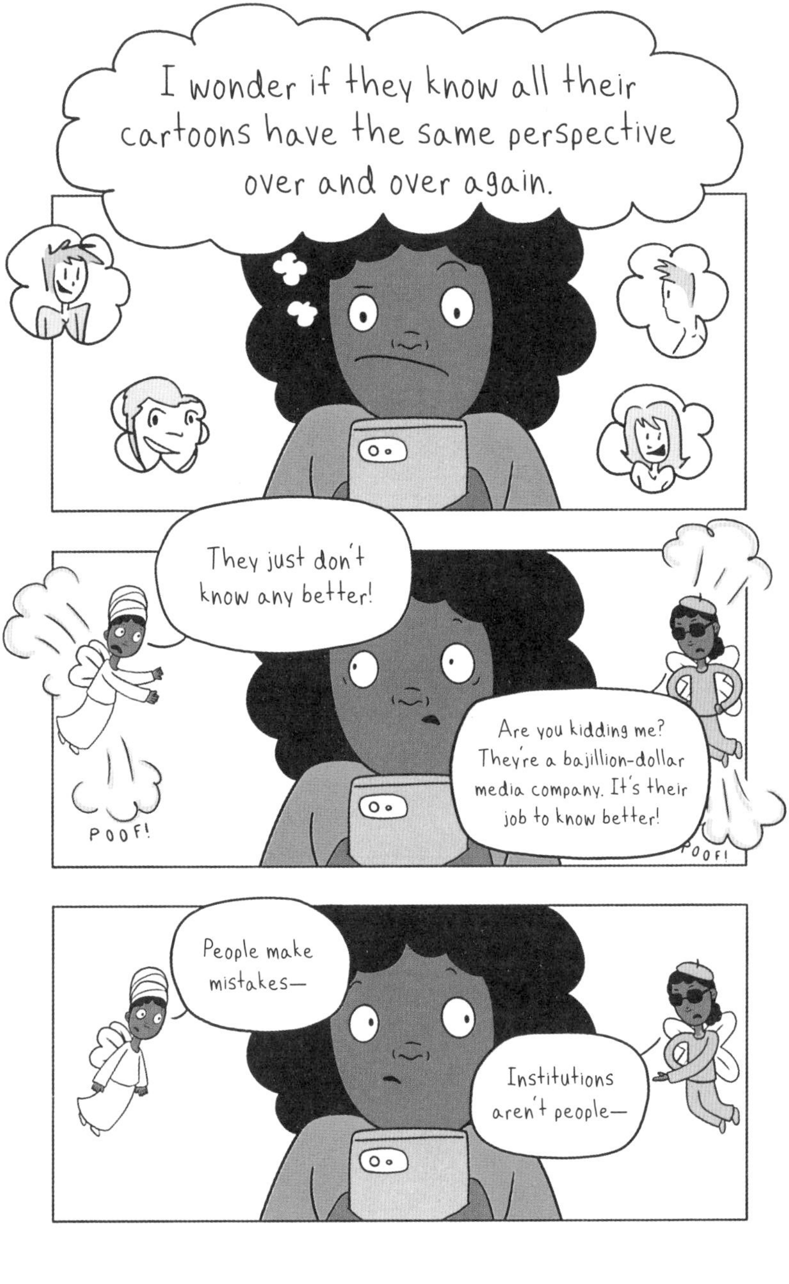
I wonder if they know all their cartoons have the same perspective over and over again.
They just don't know any better!
POOF!
Are you kidding me? They're a bajillion-dollar media company. It's their job to know better!
POOF!
People make mistakes—
Institutions aren't people—

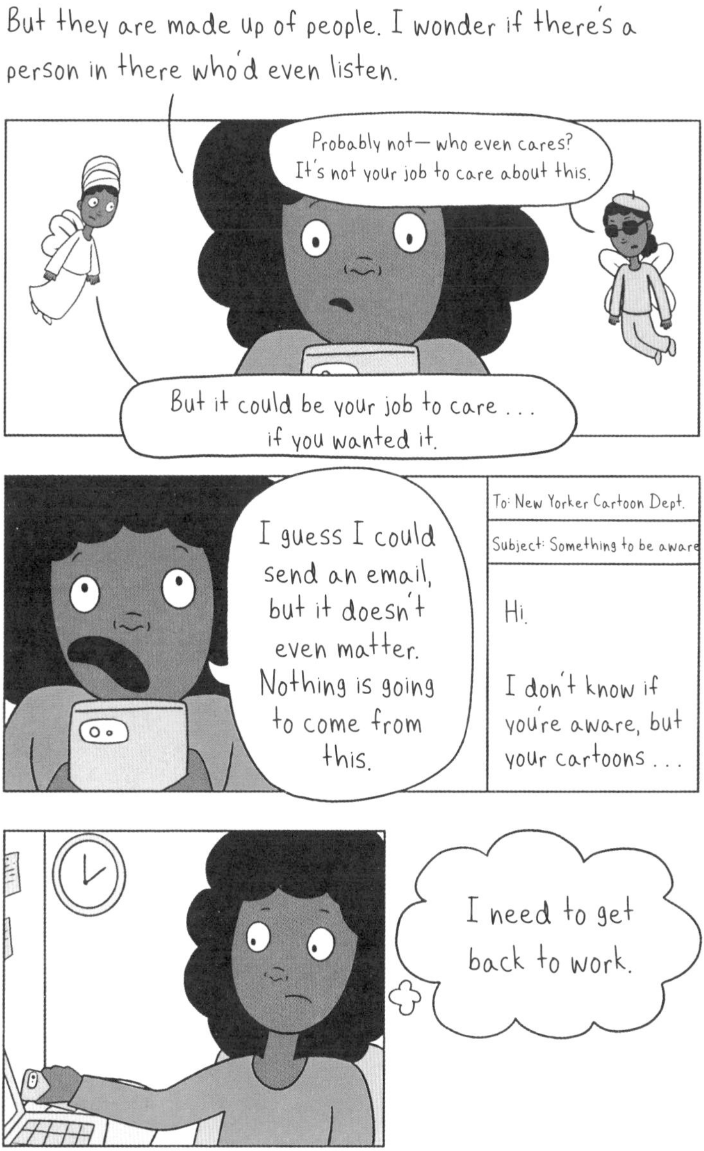

But they are made up of people. I wonder if there's a person in there who'd even listen.
Probably not— who even cares? It's not your job to care about this.
But it could be your job to care . . . if you wanted it.
I guess I could send an email, but it doesn't even matter. Nothing is going to come from this.
To: New Yorker Cartoon Dept.
Subject: Something to be aware
Hi.
I don't know if you're aware, but your cartoons . . .
I need to get back to work.

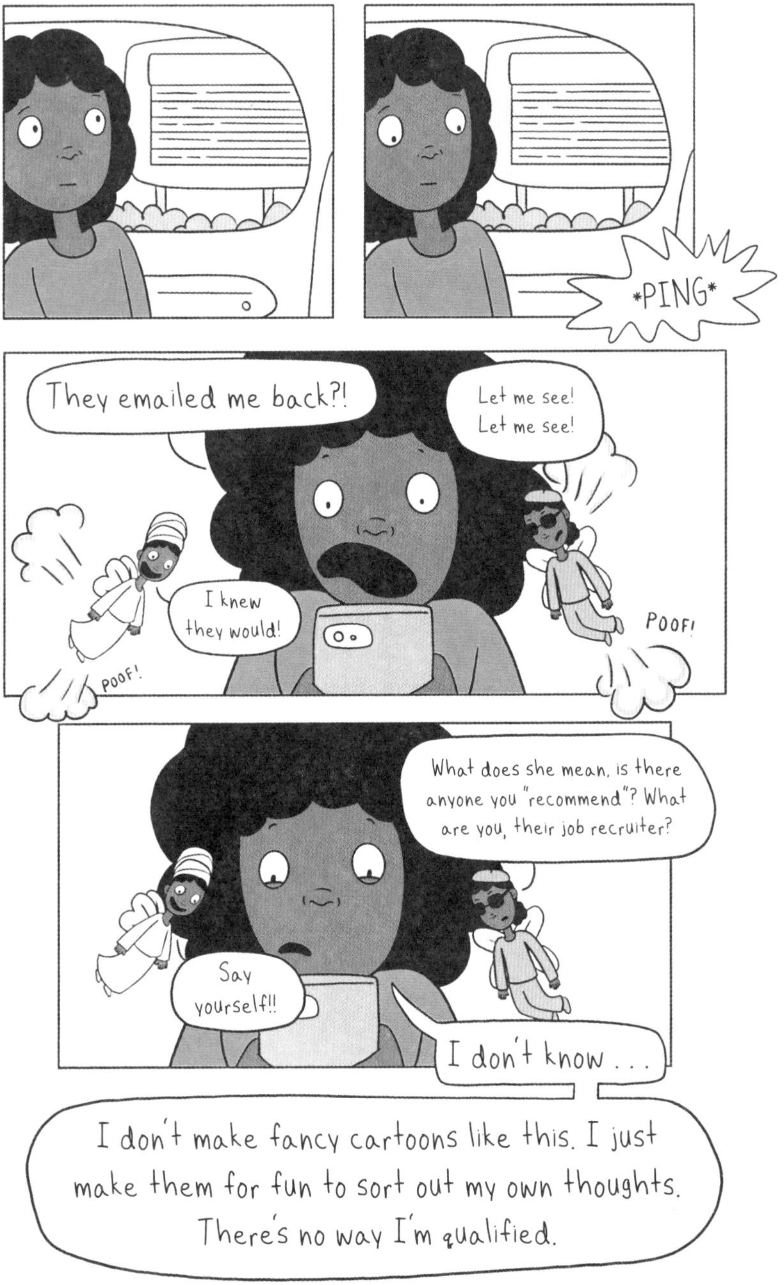
PING
They emailed me back?!
Let me see! Let me see!
I knew they would!
POOF!
POOF!
What does she mean, is there anyone you "recommend"? What are you, their job recruiter?
Say yourself!!
I don't know . . .
I don't make fancy cartoons like this. I just make them for fun to sort out my own thoughts. There's no way I'm qualified.

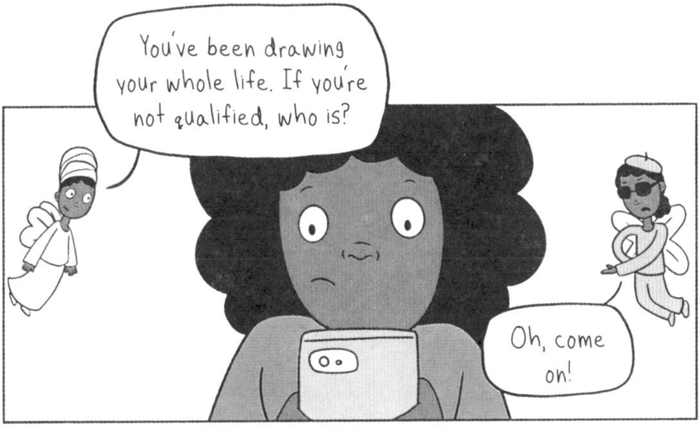
You've been drawing your whole life. If you're not qualified, who is?
Oh, come on!

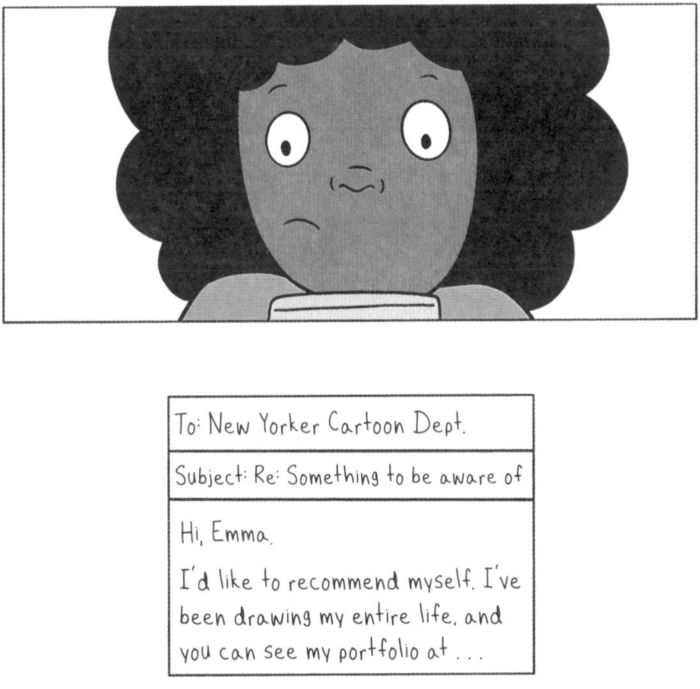

To: New Yorker Cartoon Dept.

Subject: Re: Something to be aware of

Hi, Emma.

I'd like to recommend myself. I've been drawing my entire life, and you can see my portfolio at . . .

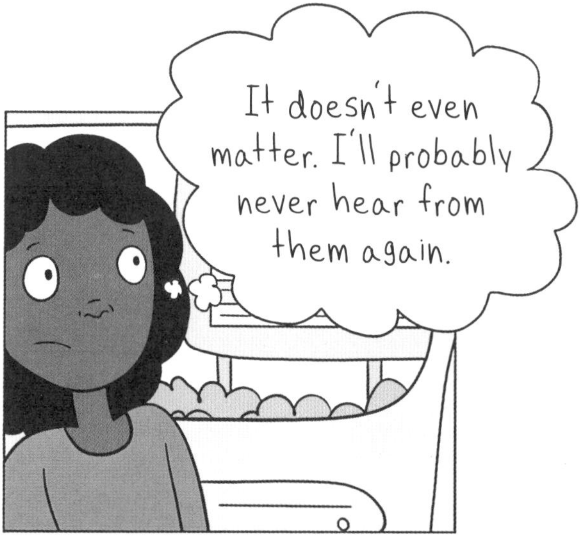
It doesn't even matter. I'll probably never hear from them again.

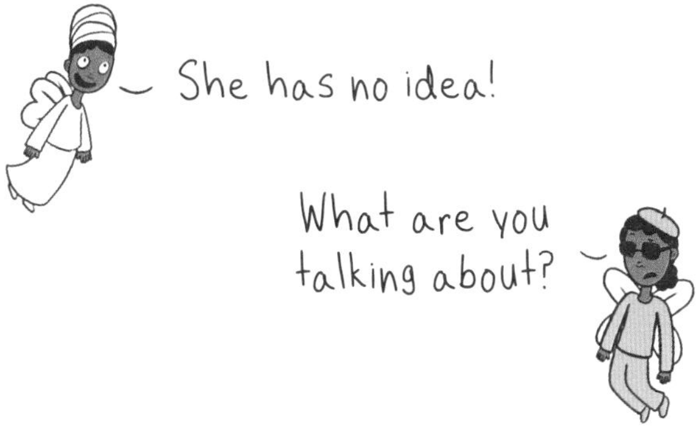

She has no idea!

What are you talking about?

MY NEW YORKER CARTOONS (!!)

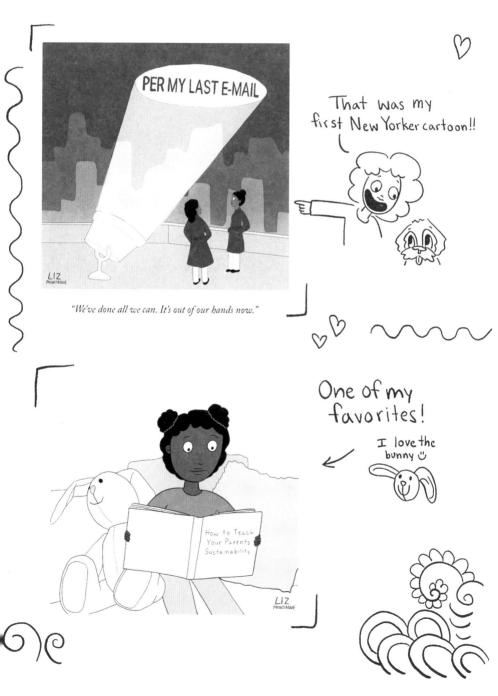

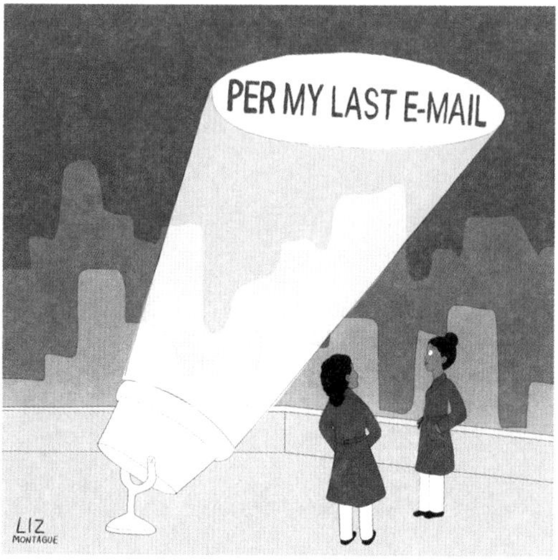
PER MY LAST E-MAIL
LIZ MONTAGUE

"We've done all we can. It's out of our hands now."

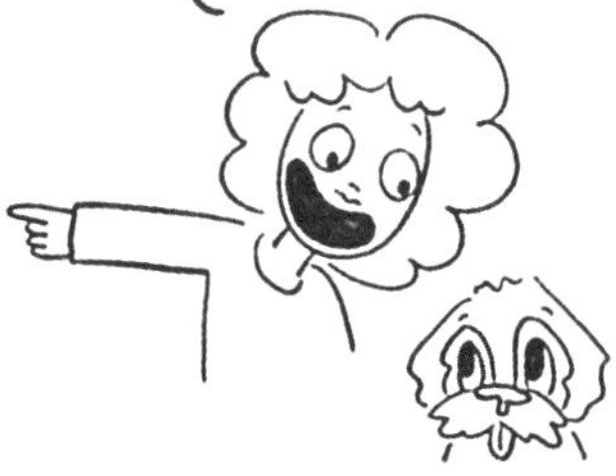
That was my first New Yorker cartoon!!

One of my favorites!

I love the bunny ☺

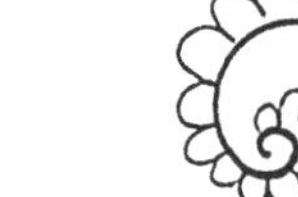

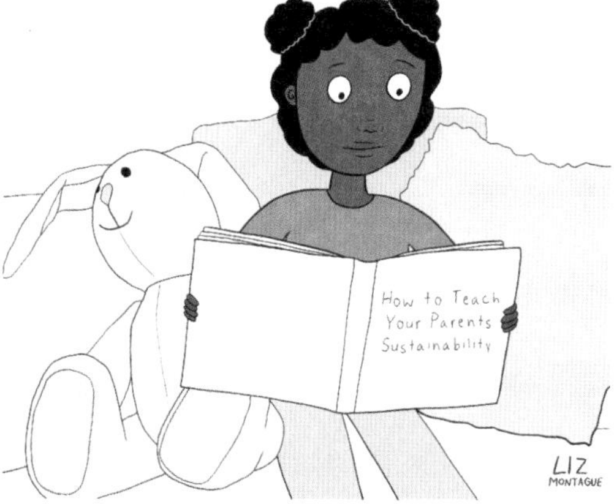
How to Teach Your Parents Sustainability
LIZ MONTAGUE

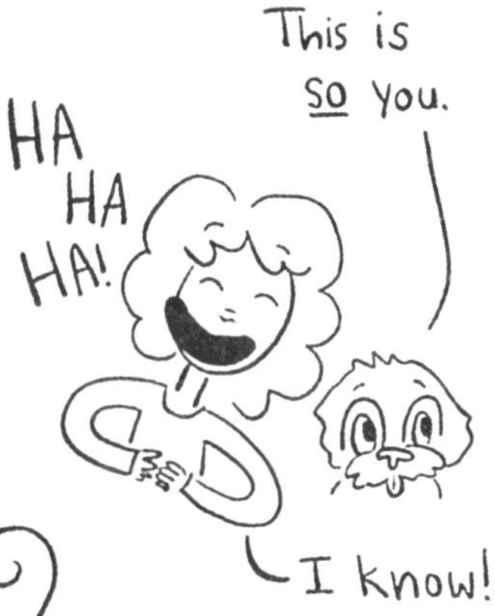
HA HA HA!
This is so you.
I know!

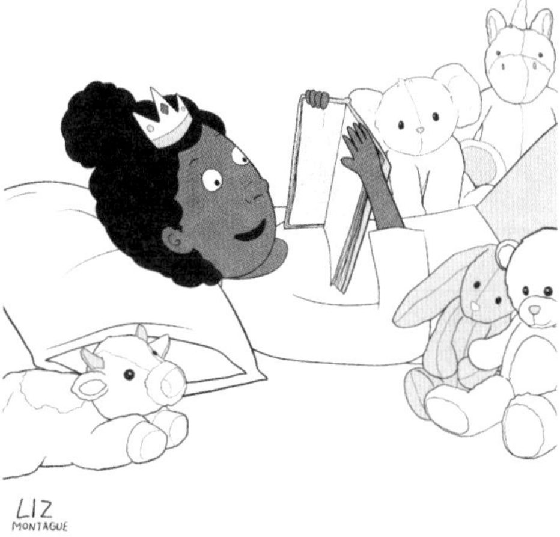
LIZ MONTAGUE

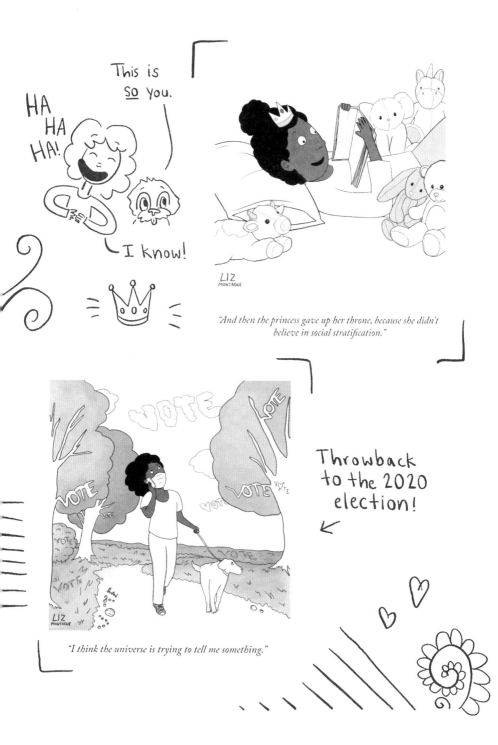

"And then the princess gave up her throne, because she didn't believe in social stratification."

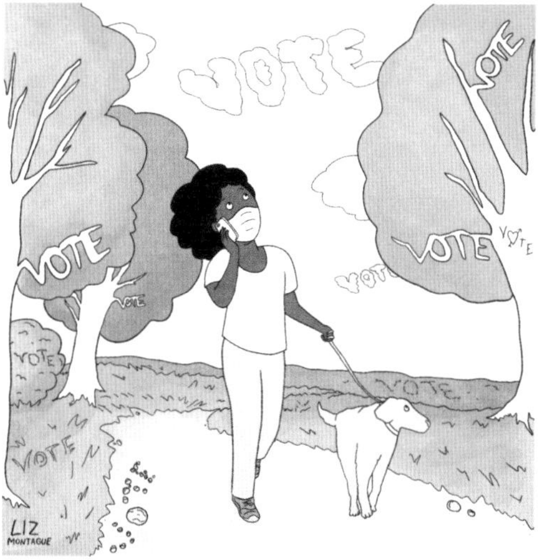
VOTE
VOTE
VOTE
VOTE
VOTE
LIZ MONTAGUE

"I think the universe is trying to tell me something."

Throwback to the 2020 election!

MORE STUFF ADULT ME DID

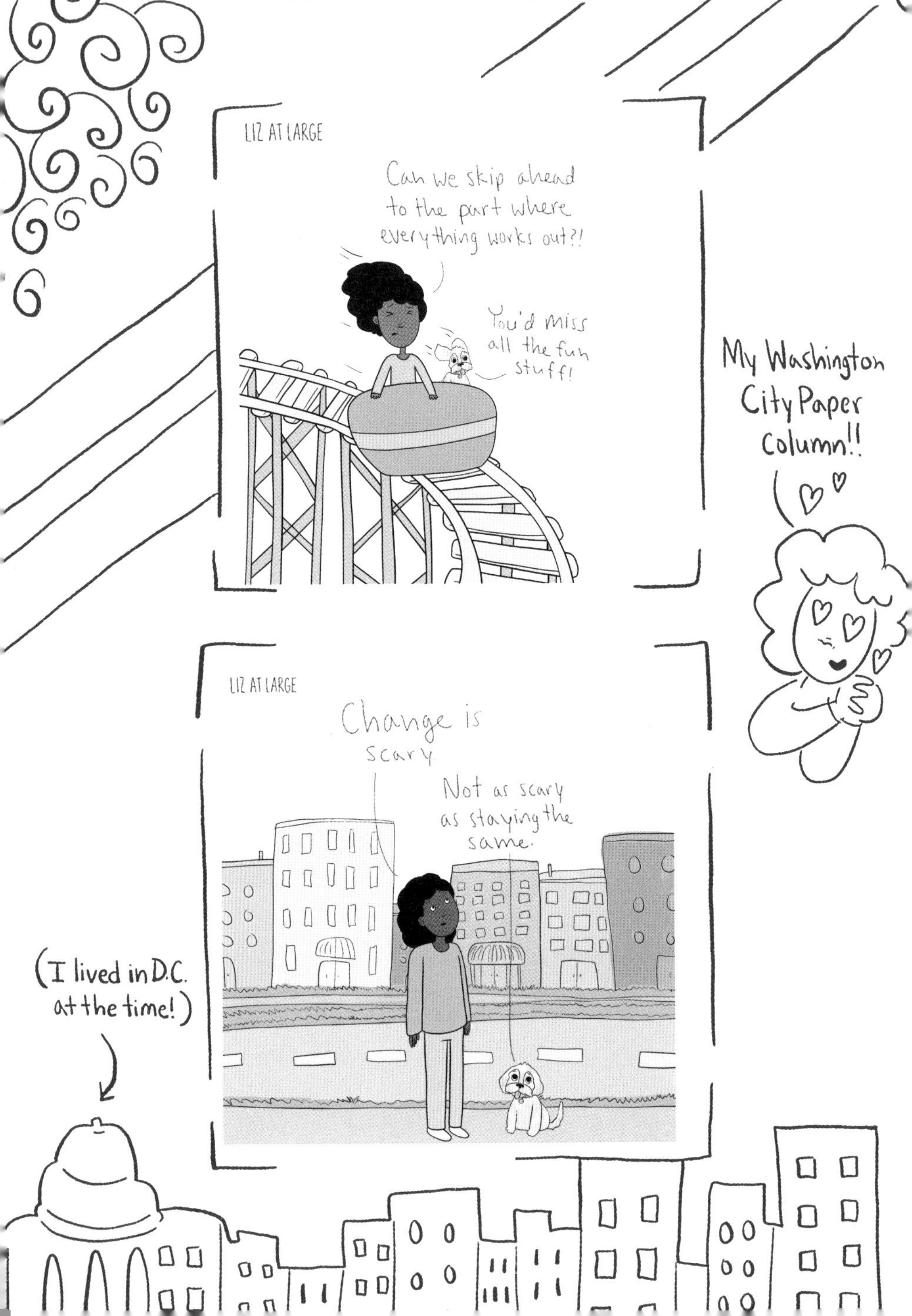
LIZ AT LARGE
Can we skip ahead to the part where everything works out?!
You'd miss all the fun stuff!
My Washington City Paper column!!
LIZ AT LARGE
Change is scary
Not as scary as staying the same.
(I lived in D.C. at the time!)

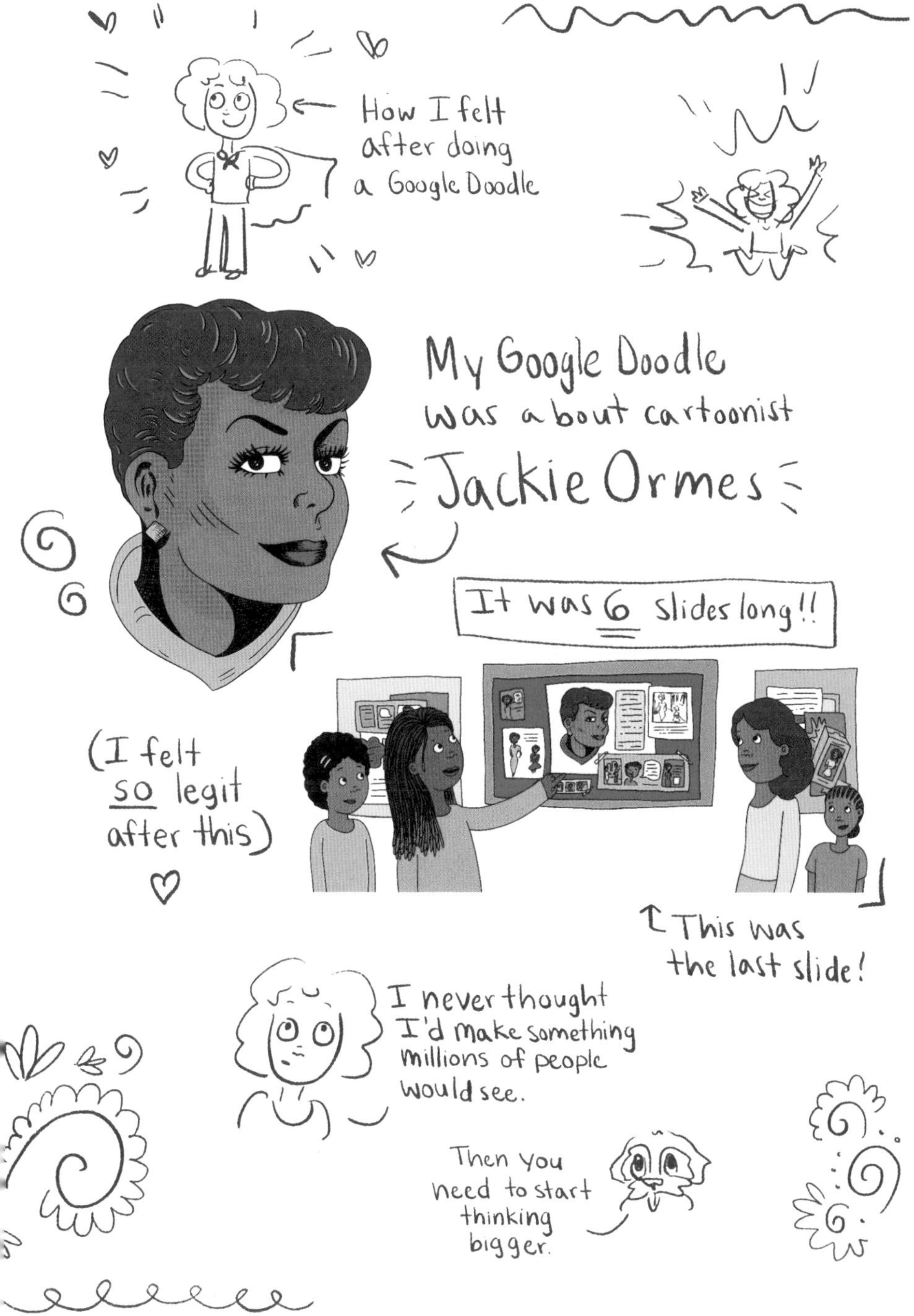
How I felt after doing a Google Doodle
My Google Doodle was about cartoonist
Jackie Ormes
It was 6 slides long!!
(I felt so legit after this)
This was the last slide!
I never thought I'd make something millions of people would see.
Then you need to start thinking bigger.

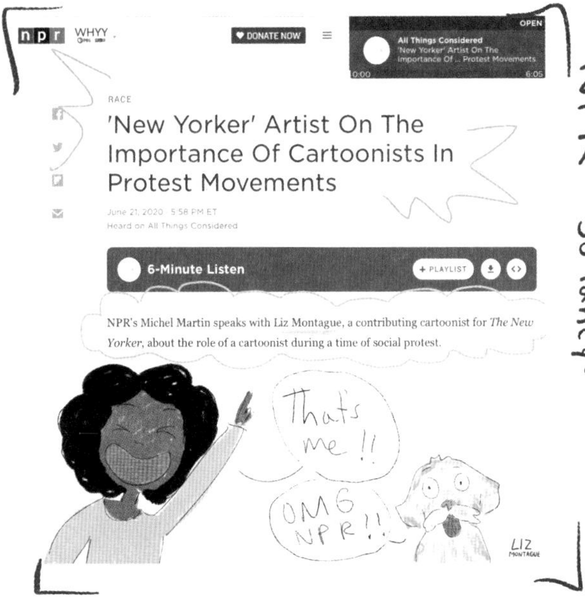
npr
WHYY
DONATE NOW
OPEN
All Things Considered
'New Yorker' Artist On The Importance Of ... Protest Movements
0:00
6:05
RACE
'New Yorker' Artist On The Importance Of Cartoonists In Protest Movements
June 21, 2020 · 5:58 PM ET
Heard on All Things Considered
6-Minute Listen
+ PLAYLIST
NPR's Michel Martin speaks with Liz Montague, a contributing cartoonist for The New Yorker, about the role of a cartoonist during a time of social protest.
That's me!!
OMG NPR!!
LIZ MONTAGUE

NPR ~So fancy~

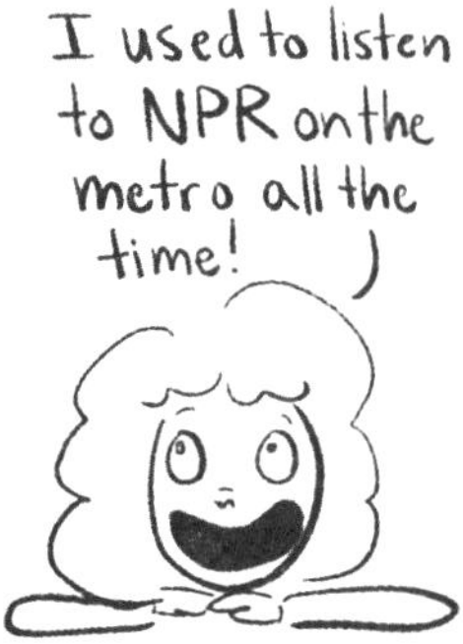
I used to listen to NPR on the metro all the time!

By now I lived in

Philly

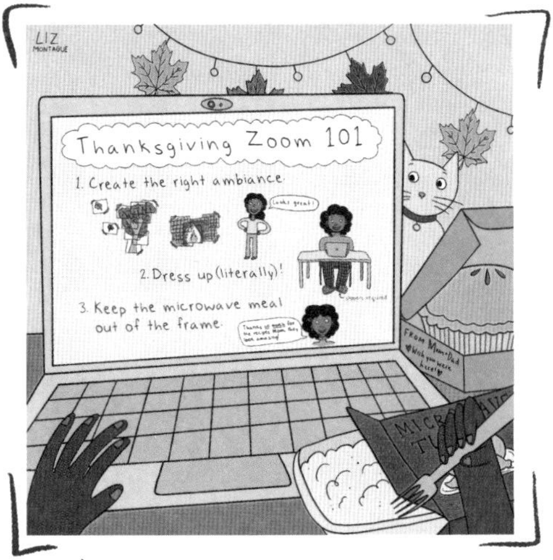
LIZ MONTAGUE
Thanksgiving Zoom 101
1. Create the right ambiance
Looks great!
2. Dress up (literally)!
3. Keep the microwave meal out of the frame

Food Network

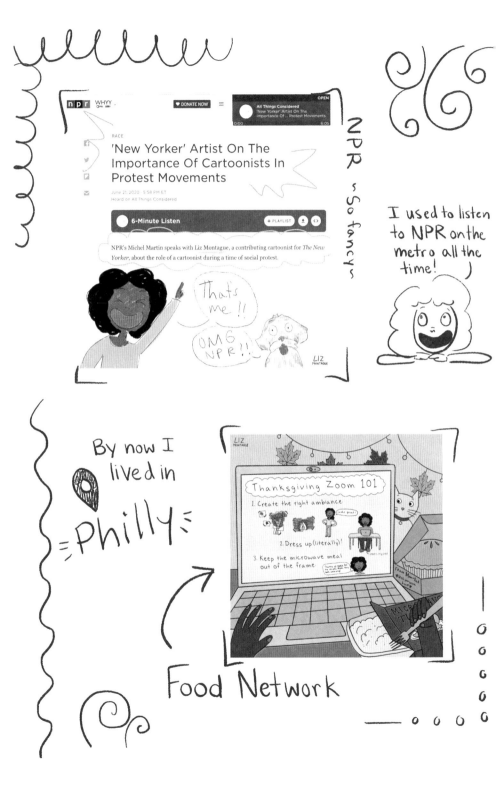

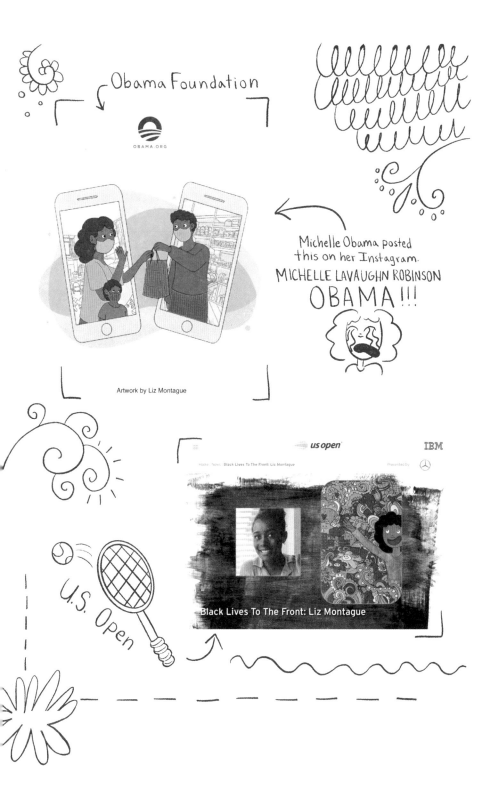

Obama Foundation

OBAMA.ORG

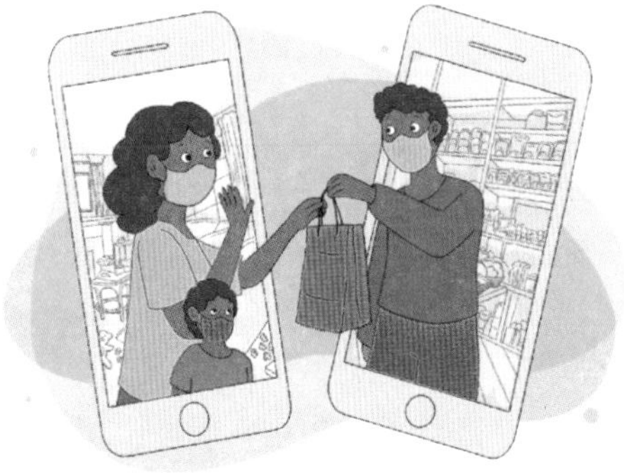

Artwork by Liz Montague

Michelle Obama posted this on her Instagram. MICHELLE LAVAUGHN ROBINSON OBAMA!!!

U.S. Open

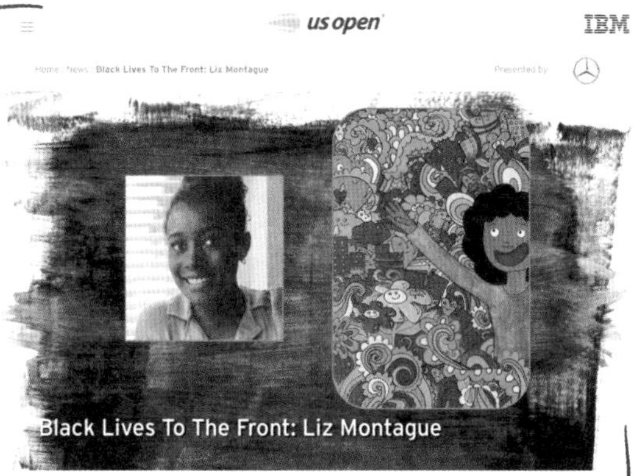

us open
IBM
Home / News / Black Lives To The Front: Liz Montague
Presented by
Black Lives To The Front: Liz Montague

ACKNOWLEDGMENTS

Thank you to this project for being there during 2020 when I really needed something to hold on to.

Thank you to Annie Kelley, my amazing editor, for your humor and unwavering confidence in me. I'm so grateful I got to do my first book with you! Thank you to Wendi Gu, my incredible agent, for always being a guiding light full of understanding and care. Thank you to Carol Ly for your hard work on this project that did not go unnoticed! You all were absolutely vital in this book coming to fruition.

Mom and Dad, thank you for keeping me in art and sports and out of trouble and putting me in a position to make good choices (even when I fought tooth and nail against it). Olivia and Rachel, thanks for always keeping it real and doing the hard stuff first so I knew it was possible. I'm eternally grateful that we all get to do this journey together, and I love you guys.

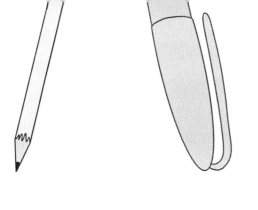

Pat, thank you for pep talks, the constant shoulder to cry on, and being the best person to laugh with. Thank you for building a life with me that makes my dreams possible.

Thank you to my amazing friends Steph, Sarah, Shelby, Nene, Whitney, and so many others for all the Facetimes, texts, and phone calls. I'm so grateful for your love and support.

Thank you to Tanja Softic, Jeremy Drummond, Dr. David Stevens, and Dr. Monti Datta for teaching me the power of craft and purpose.

Thank you to Mrs. Wilson (may she rest in peace), Mrs. Henning, Mr. Ellis, Mrs. Delguercio, and every art teacher, educator, and coach I've been lucky to have.

To anyone who reads this book, thank you for reading it. I hope it finds you at the exact place and time it's meant to.

With gratitude and love,
Liz

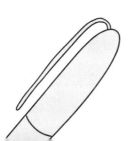

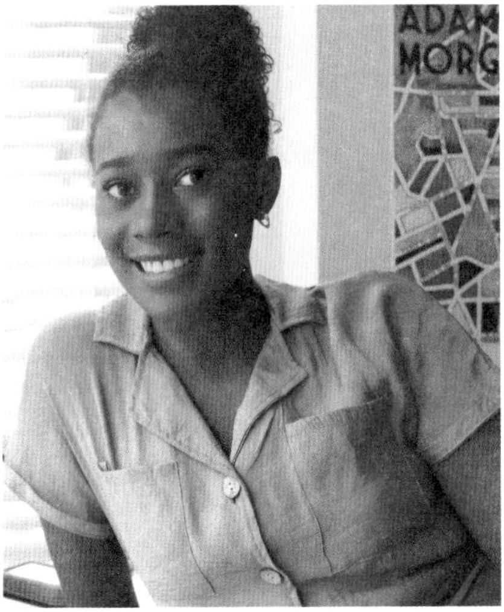

ADAM
MORG

Liz Montague is a cartoonist, writer, and illustrator whose work focuses on the intersection of self and social awareness. She began contributing cartoons to the *New Yorker* in 2019, at the age of twenty-two. She has also illustrated for the Biden presidential campaign, the Obama Foundation, Google, the Food Network, the US Open, and more. Liz is the creator of the popular *Liz at Large* cartoon series, which ran in *Washington City Paper*, and is passionate about documenting social change and social movements. She fundamentally believes in representation, accessible information, and drawing your feelings. This is her first children's book. Liz lives in Philadelphia with her husband, Pat (yes, *that* Pat!).

lizatlarge.org @lizatlarge lizatlarge